Paul Ricoeur

RHETORIC IN THE MODERN ERA

Arthur E. Walzer and Edward Schiappa, Editors

The goal of the series "Rhetoric in the Modern Era" is to prompt and sponsor book-length treatments of important rhetorical theorists and of philosophers and literary theorists who make substantial contributions to our understanding of language and rhetoric. In some cases, a book in this series is the first book-length treatment of the figure; in others, a book in the series is the first to examine a philosopher or theorist from the perspective of rhetorical theory.

The intended audience for books in the series are nonspecialists—graduate students coming to the study of a theorist for the first time and professors broadly interested in the rhetorical tradition. The series books are comprehensive introductions—comprehensive in the sense that they provide brief biographies, descriptions of the intellectual milieu, and discussions of the major scholarship on the figure as context for a detailed examination of the figure's contribution to rhetorical theory or history.

We envision these as the first books on their subject, not the last. While books in the series may exceed these modest aims, their focus is on achieving them. A complete list of the books in the series can be found at the end of this volume.

Paul Ricoeur

Tradition and Innovation in Rhetorical Theory

Andreea Deciu Ritivoi

Southern Illinois University Press
Carbondale

First edition published by State University of New York Press, 2006

Printed in the United States of America

17 16 15 14 4 3 2 1

Library of Congress Cataloging-in-Publication Data

Ritivoi, Andreea Deciu, 1970–
Paul Ricoeur : tradition and innovation in rhetorical theory /
Andreea Deciu Ritivoi. — [New edition]
pages cm — (Rhetoric in the Modern Era)
"First edition published by State University of New York Press, 2006."
Includes bibliographical references and index.
ISBN 978-0-8093-3360-8 (pbk. : alk. paper)
ISBN 0-8093-3360-0 (pbk. : alk. paper)
ISBN 978-0-8093-8622-2 (ebook)
ISBN 0-8093-8622-4 (ebook)
1. Ricoeur, Paul. 2. Rhetoric—Philosophy. I. Title.
B2430.R554R58 2014
194—dc23 2014001674

The paper used in this publication meets the minimum requirements of American National Standard for Information Sciences—Permanence of Paper for Printed Library Materials, ANSI Z39.48-1992. ♾

Contents

Acknowledgments

Writing this book has benefited significantly from the resources made available to me at my home institution, Carnegie Mellon University, Pittsburgh, Pennsylvania. A Laura Falk and Berkman Faculty Development grant provided financial support, while generous colleagues helped me to clarify my ideas and my overall strategy by offering excellent suggestions and feedback. I am especially grateful to Stephen Brockmann, Paul Hopper, Barbara Johnstone, Christine Neuwirth, David Kaufer, William Keith, Peggy Knapp, and Alex John London, as well as to series editor Arthur Walzer and to State University of New York Press editor Priscilla Ross. The doctoral students in my rhetorical theory seminar, who read one of the chapters, made me realize what the ideal audience can be like: smart, interested, demanding, and charitable. I remain particularly indebted to Jennifer Andrus, Nathan Atkinson, Thora Brylowe, John Timothy Dawson, and Heather Steffen. I am also grateful to Anthony Arrigo and Ludmila Selemeneva for their wonderful help as my research assistants. Any error in the book remains, of course, mine.

While I was writing this book my grandmother, who raised me and was my first audience ever, died. The love of my husband, Milu D. Ritivoi, helped me to continue this work through the worries, the pain, and the missing. This book is dedicated to both of them.

List of Abbreviations for Ricoeur's Books

CC	*Critique and Conviction*
FN	*Freedom and Nature*
HT	*History and Truth*
MHF	*Memory, History, Forgetting*
OA	*Oneself as Another*
PM	"Political Memory"
PSE	*Political and Social Essays*
RHP	"Rhetoric, Poetics, Hermeneutics"
RP	"Between Rhetoric and Poetics"
TJ	*The Just*
TA	*From Text to Action*
WMUT	*What Makes Us Think*
RM	*The Rule of Metaphor*
TN	*Time and Narrative*

Introduction

The books published so far in this series, Rhetoric in the Modern Era, include such well-known figures in the rhetorical tradition as George Campbell, Adam Smith, and Chaim Perelman, all three authors of treatises that bear explicitly a connection to our field. Paul Ricoeur, the protagonist of this book, is a philosopher versed in several philosophical traditions, perhaps best known and appreciated for his work in hermeneutics, yet emphatically not a rhetorical theorist proper. But, then, what makes a rhetorical theorist anyways? Is it the title of one's works, institutional affiliations, or use-value for other rhetoricians?

Ricoeur belongs to the camp of European philosophers who have "colonized" American academia in the last few decades. In this category are also Jürgen Habermas, Michel Foucault, Jacques Derrida, Emmanuel Levinas—all of them names familiar to rhetoricians, yet none a rhetorical theorist proper. The lack of disciplinary credentials has certainly not mattered in the production of valuable rhetorical scholarship that draws heavily on these authors. To give a few examples: Gerard Hauser's *Vernacular Voices*, influenced by Habermas's deployment of the public sphere; Alan Gross's analysis of peer review in science, based on Habermas's ideal speech act situation; Mary Lay's presentation of the debates around midwifery, grounded in Foucault's understanding of power; Barbara Biesecker's revision of a classic concept in rhetorical theory, *rhetorical situation*, using Derrida's notion of "différance"; or, finally, Michael Hyde's investigation of the controversial issue of assisted suicide, grounded in Levinas's philosophy of consciousness. Works like these make us take it for granted that Foucault, Habermas, Derrida, and several others matter to the field of rhetoric, so much so that it becomes irrelevant that the authors themselves did and do not write for an audience of rhetoricians. Indeed, that rhetoric has adopted them is proven by the fact that their names can be found in Patricia Bizzell and Bruce Herzberg's classic anthology, *The Rhetorical Tradition*. Although not less famous and certainly not less interesting, Ricoeur, on the other hand, is absent from a rhetoric anthology. Given others' inclusion, his omission raises an obvious but also very difficult question: how do theorists and their ideas enter new disciplines, other than the ones that have produced them?

This question is comparable to Pierre Bourdieu's query about how theorists travel across national borders. What makes Derrida famous in America, Habermas in France, and Foucault in Germany? Bourdieu's answer comes in the form of a complaint: we do not fully understand the international circulation of ideas, and indeed we often misrepresent and misuse ideas because we mistranslate them, remove them from their context, or fail to see to what particular cultural or social exigency they respond at home. The same complaint can be voiced with regard to interdisciplinary circulation: dislodged from a particular conceptual environment that produced them, separated from the influences that shaped them, and the vocabulary they employ, ideas become the vehicle for misrepresentation and obfuscation.

Rhetoric is particularly vulnerable on this front, because, as Dilip Gaonkar Parameshwar argues, it has always "relied on the kindness of strangers" borrowing concepts and methods left and right (359). Gaonkar's solution to this difficulty promotes a conservative agenda, one that would maintain the conceptual core of rhetoric firmly anchored in the ancient legacy. Whether we agree or not with him, the burden of proof lies on the shoulders of those who deal in theoretical imports. Ours is the job to explain how concepts and ideas from other disciplines fit well into an existing mold, formed over the centuries, and that they do not derail the course of rhetoric as shaped throughout its intellectual history. Yet in the current climate of interdisciplinary efforts that increasingly erode disciplinary boundaries, to foster a dialogue between rhetoric and other fields, which would also strike a balance between tradition and innovation, can pose a daunting challenge. This book assumes such a challenge by taking on the provocative case of Ricoeur and showing how his thinking, though not directed to an audience of rhetoricians, can refashion modern rhetorical theory while at the same time preserving its historical and intellectual distinctiveness.

The difficulty of my task is somewhat allayed by the fact that Ricoeur is not an unfamiliar name to rhetoricians. His reflections on hermeneutics and his study of metaphors, in particular, have been duly noted in the field. We may even be able to locate the origin of these interests. In 1983,

Louise Wetherbee Phelps edited a special issue of *PreText* dedicated to Ricoeur's theory of interpretation. In a 1987 article, Barbara Warnick continued this interest in hermeneutics, and introduced rhetorical scholars to Ricoeur's method of analysis, insisting that it is a useful framework for rhetorical criticism of a particular kind of speeches—Abraham Lincoln's Gettysburgh Address or Martin Luther King Jr.'s "I Have a Dream"—that record the beliefs and values of a culture, and hence retain a meaning and significance beyond their initial circumstances, from one generation to the next. Also in 1987, Michael Leff turned to Ricoeur's theory of metaphors to explore a notion of persuasion that does not require a separation of proof from style. In 1988, Phelps employed Ricoeur again, this time to discuss pedagogical implications of his hermeneutical ideas. More recently, Lenore Langsdorf has drawn on Ricoeur's theory of personal identity to analyze the claims involving selfhood in Alcoholics Anonymous meetings.

Valuable as these studies are, they tend to isolate and zoom in on particular aspects of Ricoeur's work, and, with the exception of Langsdorf, who has made sustained efforts to integrate Ricoeur more organically in her thinking, use him perfunctorily as he happens to support a particular analytic or theoretical goal. The tendency to appropriate isolated concepts and ideas from a body of knowledge bothers Bourdieu, who sees it as conducive to misunderstandings. Read outside a broader explanatory concept, an idea cannot be understood in its entire complexity. A particular distinction proposed at one time but amended later by its author can be taken as indicative of that author's position if the amendment remains unnoticed. A case in point is Leff's reading of Ricoeur, which attributes to him a traditionalist conception of rhetoric without scrutinizing his later work, which would reveal a more modernist one. Such limitation to out-of-context-ideas can also explain why some aspects of a thinker's *oeuvre* might receive very little attention, even when they happen to be deeply connected to those that do come under scrutiny. For instance, Ricoeur's endeavors in moral and political philosophy, or more recently in memory studies have received little attention from rhetorical scholars, although they elaborate and clarify his work in hermeneutics and in the philosophy of language.

I intend to draw largely on the less discussed (in the field of rhetoric) writings of Ricoeur, not for the sake of novelty but because they allow me to complete a rather sketchy picture of this important thinker, as I try to present his contribution to rhetorical theory in the form of a coherent set of problems. Chapter 1 addresses the question of relevance and motivation—why Ricoeur?—from the perspective of intellectual biography, introducing him to the reader as a politically involved citizen and as an intellectual concerned with social affairs, a man shaped by uniquely personal, as well as social and political experiences, and as a genuine source of inspiration for reflecting on, as well as dealing with, broad public concerns. Chapters 2–5 concentrate on particular aspects of Ricoeur's vast body of work (especially the lesser known and more recent ones), those aspects that do not simply confirm that his writings are rhetorically salient, but that allow us to redefine key rhetorical concepts. Through focused investigations of four such concepts squarely located in the classical tradition—*doxa*, *phronesis*, *polis*, and *epideictic*—and through analyses of provocative test-cases, I hope to prove that a rhetorical enterprise refashioned with Ricoeur's help enables us to raise questions that are crucially relevant to our time, yet are also grounded in the historical basis of the discipline.

Why these particular concepts? Why select them from the classical tradition? Why try to fit a twentieth-century Continental philosopher in an intellectual matrix created in another time and in another field? In this introduction I try to address these questions by defending a view of the rhetorical tradition focused on ideas rather than on figures, and especially on the explanatory value that ideas have over time, as they change in response to new influences and challenges. My investigation targets concepts that are directly impacted by both Ricoeur's philosophy and his understanding of rhetoric, even though *he does not explicitly deal with them himself.* To explain this impact, I discuss his conception of rhetoric, and I strive to pin down the interrelatedness we can begin to see among these four different notions once we consider them from Ricoeur's perspective. The selection of the concepts, then, is guided by an inductive approach that uses Ricoeur's remarks on rhetoric as the starting point of the investigation, adding as necessary, insights from his other works. Throughout the book, my goal is hardly ever exegetical. I do not aim at explaining Ricoeur's ideas, whether all of them or even only a few select ones. In the terms of Edward Schiappa, I propose a rational reconstruction of Ricoeur's contribution to rhetoric by carefully linking his ideas to basic tenets of the field, identifying consequences that his arguments have for how we conceptualize discursive interactions, and learning how to ask new questions about old problems in our discipline. This approach, too, is shaped after Ricoeur's own method of inquiry, critical hermeneutics, which furnished me with an interpretive strategy in dealing with his texts and putting them in a productive dialogue with others. I discuss this method, and the structure of the book inspired by it, in the last two sections of this introduction.

Defending the Disciplinary Turf

In an essay devoted to the difficult problems raised by any attempt at identifying a rhetorical tradition, Gross argues that a historical criterion simply does not work. Taking Bizzell and Herzberg's anthology as a case in point, Gross ponders the large temporal gaps separating canonical figures in the historical trajectory proposed by the editors: three centuries between Aristotle and Cicero, a thousand years between Boethius and Erasmus, and a century between Richard Whateley and Kenneth Burke. "A history with such lacunae seems no history at all," Gross justly complains ("The Rhetorical Tradition," 32). In lieu of the historical criterion of continuity, he proposes that we focus on a series of concepts that originate in classic and preclassic times and continue to generate over time scholarly quandaries. Such emphasis, Gross believes,

> turns such texts as *The Rhetorical Tradition* from scrapbooks of selections into exemplary disciplinary documents. The rhetorical tradition is now legitimately unified: its unity consists in attempts over two and a half millennia to grapple with one or another scholarly quandary that its conceptual system generates. Some thinkers, such as Aristotle, Campbell, Burke, and Perelman, address these questions directly; others, like Nietzsche, Locke, and Derrida, address issues that bear directly on the answers to these questions. This latter group forms an open set of thinkers who are not rhetoricians but whose fields of study—philosophy of language and cognitive psychology might be examples—legitimately influence rhetorical theory and can help form and re-form the rhetorical tradition. (36)

In this book, I pay heed to Gross's proposal, which has the advantage of moving the discussion of disciplinarity away from the counterproductive strategy of boundary drawing and toward genuinely intellectual concerns that enrich a discipline. His understanding of a rhetorical tradition allows us to consider interdisciplinary influences as substantive cross-fertilization, not as fads. Unlike Bizzell, who views Derrida, Habermas, and Foucault as the "dot coms of the rhetoric stock market" (Bizzell, 113)—a profoundly unfair statement, as easily proven by even the most cursory look at the bibliographies of most books and articles published in the field—Gross sees theorists from other fields as potential participants to an intellectual conversation centered on "a set of problems, initiated by an exemplar, and subsequently addressed, directly and indirectly, by various thinkers" (42).

It is as a participant to such a conversation that Ricoeur can be included in the rhetorical tradition. The four concepts I mentioned before—*doxa*, *phronesis*, *polis*, and *epideictic*—are at the core of our discipline, and they emerge as particular problems in his comments on rhetoric. Although Ricoeur has not produced a systematic or ample body of work that deals explicitly with rhetoric, he has written two essays on rhetorical topics. "Between Rhetoric and Poetics" (RP) and "Rhetoric, Poetics, Hermeneutics" (RPH) will constitute my point of entry in this investigation. A careful reading of these essays reveals a true disciplinary credo, which leads to a series of interrelated questions directly related to key concepts in the rhetorical tradition. Based upon Ricoeur's comments in these two essays, I develop inductively a rhetorical problematic centered on the classical tradition, but one that has continued to engage the attention of theorists. Adding Ricoeur to the expert voices that have spoken on these issues will have both theoretical and analytic implications, as this book attempts to demonstrate.

Reading Ricoeur's "Rhetoric"

Ricoeur understands rhetoric from an Aristotelian perspective, which leads him to contrast it to poetics and hermeneutics, seeing it as a discursive domain predicated on convention, and not on innovation—unlike poetics—and on production and not on interpretation—unlike hermeneutics. But Ricoeur is no instrumentalist. He grants rhetoric an imaginative, creative dimension.

"The history of rhetoric is one of diminishing returns," complained Ricoeur in an essay devoted to Aristotle's theory of metaphors (RP, 319). Like another famous Continental philosopher, Hans-Georg Gadamer, in this essay Ricoeur uses the term *rhetoric* primarily, if not exclusively, in reference to the ancient rhetorical tradition. Deviations from this tradition strike him as either impoverishment, such as the reduction of rhetoric to style or tropes handbooks, or as unjustified aggrandizement, such as the expansion of rhetoric to a generalized theory of discourse. If called upon to participate in current debates regarding the status of the discipline and of its "true" intellectual mission, Ricoeur would probably side with those who, like Gaonkar, bemoan the misappropriation of rhetoric, as a productive art, into interpretive endeavors. To prevent such derailment, and to protect the classical heritage, Ricoeur insists on the necessity of finding ways to delineate rhetoric not only from hermeneutics, the study of interpretation, but also from poetics, the art of composing literary discourse. In a lecture delivered at the Institut des Hautes Études in Belgium under the presidency and in the presence of Perelman, Ricoeur submitted that "one must leave each of these three disciplines [rhetoric, poetics, and hermeneutics] in their three respective birthplaces, which are irreducible to one another" (RPH, 7). He cautioned those who are keen on abolishing disciplinary boundaries: "there is no superdiscipline which would totalize the whole field covered by rhetoric, poetics, and hermeneutics. Lacking this impossible totalization, one can only locate the noticeable points of intersection between the three disciplines. But each discipline speaks for itself" (RPH, 7).

As disciplinary credos go, principles of exclusion and separation are just as important as those of inclusion and association. To see why Ricoeur insists on maintaining rhetoric separate from poetics and hermeneutics is to get a sense of his conception of rhetoric beyond an allegiance to texts or authors. With such an understanding, I hope to show, comes the ability to harvest salient insights into rhetorical theory even in the work that was not intended by Ricoeur to be a direct contribution to rhetoric. While he wants to preserve disciplinary boundaries, the "uncontaminated" rhetoric he envisions is not fully articulate in his account without recourse to its "points of intersection" with poetics, and respectively, with hermeneutics. Through forays in his other works, designed to allow us to understand more comprehensively the key notions Ricoeur employs to define rhetoric in counterdistinction to poetics, I plan to seek out and detail what is involved in these "noticeable points of intersection," and to show how his scholarship forges a rhetorical view articulated at such critical junctures.

One of the difficulties involved in tracing Ricoeur's rhetorical views is that the relevant information is scattered across several texts. This is not only a challenge for data gathering, but also a genealogical question of assuming a continuity and compatibility of positions and intentions across an author's body of work, and the contexts in which it was produced, the audiences for whom it was intended, and the exigencies to which it responded. I am prepared to deal with this latter, more conceptual difficulty, by grounding my investigation in the two texts in which Ricoeur tackles explicitly and directly rhetorical problems and then following the intellectual history of the key concepts he employs in his other works. At the same time, however, I will not assume that this intellectual history is linear and perfectly progressive: I will read specific claims from the perspective of the logic of the text in which they appear, and then link them to other claims.

The virtual bridge between texts will be grounded in what Louis Althusser would call signifying absences—the inconsistencies, contradictions, and loose ends in one text turned by the author into foci of inquiry in another. I do so not out of an uncritical, charitable assumption that there must be coherence underneath confusion, or cohesion beyond incoherence, but because Ricoeur has confessed that he is inclined to develop ideas in a two-tier structure, with a major theme echoed by undercurrents that demand critical scrutiny themselves, and therefore are submitted to examination when they take central stage in other works. At the same time, his expository and argumentation style—very *French* in all senses of the term—is more often than not allusive and tentative, resorting to understatement at crucial moments when more analytically oriented readers would prefer no ambiguity and as strong an emphasis as possible. French theory, as American critics have come to acknowledge, treats language performatively, and if it favors metaphor and analogy over syllogism it is because it believes that "expressions can give birth to thoughts" (Judt, 249). Therefore, I use Ricoeur's turns of phrase, ambiguity and figuration—all potential moments of frustration for an Anglo-American reader—as centers of gravity in the argument and as means of navigation through his work, pondering and articulating them, and therefore continuing or extending arguments beyond one specific text's boundaries. Most importantly for my approach, I create a conversation between Ricoeur and rhetorical theorists concerned with similar issues in order to clarify and give a context for Ricoeur's contribution to rhetorical theory.

Critical Hermeneutics as Method of Inquiry

French theory is sometimes met with resistance because of the nagging suspicion that underneath its stylistic flourish the conceptual field lies barren. How many times has Derrida been called an impostor, or Foucault's historical claims proven inaccurate? Much of the skepticism vis-à-vis French, and indeed poststructuralist theory in general, comes from a method-oriented perspective that seeks epistemic results and worries about the *terministic screen effect* of theory—the subordination of the inquiry to a set of premises allowed to inform every step of the process and to adjust results to fit a master schema. Since he admits that ideology lies at the origin of theoretical inquiry, Ricoeur, too, would seem to be vulnerable to such criticism. But he has never abandoned the search for accuracy and significance in his deployment of theory. Indeed, I argue, Ricoeur has patented his own method of inquiry, known as *critical hermeneutics*. His epistemic commitment is ultimately a question of professional ethics: to envision theory as inescapably a projection is tantamount with giving up on the possibility of research, reducing inquiry to a kaleidoscope of theoretical perspectives, none capable of claiming priority over another. Without understanding the parameters, standards, and goals of theoretical inquiry, we cannot formulate meaningful hypotheses, make analytic decisions, or draw conclusions. But simply positing the possibility of an analytic vantage that is theory-free amounts to nothing more than intellectual prestidigitation.

According to Ricoeur, a solution to this dilemma is to be found in hermeneutics. Theory, in his view, evolves over time. Like ideology, theory has a historical dimension that serves as a link across generations of scholars and intellectual communities, all temporally distributed groups of individuals. Reflection upon the historical matrix that holds myself and my contemporaries together is preceded, in Ricoeur's view, by a "relation of *belonging* upon which we can never entirely reflect. Before any critical distance, we belong to a history, to a class, to a nation, to a culture, to one or several traditions. In accepting this belonging that precedes and supports us, we accept the very first role of ideology, . . . the self-representation" (TA, 267). We can make a similar comment on theory: any attempt to gain reliable knowledge through theoretical lenses is filtered through the process of belonging to an intellectual and disciplinary tradition. But does that not mean that some degree of autonomous reflection is not possible? Such autonomy is inevitably relative, rather than absolute, and it is afforded by what Ricoeur calls, in the vocabulary of Gadamer and Heidegger, *distantiation*—a self-effacement or estrangement caused by the encounter with a radically different other, like another discipline. Distantiation offers temporary relief, so to speak, from the pressures of belonging, yet ultimately the knowledge afforded by a theoretical perspective remains partial and fragmentary, as the theory itself is always guided by a specific interest. How can one theoretical standpoint, then, be preferred over another?

Ricoeur's response to this question is unashamedly normative, indeed deontological:

> Knowledge is always in the process of tearing itself away from ideology, but ideology always remains the grid, the code of interpretation, in virtue of which we are not unattached intellectuals but remain supported by what Hegel called the "ethical substance," *Sittlichkeit*. . . . nothing is more necessary today than to renounce the arrogance of critique and to carry on with patience the endless work of distancing and renewing our historical substance. (TA, 269)

The epistemological incompleteness of theory has important consequences for our understanding of rhetoric, as does the deontological imperative issued by Ricoeur in his call for constant distantiation and renewal of "historical substance." In this book, distantiation will function in two ways: on the one hand, by reading classical concepts through Ricoeur's lens I hope to create a critical vantage from which the scrutiny can yield more reliable results, while on the other hand by reading Ricoeur himself from the perspective of rhetorical theory I hope to create a vantage from which his concepts can be more thoroughly examined. At the center of such a twofold effort is an epistemic concern that defines the hermeneutical project: how can we make sure that our interpretations advance knowledge systematically and reliably?

Throughout an intellectual history that began in the seventeenth century with Friedrich Schleiermacher; continued in the Enlightenment with Wilhelm Dilthey; and in the modern era with Heidegger, Gadamer, Habermas, and Ricoeur himself—to mention only the most influential writers—hermeneutics has tried various approaches to this epistemic question. From answers that focused on textual or contextual evidence, to those geared to the author's intention or to the readers' expectations, including combinations of the ideals of these writers, hermeneutics has been influenced by developments in other fields, philosophy, of course, but also history, psychoanalysis, literary criticism, and more recently, social thought and political theory. From philosophy's viewpoint, it has been chiefly informed by phenomenology, especially in Gadamer's *Truth and Method.* Although also influenced by phenomenology, Ricoeur's contribution draws on many other fields as well—the reason it is perhaps more compelling but also less pellucid than others'. His original position has evolved primarily in relation to the Gadamerian notion of "historical consciousness" defined as an awareness of how the past and tradition shape our existence and perceptions in the present. Ricoeur had an opportunity to clarify both his indebtedness to, and departure from, Gadamer's position when he intervened in the former's debate with Habermas. In 1965, upon reviewing Gadamer's *Truth and Method*, and issuing generally positive comments, Habermas reproached the author for his failure to see that tradition can systematically distort, rather than inform, one's understanding. Ricoeur recognized this limitation, but unlike Habermas, who sought to replace hermeneutics with his own theory of ideology as communicative practice, he tried to reform the hermeneutical project upon the foundation set by Gadamer. The result was an original system of thought, known as "critical hermeneutics," based on a rehabilitation of the epistemological question (Thompson). In sum, his critical hermeneutics contends that understanding is a result of the ability to understand the cultural world to which a text attests by carefully explaining the choices reflected in the text at the level of argument, style, and composition, and then comparing the world they reference, to the interpreter's own realm of reference.

Critical hermeneutics marked a change in the history of a discipline that was animated for a long time by the ambitions of deregionalization and radicalization, as Ricoeur calls them. Deregionalization describes hermeneutics' ambition to expand the study of interpretation beyond a particular set of texts (historically these were legal, scriptural, and philological texts), and to discover universal, general principles of interpretation applicable to a broad range of texts and even to the nontextual. Radicalization refers to transformation of the epistemological concern into a broader, ontological issue, that of historicity as a defining feature of human existence.

Ricoeur sees Schleiermacher as the first to launch a series of efforts dedicated to the "globalization" of hermeneutics. Interested in scriptural and philological texts, Schleiermacher wanted to formulate a hermeneutical project defined as the art of preventing misunderstanding, and he estimated that this would enable the interpreter to "rise above the particular applications and discern the operations that are common to the two branches [scriptural and philological]" (TA, 55). Schleiermacher's work, as described by Ricoeur, aspired to systematicity, to becoming a genuine method (*Kunstlehre*) for reaching "the subjectivity of the one who speaks, the language being forgotten" (TA, 57). But the two categories of texts that were supposed to fuse in a general theory of interpretation did not seem to have much in common: the interpretation of biblical texts used chiefly a "divinatory" approach, as the comprehension of the text relied on "guessing" the intentions of the author. Philological interpretation relied on applying "grammatical" techniques, oriented toward uncovering characteristics common to a culture and reflected in semantic and syntactic patterns. Thus, in one instance of interpretation, language was viewed as the expression of a divine entity irreducible to anything human and at best likely to be approximated through some intuitions, while in the other instance of interpretation as a medium of shared experience. How, then, to reconcile such seemingly opposed approaches into a general theory of interpretation?

Instead of reconciliation, Schleiermacher resorted to a conflation, reducing "divinatory" to "grammatical" rules, and thus defining language as "an instrument at the service of individuality" (TA, 57). This was a mistake, believes Ricoeur, arguing that the comprehension of the intention behind a text "is never restricted to establishing an affinity with the author . . . [because it] implies critical motifs in the activity of comparison: an individuality can be grasped only by comparison and contrast. . . . We never directly grasp an individuality but grasp only its difference from others and from ourselves" (TA, 57). This principle gives credence to Gross's notion of tradition as conversation, and justifies my method of putting Ricoeur in dialogue with other theorists.

Should we be concerned, in staging this dialogue, with recapturing the exact intentions of the authors? By approaching texts solely as the expression of an individual mind, Schleiermacher de-emphasized the role of language in establishing cultural commonality. He thus shifted the focus of interpretation on the question of intention per se (rather than how the intention is manifested). Later on, in Dilthey's work, the intention of the author became a purely psychological concern. As Ricoeur explains, Dilthey connected the interpretation of texts to "a primordial capacity to transpose oneself in the mental life of others. . . . Man is not radically alien to man, because he offers signs of his own existence. To understand these signs is to understand man" (TA, 59). By positing a direct relationship of containment between thought and expression, Dilthey capitalized on the etymological sense of the term *hermeneutics*: for the Greeks, *hermeneia* (utterance) was "a translation of inner thoughts in externalized language" (Grodin, 21). In his view, the focus on recapturing authorial intention as an "inner thought" is based on the premise that "life produces forms, externalizes itself in stable configurations; feelings, evaluations, and volitions tend to sediment themselves in a *structured acquisition* that is offered to others for deciphering" (TA, 60). Ricoeur's emphatic deployment of Dilthey's method as one based on deciphering the "structured acquisition" of an individual's mental life might suggest that there was some protocol in place for such decodification. Quite the contrary, as Dilthey radically redefined the notion of method as specific to the hermeneutical enterprise. A hermeneutical *Kunstlehre* (Eng. methodology), for him, was different from a scientific method based on explanations and focused on generalizations and predictions. The goal of the humanistic pursuit in general, and of hermeneutics in particular, was understanding not explanation, and to Dilthey understanding involved empathic identification with, and transposition in, the mind of another human being. By his own maxim, "we explain nature; we understand mental life" (Dilthey, 176).

In Dilthey's own time, this attitude was a strategic response to positivism—an increasingly popular philosophy, which demanded that the model of all intelligibility be the empirical explanation cultivated by natural scientists. But beyond its epoch, the psychologization of intention radically changed the course of the discipline. In a first instance, it led to an emphasis on the biographical persona of authors as a location of their authorial intentions, to the detriment of other analytic and interpretive techniques more broadly focused on context, influences, or textual evidence. No wonder, then, that the psychologization grew old and left room for an interdiction on discussing authorial intent under New Criticism.

In this book, I discuss the key texts that inform my analysis not by focusing on recovering some pure individual intentions, but also not dismissing the validity of authorial choice and strategic communication. My approach is dialogic as well as historical. By giving Ricoeur a voice in a larger conversation, I hope to define his contribution to explaining a set of problems in a way that is both consistent with his overall body of work, and affine with the conceptual inclinations of rhetoric. I resort to intellectual biography in chapter 1 because I want to position Ricoeur in a context that can explain his beliefs and interests as socially, culturally, and politically situated responses. Critical hermeneutics, as I employ it in this book, relies on explicit interpretive moves that can be defended through recourse to textual evidence as well as to contextual data.

The Structure of the Book

Ricoeur deems rhetoric the oldest in the classic trio of disciplines (along with poetics and hermeneutics) concerned with "the discursive usage of language" (RPH, 61). Seniority, however, is not in his view rhetoric's main distinguishing trait. Analyzing the characteristics of the ancient legacy in rhetoric, Ricoeur finds three enduring dimensions that uniquely define the intellectual domain of rhetoric. First, he considers rhetorical discourse bound to a set of situations, and correspondingly, to the audiences most likely to participate in such situations: "Aristotle defines three [situations of discourse] which regulate the three genres of the deliberative, the judicial, and the epideictic. Three locations are thus designated: the assembly, the tribunal, and commemorative gatherings" (RPH, 7). Although differentiated by situation as well as by specific purpose—to make decisions concerning a future course of action, to establish guilt or innocence, and to impart shame or praise—the three rhetorical genres share, in Ricoeur's view, an epistemic concern. They all involve making one judgment prevail over others, and "in each of these situations, a controversy cuts forth the cutting edge of decision. One can speak in a broad sense of litigation or of a trial even in the epideictic genre" (RPH, 7).

With controversy singled out as the epistemic fulcrum of all rhetorical discourse, the second distinctive feature follows as a natural correlate:

rhetoric operates through argumentation, a mode of demonstration "situated halfway between the constraint of the necessary and the arbitrariness of contingency" (RPH, 8). Third, what keeps rhetoric distinct from communication in general is its orientation to the audience. In Ricoeur's view, persuasion is possible only when the communication focuses on the audience. The rhetor's golden rule, by his account, is to ground arguments in conventional ideas shared with the audience; these are hence safe from becoming a potential source of controversy themselves. To argue persuasively, then, is to transfer "the agreement granted to premises onto conclusions" (RPH, 9) in specific situations and for a specific audience. Without the initial agreement (real or presumed) the entire process is rendered moot, as rhetoric's very condition of existence no longer applies.

In the terms of classical rhetorical theory, *doxa* is critical to such an understanding of rhetoric: it identifies the conventions of a community as the foundation for shaping persuasive discourse. To start an investigation of Ricoeur's contribution to rhetoric with the concept of doxa might seem to suggest that, typically for a philosopher, he falls in the camp of those who regard rhetoric as epistemologically inferior to other domains. But Ricoeur is committed to an Aristotelian legacy that tried to elevate rhetorical discourse from "undisciplined common speech," by grounding it in a series of theoretical concepts and distinctions (RP, 325). Of these, doxa contrasted the realm of the probable in distinction to that of certainty, but also identified particular premises or *topoi* likely to be widely accepted in the Greek culture (revenge is sweet, young people are passionate, etc.). Such premises held the community together, the shared belief acting as social glue that also made persuasive communications possible. But by the same logic, doxa also explains why discourse directed against shared convictions risks not reaching its audience. How, then, does rhetorical discourse effect change, or is rhetoric doomed to alter only minor aspects of an existing state of affairs?

An answer to this question can be considered if we revisit Ricoeur's comparison of rhetoric and poetics. In his view, the very reversal of the doxastic mechanism of persuasion is the engine of poetic expression, which relies on imaginative leaps that depart from the "universe of sedimented ideas." When he articulates the points of disjuncture between rhetoric and poetics, Ricoeur explicitly contrasts persuasion with catharsis: one draws upon what is already accepted as true by an audience; the other prompts recognition of something that does not exist at all in reality. According to Ricoeur, "poetics stirs up the sedimented universe of conventional ideas which are the premises of rhetorical argumentation" (RPH, 12). Poetic expression, in other words, expands endoxa, the set of premises that enable rhetorical persuasion, through recourse to imagination. This chapter further develops a twofold concept of rhetorical imagination that can reinforce a community's allegiance to a shared set of premise, or that challenge them to accept alternatives or to revise existing commitments. To illustrate what is at stake in such a revision of doxa, I draw on the example of Martin Luther King Jr.'s speech, "I Have a Dream," an excellent illustration of a rhetor's ability to encourage imaginative projections into a future time of racial desegregation in order to challenge the existing beliefs according to which segregation is acceptable. If conventional ideas are crucial to persuasion, how could King (or other rhetors going against the grain) manage to convince his audience to take such an imaginative leap, and then pursue the vision in their own real lives? The answer I offer is based on Ricoeur's conception of imagination, one that has both rhetorical salience and originality.

Hardly the first to allow imagination to have a role in rhetorical discourse, Ricoeur departs from the more common approaches that treat imagination as a stylistic matter with some impact on perception. Drawing on a philosophical tradition that views imagination as a volitional act intended to represent a state of affairs for a particular reason, Ricoeur locates imaginative practices at the origin of communal life. To live with others in meaningful ways, he argues, I employ analogies between me and them, which lead to the creation of a space for social interaction. "The truth of our condition," according to Ricoeur, "is that the analogical tie that makes every man my brother is accessible to us only through a certain number of *imaginative practices* (TA, 181). Such imaginative practices function poetically. They constitute a community-integrating element that would otherwise be deemed disparate, just as poetic imagination draws the spectators into an imagined community at the center of which is the tragic hero.

But the integrating function of imagination is counterbalanced, according to Ricoeur, by its centrifugal force, which allows the members of a community to envision worlds different from the one they inhabit, and to model a changed existence on such other realms. Imagination, then, as construed by Ricoeur, operates along two complementary dimensions, one that draws individuals back into constituted matrices, and thus cements their shared beliefs and conventions, and the other that enables individuals to challenge conventions and to refashion the community to which they belong. King relied on a utopian projection—his dream—to make available to his audience images and beliefs that were not part of their doxa, and then urged them to adopt the beliefs and to make the projection real.

The link I try to establish between imagination and doxa is important because it shapes a more exciting view of our discipline, as a conceptual setting for analyzing and producing innovation, rather than consolidating existing beliefs and reinforcing accepted opinions. To ground rhetorical theory in doxa risks divesting rhetors of precisely the creativity that we, as critics, so often identify in their speeches and interventions. After all, if persuasion is so deeply entrenched in convention, then how much creativity do we allow for rhetorical discourse? But Ricoeur's deployment of imagination as a corollary to doxa—inasmuch as it can reaffirm the social bond and confirm the shared premises, but also facilitate change—brings individual creativity back into focus. To emphasize the ability that individual rhetors have to challenge, indeed speak against the doxa (and dogma) of their community, I conclude the chapter by analyzing Václav Havel's appeal to imagination as a form of criticizing publicly but indirectly the official Communist regime.

But my redefinition of doxa raises a question of resources: how do certain individuals manage to break free from the influence of shared beliefs and see alternative perspectives? Ricoeur's depiction of imagination as ideological as well as utopian only suggests that such emancipation is possible, without, however, offering insights into its development or emergence. Classical rhetorical theory viewed *phronesis*, or practical wisdom, as the source of a rhetor's ability to respond promptly to various social and political exigencies. Aristotle maintained that there is a particularly *rhetorical* form of rationality that enables such interventions and makes them effective. Thus, *rhetorical reason*, as later argued by theorists, "broadens the idea of what is reasonable well beyond the analytical, the demonstrative, and the calculable" (Gross and Dearin, 28); "its investigation bears upon discourse which allows a place to the non-conventional, to the implicit, to the indeterminate . . . which affects ideas and which is manifested when the meaning attributed to these latter finds itself contested either by a new truth or by a new situation" (Loreau, 457–58). But such definitions still leave the question in part unanswered: how is rhetorical reason achieved? what allows it to function efficiently? can it be taught or is it completely ad hoc and intuitive?

To address this cluster of questions, chapter 3 draws on Ricoeur to develop a concept of *phronesis* that is historical and interpretive in nature. He defines practical reasoning as the ability to account for one's actions both from one's own perspective, or from a particular point of view and from the perspective of others. The first requires what Ricoeur calls "conditions of intelligibility," while the second requires "conditions of desirability" (TA, 189, 193). King, for example, argued for desegregation from his own perspective as a black man living in 1960s America, but then also explained his vision as desirable in the context of the Founding Fathers' vision of a country created on the principle of equality. He was able to identify social change, which was intelligible to him as a black man whose life was directly affected by racial discrimination, as desirable also to millions of others by putting equality between white Americans and African-Americans in a broader historical context. Practical reasoning is what allowed him to move back and forth from the public to the personal, and from history to the present.

It was not an isolated incident that history informed practical reasoning in King's case. By some accounts, "nearly all twentieth-century presidents (in the United States) have turned to history to find justification for the policies they have wished to pursue" (Stampp, 17). Why history? One answer might be that history is "a way of getting out of the boundaries of one's own life and culture and of seeing more of what human experience has been" (Latham, 12). Or, it could be because we tend to invest the figures of the past with authority out of a sense of indebtedness and gratitude for what they have passed on to us. Ricoeur's own answer is influenced by Gadamer, and it locates *historical consciousness* at the origin of our capacities for comprehension and action. But although history might inform practical reasoning, even help make decisions in the present and prompt action, history is also subject to competing reconstructions. Though practical reasoning is frequently equated with life experience, and hence associated with old age, we should not think of history as an old sage who gives advice to whoever happens to listen. History requires an interpretive effort, and the interpretation can be disputed, replaced, or dismissed. In 1858 during the series of debates between Abraham Lincoln and Stephen Douglas, for example, both men relied on history to explain their political positions. Neither succeeded in making history his ally, because neither managed to present his own standards of rationality and criteria of intelligibility as generally recognized principles. To be sure, there were segments of the American public that accepted the argument, some Lincoln's and some Douglas's. That there was no consensus on the issue could be explained in various ways: perhaps nineteenth-century America was undergoing a crisis of its own cultural identity (which ultimately led to the war) that made many things become contentious, including history. Or perhaps history constitutes a plane of generality that insists on being too inclusive for a domain—rhetorical discourse—that is fundamentally committed to the particularity associated with contingency.

To inform practical reasoning, history must be strategically interpreted so as to provide a context of intelligibility but also one that recommends a desirable course of action. In the actual examples of rhetors who have invoked history, the challenge seems to be as follows: how to justify their particular interpretation of the past, presenting it as both reliable and useful for the particular task at hand. This double requirement of reliability and use-value has been at the center of the discipline traditionally in charge with interpretation, hermeneutics. This discipline has always been concerned with standards of correctness, and with finding grounds of adjudication that would weed out inadmissible interpretations. Ricoeur's particular contribution to hermeneutics has centered on the so-called conflict of interpretations, and the distinctions he proposes are predicated on the assumption that "it behooves [hermeneutics] to settle interpretations, and even rival traditions" (RPH, 69). In the remaining part of chapter 3, I explain how it might be possible to select strategically one interpretation over competing ones; my account draws on Ricoeur's concept of the *matter of the text.* For Ricoeur, texts are the master model for determining how we interpret history. In his view, texts have a *matter* that transcends the author's intention, while also constraining the interpretive idiosyncrasies of readers. The "matter" of the text is a space of intersection between two realms of reference—of the author's and of the reader's. What we seek to understand in a text is a "proposed" world, and our understanding depends on the extent to which we manage to see this world as a place "wherein [we] could project one of [our] utmost possibilities" (TA, 86). Through this imaginative self-projection the quasi world of the text is "appropriated," and to explain how such appropriations might actually unfold in rhetorical practice, I turn to an example: Bill Clinton's speech delivered in Memphis in 1993 to an audience of African-American ministers. Clinton asked the ministers to imagine that King was standing next to him, demanding an explanation for why the black community had turned against itself (in numerous acts of gang violence) after he and others had fought so hard for its freedom. Clinton used history to plead against violence among African-Americans, and he "defended" *his* version of history not just by invoking King but also *sounding* like him, using not just his arguments but also his language, images, and biblical allusions. He *performed* King, and thus created an appropriation of history that justified his views as not only meaningful to the audience, but also to long-standing desiderata still waiting to be fulfilled.

In chapter 4, I continue the inquiry into the rhetorical value of history, this time under a different rubric. I develop a concept of epideictic relying on Ricoeur's ideas about the formative role of the past in shaping and maintaining national identities. The connection between epideictic and group identity was well established in the classical tradition, which defined epideictic as a set of celebratory or condemnatory practices designed to reinforce the values of a community at critical moments in its history. In her influential study on the political role of rhetoric in ancient Greece, Nicole Loraux argued that *panegyrics*, *encomiums*, and *epitaphs*—the classic manifestations of the epideictic genre—functioned as a way of making the audience aware of, and increasing their allegiance to, the social space they inhabited together. This space was not just a concrete location, the city-state of Athens, but rather "something like an ideality, well beyond the sum of concrete experiences that made up [the Athenians'] political life" (Loraux, 328). In articulating and maintaining this ideality, the past played a vital role. Populated by heroes and by their glorious deeds, the past was a source of myths and triumphant narratives that could mobilize energies in the present, provide a needed point of reference, and sustain a community's confidence in its ability to overcome times of hardship. Simultaneously, the past could be deliberately manipulated for the purpose of justifying particular policies in the present, or rendered heroic in a way that would cover up dishonor, injustice, or abuse. As a purveyor of ready-made "golden ages," epideictic seemed equally prepared to provide enlightenment or deception. As Perelman and L. Olbrechts-Tyteca would note, ever since its conceptual inception, the genre walked a thin line between education and propaganda. And the distinction seems all the more difficult to maintain in contemporary rhetorical theory, influenced as it is by a constructivist agenda that recognizes the inescapable hermeneutics of any account. If we acknowledge that the past is always constructed—as virtually every historian after Hayden White urge us—what role can we still assign epideictic discourse?

To stress the poignancy of this question—otherwise easy to write off as a naive realist's dilemma—I focus on the problematic case of postwar Germany. Was there any room or need for an epideictic discourse supposed to glorify the past in the country that had the death of millions of Jews on its collective conscience? Insofar as Germany was to remember its past, could it do so other than to remember it as one defined by perpetual shame and inescapable guilt? How can we fashion a conception of epideictic that allows a national community to maintain an ideal self-image anchored in past deeds even when such deeds include horrendous crimes that cannot be simply bracketed or excused?

In his reflections on the ends and standards of historical inquiry, particularly in the case of Germany, Ricoeur provides an answer that enables me to propose a revised conception of epideictic. Unlike other philosophers of history, he insists on the epistemic dimension of historical writing, emphasizing the importance of connecting events in sequences and of establishing contingent patterns that can be read as explanations of particular actions and provide insight into the intentions of agents. But Ricoeur also stresses the singularity of historical events, and cautions against the possibility of their manipulation for ideological reasons. This was the case in West Germany, when several historians led by Ernest Nolte tried to argue that the crimes of the National Socialist regime were not unique and that they originated as an attempt at facing the danger posed by the Soviet Union. In the 1980s, when such arguments were first proposed, they could easily be read as a condemnation of communism, which in the larger context of the Cold War made them plausible. That such revisionist historiography—as it was labeled by critics—had an epideictic stake was acknowledged by one of the historians in question, Michael Sturmer, in his statement that "in a country without history, he who fills the memory, defines the concepts, and interprets the past, wins the future" (qtd. in Habermas, "Apologetic Tendencies," 213). In opposition to such a perspective, Habermas insisted that the past must only be remembered for expiatory purposes, as a point of departure and not as a platform for shaping national identity in the present. Habermas went as far as to argue that insofar as national identity is anchored in the past, it risks being founded on vacuous myths and pernicious glorifications that can make the most atrocious actions justifiable. For him, then, epideictic is doomed to be morally pernicious.

Ricoeur has a different position. In his view, history can sustain a positive sense of national identity by representing the events of the past as exemplary. He employs the term *exemplary* in the sense of legal trials that sanction the actions of particular individuals—like Klaus Barbie or Maurice Papon—as a way of setting up examples for an entire category and expressing a general condemnation of a particular type of action. Departing from both revisionism and Habermas's response, Ricoeur argues that even the worst moments in a community's past can be used to reinforce an ideality, because the component of blame in epideictic discourse has the same function as that of praise—to signal the irreducible gap between a particular group of people and the abstract principles and values organizing their sense of themselves as a community. Simply put, by his logic Nazi Germany did not murder millions of people in the name of ideas that cumulatively define German identity throughout the centuries. Rather, the crimes of the war can be seen as radically departing from, indeed violating principles upon which the German nation articulates its identity. To explain the gap between national identity as an ideality and its particular actions at a given time, Ricoeur describes the first as unfolding according to the logic of superabundance: no amount of wrongdoing can render void the resources of self-esteem available to a community through recourse to its past construed as the repository of an ideality.

The advantage of this perspective is that it enables an understanding of epideictic that does not equate it with manipulation. At the same time, as I explain in the conclusion, Ricoeur's perspective has its risks: it can be read as exculpatory. To pin down the difference between using and abusing epideictic, I use Ricoeur's concepts as a heuristic for analyzing two commemorative speeches delivered in West Germany in 1985 by the American and German presidents at that time, Ronald Reagan and Richard von Weizsäcker, respectively.

The concept of epideictic that we can envision with Ricoeur's help reminds us that the past comes to life in commemorative acts that need not always be triumphant and celebratory. But does the past thus re-created sustain a homogeneous community in the present, promoting the same identification with another era's heroes for every member of the community? We don't usually think of national identity as a matter of degrees, but we do recognize that participation or active involvement in the political arena of a nation-state may vary across issues of status, race, gender, and other such variables. While chapter 4 drew on Ricoeur's work in the philosophy of history in order to present a way of understanding the role played by doxa in the formation of national identities over time, chapter 5 takes on Ricoeur's work in political philosophy to discuss the political mechanisms that control a nation-state. Using the rhetorical concept of polis as the center of the argument, chapter 5 turns to Ricoeur's ideas to address questions that rhetoricians interested in political participation have still to answer.

The Greek polis emerged as an attempt at creating a discursive political sphere in which rational deliberation and publicity were virtually synonymous. As historians and classicists have argued, the polis was predicated on the assumption of uniformity among its members. Hence, the deliberation was likely to bring together similar points of view and to end in consensus without risking prolonged conflict or continuous disagreement. This assumption of likeness among the members of a polity has persisted through the centuries and reemerged in various historical contexts, often enforced normatively as a way of silencing or dismissing dissenting voices or opinions distinctly different from the (presumed) prevalent opinion. The work of Habermas has been both a major source of conceptual clarification for those interested in the public sphere, and the main target of criticism insofar as it validated, on several levels, this assumption of homogeneity and likeness. Since the publication of Habermas's *Structural Transformation of the Public Sphere* in an English translation, an entire field has emerged, public sphere studies, moving beyond the founder's ideas, particularly his notion that deliberation within a public sphere must end in consensus. Among others, Hauser has devoted a book and many articles to argue that consensus is a normative term that can trump discursive difference.

The concept of a public sphere emerged as a way of engaging critically the assumption of homogeneity, scrutinizing the mechanisms that control political participation, and increasing the opportunity for active political involvement for a variety of actors. As Nancy Fraser explains, "a public sphere is supposed to be a vehicle for mobilizing public opinion as a political force. It should empower the citizenry vis-à-vis private powers and permit it to exercise influence over the state. Thus, a public-sphere is supposed to correlate with a sovereign power, to which its communications are ultimately addressed" (2). Ricoeur's main contribution to an understanding of the public sphere lies in how he views this correlation to a sovereign power. In a 1955 essay written in reaction to the Hungarian Revolution, he argued that the state is a profoundly paradoxical political entity: it reflects the need for communal life, allowing individual human beings to coexist within specific communities, but it is set up from the very beginning to maintain its existence precisely by imposing uniformity in the guise of common submission to its authority. On the basis of various historical examples, Ricoeur points out that states tend to be repressive even in their most enlightened or democratic forms, insofar as they operate normatively, sanctioning public behaviors, establishing criteria of validity, and systematically reducing individuals to categories. When the Hungarian population rose up against the Communist regime—which at that point was still seen in the West, particularly in red France, as highly Democratic—the response was unambiguously violent. In the name of a presumed majority who had opted for a Communist ruling, those who rebelled were killed. But behind the Iron Curtain, the presence of Soviet tanks on the streets of Budapest could still be explained as an effort to maintain a political order that reflected people's wishes. Drawing on Rousseau and Aristotle, Ricoeur maintains that states derive their legitimacy from a virtual pact assumed to function among their citizens, a pact that expresses their willingness to share their lives within a community. The assumption of uniformity underlying many historical public spheres is a direct consequence of this virtual pact, which becomes reified in institutions and in forms of government supposed to reflect equally well the views of any of the individuals who entered the pact. Because the pact represents the foundation of communal life, at the level of the sovereign power supposed to represent the pact, dissent tends to be seen as subversive or destructive. Indeed dissent can be destructive: it can lead to chaos and erode the very social fabric of a community. Political scientists recognize this problem when they seek to articulate a conception of the public sphere "supposed to assure (at least some degree of) moral-political validity," in other words, which can make sure that the opinions allowed to be heard indeed benefit the community (Fraser, 2). The political paradox, as Ricoeur calls it, is as follows: what enables individuals to live as a community—particular regimes and the institutions on which they rely—is also what limits their capacity of " engendering the political sphere for themselves" (CC, 102).

Insofar as the concept of a public sphere is designed to correlate individual agents with the sovereign power, Ricoeur draws our attention to the genuine dilemma of how to find strategies for evading the state's authority in order to empower citizenry. Much work on the subject tends to focus primarily on increasing political participation and assumes that a democratic organization is in principle open to such desideratum. While this work readily concedes that there are many forms—from explicit violence to more subtle manipulation—in which a polity can keep out dissenting voices, it still invests its energy in devising ways to increase participation but does not take the time to understand and then address the very conceptual mechanism that forces an equation between participation with likeness. By explaining the encounter between individuals who concretely make the public and a sovereign power supposed to abstractly represent the public in the terms of a political paradox, Ricoeur urges us to develop a conception of the public sphere that remains alert to the imbalance between state or institutions and individuals. His own writings on moral and political philosophy provide a solid foundation for such a revised conception of the public sphere. Particularly important to such a revision is Ricoeur's idea that a community can enter an *actual* pact, forging solidarity among its members by allowing them to engage one another directly, not through the mediation of institutions. Shifting the emphasis from participation—often envisioned as a symbolic opening of the gates, which only reinforces the existence of gatekeepers, to solidarity, reminds us that on some level people are already inside the community to which they belong. But this shift also requires a departure from the focus on difference and a return to what the members of a community have in common, without also committing us again to consensus as the goal of deliberation in a public sphere. Ricoeur offers an understanding of solidarity as a *personal* rather than only or primarily a social bond, which is shaped through consent. He defines consent as a form of deliberation with very high stakes, one through which the decision maker is transformed to the point where she deems the decision, once made, as an absolute necessity. By this account, individuals who express their solidarity with others consent to a necessarily shared existence that defines who they are.

THE BASIS OF THEORY

In his *Praise of Theory*, Gadamer defines conceptual explorations of the sort on which I embark in this book as manifestations of what the ancients called *vita contemplativa* (Eng. contemplative life). Indeed, many think of theory as an alternative to, even delay of, action (16). I prefer to think of it as a prelude to, and justificatory basis of, action. For this reason, the instances of rhetorical discussed in chapters 2–5 represent more than illustrations of abstract notions, or attempts at making theory more concrete and palpable. King's speech, Václav Havel's eulogy, the Lincoln-Douglas debate, Clinton's Memphis address, the historians' debate, the Bitburg affair, and Adam Michnik's role in the Solidarity movement represent the basis upon which the theory presented in this book can be assessed for explanatory value. I have selected them because they raise difficult and interesting questions that can now be adequately answered. As such, my goal is to show the integration of theory with these examples of public and political discourse in a fashion usually characteristic of full-fledged case studies. While the scope and goal of this project makes it impossible to develop true case studies, the analyses are intended to follow common rules for "casing" particular instances into highly salient objects of inquiry: comparison and contrast, broad contextualization, and close reading (cf. Ragin and Becker). Together, these strategies try to balance the microscopic focus usually associated with rhetorical analysis and the macroscopic level of theoretical relevance. Thus, in chapter 2 I turn to King and Havel for the radical difference in their political context and comparable effect in articulating a political vision at odds with the conventions of the place and period. In chapter 3 I rely on the contrast between the uses of history in the Lincoln-Douglas debate and in Clinton's speech. In chapter 4 I attempt to create a broad context for analyzing the conditions for, and constraints upon epideictic discourse, by looking at arguments made across professional communities (by scholars and politicians) and national lines (by Germans and by an American president). Finally, in chapter 5 I pay close attention to a particular text written by a Solidarity leader, trying to match its discursive strategies with the features of the movement, as identified by historians and political scientists. Obviously, in the end these analyses have to remain rather succinct, as the book centers on Ricoeur and not on any of the prominent public and historic figures featured in the case studies. But my goal in writing this book has been to do more than to have as its protagonist a philosopher: I hope to provide conceptual clarification to serious problems, and to articulate an analytic framework that can shed light on important issues.

Chapter One

The Vagrant Scholar

Why this particular author?—asks Karl Simms in the introduction to his 2000 intellectual biography of Paul Ricoeur. His response comes enthusiastically: "Paul Ricoeur is probably the most wide-ranging of thinkers alive in the world today. Although nominally a philosopher, his work has also cut across the subjects of religion and biblical exegesis, history, literary criticism, psychoanalysis, legal studies and politics, as well as having implications for sociology, psychology, and linguistics" (Simms, 1). In this chapter, I address the same question of relevance and motivation—why Ricoeur?—and my answer draws largely on the interdisciplinarity noted by Simms, but also on the portrait of a remarkable individual, with a fascinating life that has inspired a philosophical *oeuvre* deeply concerned with the major social, moral, and political problems of our time. In this brief sketch of Ricoeur's intellectual biography, my goal is to present him as a scholar as well as a citizen, a man shaped by personal, as well as by social and political experiences, and in his turn he's a genuine source of inspiration for reflecting on, as well as dealing with, broad public concerns.

It was perhaps prophetic that the Frenchman whose philosophical career would take off, by his own admission, on the Anglo-American scene, should come into this world as the son of a high-school English teacher from Normandy. Born on February 27, 1913 at Valence, Jean Paul Gustave Ricoeur grew up among elderly people, raised by his grandparents after the premature death of his mother (when he was only seven months old), his father's fall in battle during World War I, and his younger sister's demise from tuberculosis at age seventeen. This series of losses certainly marked Ricoeur's entire life, as he confesses, and it may also be responsible for some of his more somber intellectual interests in tragedy, guilt, and fallibility. In the stern Protestant environment of his grandparents' household, childhood games were replaced by reading. As a boy Ricoeur also read a lot in bookstores, peeking through the uncut pages with which books came in those days—all the guessing and deducting involved probably shaping the creativity of the future thinker. For Ricoeur and his sister Alice, the memory of their father became a standard of discipline and authority, his symbolic presence invoked more reproachfully than affectionately as a way of reminding the children to behave: "I was always told," Ricoeur remembers, "'What if your father could see you!' I had to satisfy an absent viewer, who, what is more, was a hero" (CC, 3). A maternal figure was absent from their lives. Although they were raised by a grandmother whose place was later taken by an unmarried aunt, Ricoeur recalls that he only understood what a mother figure meant by observing his wife with their children. "The word 'mama' was a word pronounced by my children but never by me" (CC, 4). Because he was studious, and perhaps because he was the boy, Ricoeur received preferential treatment for which he felt deeply remorseful when his sister died:

> . . . her youth was in a sense eclipsed by mine. I have regretted this all my life, with the impression that she received less than her due, while I received more than mine; I still struggle with the feeling of an unpaid debt, with the feeling that she suffered an injustice from which I benefited. This must have played an important role in my life: the "unpaid debt" is a persistent theme, turning up frequently in my work. (CC, 4)

Yet it is hard to see Ricoeur, a "*Pupille de la Nation*" (orphan of the state) who by the time he turned twenty had almost no close relatives left, as someone who received more than his due. He made, however, the best of what he did receive: absorbed the religious fervor of his grandparents to develop a spiritual side early on in life; internalized the remarkable penchant for inquiry and intrepidness of his first philosophy teacher, even though his own nature was rather shy and hesitant; and married his and Alice's closest childhood friend, Simone Lejas, with whom he had six children and lived with until her death in 1998. Ricoeur also made the most out of the educational opportunities made available by the government to orphans of war heroes. A small yearly stipend allowed him to buy books and to pay for other school expenses as a student at the University of Rennes. But when he tried to leave the provincial university for the more prestigious (and Parisian!) *Ecole normale superieure*, he failed the philosophy exam by giving an Aristotelian response to the Cartesian dictum, "The mind is easier to know than the body." Under pressure to complete his studies, so he would not spend too much of the government money, Ricoeur obtained his diploma at age twenty, and was certified as a high-school teacher and examiner. He finished his graduate education at the Sorbonne, with a thesis written under the direction of Leon Brunschvig. While at the Sorbonne, Ricoeur met and befriended Gabriel Marcel, who became his Socratic mentor: weekly Friday sessions with the founder of existentialism critically influenced both his philosophical beliefs and outlook on life. Ricoeur remembers Marcel's one and only rule: "never quote authors, always start from examples and reflect by oneself" (CC, 10). Even in the absence of direct citations, this happens to be a rule the later erudite would hardly follow, as Ricoeur's work is often structured as a true palimpsest.

Through Marcel, Ricoeur discovered German philosophy, Karl Jaspers and Edmund Husserl in particular. But it was not until 1939 that he made a real commitment to studying German, and was able to take advantage of a small grant that allowed him to go to Munich and to improve both his German and knowledge of German thought. The stay in Germany was cut short by the impending war, and although reluctant to leave, Ricoeur returned to France only a few days before the war officially began. He had completed his mandatory military service right after college, and was mobilized to serve with an infantry regiment on the northern coast of Brittany. The year spent there, before Germany invaded France on May 10, 1940, was marked by boredom (since there was not much to do at the time) and "profound hostility with respect to the military" (CC, 10). The hostility dated back to the conscription period—which Ricoeur had spent mostly reading Marx—but was now intensified by his noninterventionist and pacifist convictions. Before the war, Ricoeur subscribed to socialism, a doctrine he found most compatible with his moral and religious beliefs. This political affiliation—which made him impervious to the lures of Soviet communism, since French socialists and communists were in competition—and his philosophical interest in Germany, made him oblivious to the imminence of World War II. He regretfully admits:

> The error of people like me was first of all not to perceive the approach of the war and then, when we knew it would occur, to think of it in terms of the First. . . . We did not understand that the Second stemmed from an entirely different set of problems, that it resulted from the rise to power of totalitarianism. But what made it less possible for us to have a clear vision of things was that we had become the allies of one totalitarianism against the other. (CC, 14–15)

This confession is not merely an act of intellectual self-criticism, but also and more importantly, a moral reflection. Ricoeur led a regiment that was captured at Dormans, not far from Reims, after having held out to the Germans for days. "I remember clearly," he recounts,

> that after three days under the bombardment of the German stukas, without artillery, without aircraft, crushed, we heard at 3 a.m. the German loudspeakers saying in French: "At six o'clock we will attack and you will all be killed." The chaplain and I made the decision to wake up the twenty-five or thirty unfortunate soldiers huddled in the trenches and to surrender, not without a certain feeling of guilt; my earlier political choices seemed to have led to this disaster, and I myself sanctioned it by a surrender. (CC, 16)

Ricoeur became a prisoner of war on June 7, 1940, and spent nearly five years of captivity in Pomerania, in the far northeast of Germany. His daughter Noelle, the couple's third child, was born in the meantime, but for several months Simone did not even know whether her husband was still alive. In the prison camp, Ricoeur spent most of his time with Emmanuel Levinas, Mikel Dufrenne, Roger Ikor, Paul-André Lesort, and other intellectuals, prisoners of war like him. Together, they created a cultural and intellectual environment trying to enjoy, as much as possible, freedom of thought during their captivity. As a result, it was in the camp where Ricoeur began to translate Husserl's *Ideen I*, and to draft in his journal what later became his first major philosophical work, *Freedom and Nature*. In this ad hoc intellectual oasis, the prisoners studied foreign languages, attended lectures on philosophy, and read landmark texts in literature and history, and according to Paul-André Lesort, Ricoeur taught a course on Nietzsche. By 1943, what had begun as a pastime activity became a fully accredited academic endeavor. The Vichy minister of education gave the group permission to offer examinations and university degrees that were validated after the war ended.

The phenomenon known as *L'université de l'oflag* (The University of the Prison Camp) can be read as a triumph of the spirit over the body, a sort of vindication of that failed examination from Ricoeur's youth. But it can also be seen as outrageously luxurious and hence dubious by the more commonly known standards of the German camps. Indeed, as Charles Reagan explains in his monograph, a Russian camp was only 500 meters away from the French camp where Ricoeur delighted in the poems of Valéry and Claudel. Because France had signed the Geneva Accords and Russia hadn't, the treatment accorded to the prisoners was radically different. "The French could see the horrible physical condition of the Russian prisoners and could see them daily burying their dead in a trench-grave at the back of their camp. According to Roger Ikor, only 1,400 Russian prisoners remained alive out of the 4,000 who were initially imprisoned there" (Reagan, 12). Ricoeur also saw the death camps. After liberation, his regiment traveled to Bergen-Belsen, where they all witnessed in horror the release of the survivors, many of whom "dying after taking their first steps, after eating jam or something" (CC, 19), a sight that was particularly unbearable for his Jewish friends, like Ikor or Levinas, who basically survived because they were interned in camps that were not under the jurisdiction of the SS.

Ricoeur's own take on this period of his biography is interesting. He has refused to visit the place of his captivity, as some of his comrades did. He has declared that it was important for him to escape the memory of that time by seeking refuge in intellectual work, and has argued that his intellectual incursions in Goethe and Schiller while in the camp played a major role in shaping his attitude toward Germany. "The first and the second Faust, among others, helped me to preserve a certain image of Germans and of Germany—the guards finally no longer existed, and I was living in books, somewhat as I had done as a child. The true Germany was there, the Germany of Husserl, of Jaspers" (CC, 20). Yet it probably was precisely this differentiation that did not quite endear him to Jaspers, whom Ricoeur frequently tried to approach after the war, while living in Strasbourg from where he could easily travel into Germany. From Ricoeur's perspective, Jasper's insistence on a collective confession of guilt on the part of Germany was too rigid and unrealistic in the postwar context. With Mikel Dufrenne he wrote his first published book, *Karl Jaspers and the Philosophy of Existence*, which came out with a preface by Jaspers himself, who apparently did not have much appreciation for the book, even though he praised it (CC, 21).

The experience of the war undoubted shaped Ricoeur's moral and intellectual profile. But how it did so is far from obvious. Concerning the influence of the First World War on Marcel, for instance, Ricoeur suggests that there is a connection between the existentialist's extreme attention to people and his work as the person in charge of collecting information about missing soldiers, a detective of "individual destinies" (CC, 24). Can there be a similar link between Ricoeur's commitment to intellectual values and his moral stance, or between his sense of political failure (to have anticipated the war) and his willingness to assume responsibility for others? If nothing else, the war inaugurated these links as foci of tension that would explode repeatedly in Ricoeur's life, demanding answers and solutions that were not always conspicuously consistent.

After the war, Ricoeur's first academic appointment was at the University of Strasbourg, where he taught the history of philosophy between 1948 and 1956. Simone Ricoeur recalls this period as "the happiest days of our lives" (Reagan, 16), but a provincial university could only be a starting point for any young and ambitious philosopher. In France, to have a true academic career was virtually equivalent to being in Paris. So in 1956, Ricoeur left Strasbourg for the Sorbonne, joining a department that could boast about its famous names such as Raymond Aron, Vladimir Jankélévitch, Georges Canguilhem, and Gaston Bachelard. Jacques Derrida was his assistant, but Ricoeur has kept oddly quiet on the topic of their relationship. At the Sorbonne, he taught courses on Husserl, Freud, Nietzsche, and Spinoza, yet disliked what he calls the "intangibility" of the students caused by their sheer number, as he often lectured to audiences of one thousand! His impression was that "the task of creating a community of students and teachers was being entirely neglected" (CC, 28). Nor did he find a welcoming or stimulating community of peers: his reputed colleagues remained just names, each an author the others knew from books and articles, rather than a person to whom they could relate. "I felt like a foreign body there," Ricoeur recounts, "working mostly for myself" (CC, 28).

Politically, the Sorbonne period was also marked by the breakout of the Algerian Civil War. Ricoeur publicly opposed the French actions, through articles and letters published in the popular press, as well as in meetings held in academic circles. In 1961, an anonymous letter sent to the police accused him of hiding arms for the Algerian nationalists. In response, the Ricoeurs' apartment was searched and he arrested. Thanks to the intervention of a former student, Ricoeur was released shortly before other detainees were sent to a prison near Lyon. He was put under house arrest, but the arrest was lifted a few weeks later at the protests of the media.

While Parisian life got him involved in important political causes, Ricoeur eventually left the Sorbonne, disappointed by the artificiality of its teacher-students relationships. Even when still at the Sorbonne, he published several articles that criticized the French system of higher education, in which he lobbied for the decentralization of the curriculum, increased housing opportunities for the students, and a more personalized rapport between students and their professors. In 1967, Ricoeur accepted a position at the University of Paris IX, Nanterre, a new institution that promised to put into practice some of his own pedagogical philosophy. Nanterre was designed as an educational experiment, and its novelty lay in the fact that it marked a departure from the traditional French university, approaching rather the American and British model in which the campus is the locus of academic life. With its new classrooms, residence halls, library, cafeteria, and sports fields in one location, Nanterre held the promise of a true intellectual community. It is ironic that it became instead the hotbed for the events of 1968, and a bitter irony that the riots ended up targeting many protesters, in particular Ricouer.

At first, the students' protests had nothing to do, according to Ricoeur, with academic matters, and were rather focused on the creation of a coed dormitory: "At bottom," comments Ricoeur, "it was the 'sexual revolution' that was its detonator" (CC, 35). But what the students had in common, what differentiated them, and eventually sparked the conflict, were social and political positions: among the humanities students was a strong leftist faction that clashed deeply with some of the rightist beliefs shared by law students. In addition, some of the students came from bourgeois suburban families, while others were from a working-class background. Ricoeur explains:

> The sons and daughters of the bourgeois were leftists; the others, communists, were very attached to the proper functioning of the institution—for them, the university was still a traditional way of rising, offering knowledge and the prospect of social success. On the side of the bourgeois, however, it was felt that the university was no longer a privileged factor in social ascension. Since their parents had already conquered these positions, the young bourgeois could ally themselves with those who found themselves at the university without any real means of succeeding there and could dream only of destroying the instrument which was no longer, for them, a reliable means to future success. When I became Dean in March 1969, I benefited from two ideological supports, so to speak: the anti-leftist communists and the socially committed Catholics; my adversaries, paradoxically, were the traditionalist bourgeois and the leftist bourgeois. (CC, 36)

According to Reagan, Nanterre became a true center of attraction for leftist protesters, including those who were initially silenced at the Sorbonne. A series of incidents occurred between the initial outbreak and January 1969, when a group of students forbade professors and administrators from using the cafeteria, as a provocation. Defiant, Ricoeur went to the cafeteria, accompanied by a few colleagues, and as he was about to enter, a student approached and placed the lid from a trash can on his head. It was not the only humiliation he would suffer, however. A group of students tried to boycott his classes, questioning his intellectual authority, while somebody smeared the chalkboard with the words, "Ricoeur, you old clown." The situation had got out of control, and after a few failed attempts to avoid a violent escalation, Ricoeur resigned. For as long as he was in office, his main concern was to keep the police away, in order to prevent an explicit politicization of the events. While in retrospect such efforts might be considered naive, they are consistent with Ricoeur's more general pacifist orientation. But eventually the entire faculty was forced to vote in favor of a revised campus policy that allowed for official armed intervention, and Nanterre went under police control for three full days after which Ricoeur was no longer dean.

The Nanterre episode was still a painful memory for Ricoeur in 1991, when the French Television Network Antenne 2 made a film about him. In the meantime, his friend and main ally Réne Rémond had written a book about the students' revolution, in which he argued that Ricoeur could have faced the challenge successfully if only he had resisted a little longer and had not resigned. Yet from Ricoeur's own perspective, the sense of personal failure must have been overwhelming at the time. On the television show, he was interviewed by Olivier Abel, one of his friends and a professor at the Institut Protestant in Paris, and recounts how one day, after a student stood up in the middle of the lecture and said, "It's over for you, Ricoeur," every single person got up and left the room. Ricoeur viewed the incident as "a lesson in the power of the word" (Reagan, 69). In a published conversation with François Azouvi and Marc de Launy, he further described the lesson of the Nanterre period as a realization of the distinction between the hierarchical level of society and horizontal relations based on mutual respect and consideration: "At a deeper level," he confesses,

> I believe that it produced in me—in a lasting way—an unstable mixture made up of a utopian dream of self-management and the very precise, very positive experience of the American university campus, to which would have to be added the German university, which formed an intermediary reality. I have always found myself caught between nonviolent utopia and the feeling that something irreducible subsists in the relation of commanding, of governing; this is what I rationalize now as being the difficulty of joining together an asymmetrical relation and a relation of reciprocity. . . . In trying to understand the reason for my failure, in making more specific the anatomy of the institution, I became better

> aware of the squaring of the circle proper to politics: the impossible dream of combining the hierarchical and the convivial; such is, for me, the labyrinth of politics. (CC, 39–40)

Was the American university a better place for Ricoeur? Two weeks after resigning from Nanterre, he left for Chicago, where he had been invited to lecture since 1954 and where he had received a doctor *honoris causa* in 1967, along with Aron and Claude Lévi-Strauss. Ricoeur has rejected Azouvi and De Launay's suggestion that such a departure could possibly indicate that he was abandoning the French system, yet the fact that he became a full time faculty member at the University of Chicago *after* 1969 can hardly be coincidental. At Chicago, he was chosen to succeed Paul Tillich as the John Nuveen Chair and became actively involved in both the Philosophy department and on the Committee on Social Thought founded by Hannah Arendt. Although his English was not quite fluent when he first arrived in the United States, Ricoeur did teach prior to the Chicago appointment, at the Quaker college of Haverford, Pennsylvania, where he was most struck by the religious tolerance and by the simplicity of the Quakers' lifestyle. He found a different atmosphere in Chicago, but one he enjoyed nevertheless particularly insofar as it reminded him of the years spent at Strasbourg—even more nostalgically remembered from the perspective of the subsequent experiences at the Sorbonne and Nanterre. The friendly and relaxed relations among faculty and between students and their professors were something he had fought for in France. But they were also somewhat different. "I have always been astonished," he admits,

> by the very subtle mixture of familiarity and respect in the relations that the students have with their professors. Even in the 1970s, at a time when their relations with the institution were the most strained, they always maintained their sense of a vertical acknowledgment without forfeiting the horizontal dimension of conviviality. American students seem to me to have the consummate art of guiding themselves in these subtle, delicate relations. (CC, 46)

But such enthusiasm did not preclude more critical observations, such as the ones about the emotional immaturity of American students, which Ricoeur attributes to the insufficiency of intellectual stimulation during secondary education, and sometimes to the tensions between cultural heritages and professional development shaped in accordance with strictly Western values.

When invited to comment on cultural differences between France and the United States, Ricoeur responded prudently by insisting on the distinction between America and the American academe—the latter being the only one with which he is willing to claim familiarity. Yet the distinction alone indicates a broader awareness of cultural specificity, and is the basis for some fascinating insights into the nature of American democracy, multiculturalism, and political correctness. In Ricoeur's view, the American national identity was formed "from the bottom up . . . on the basis of strong communitarian experiences" (CC, 58)—a very different model from the European models of nationhood that usually came from above and were associated with a particular individual or group's agenda. Multiculturalism, for Ricoeur, is simply a historical phenomenon that describes this process of formation, and it is predicated on the "constant generative force of associative life, and [on] the priority of local powers over federal power" (CC, 59). The communitarian basis of American politics is further grounded, he argues, in religion, which in its turn represents "an antiauthoritarian and pluralistic history" (CC, 64). "It is particularly important," in Ricoeur's view,

> that the idea of tolerance was from the outset a religious idea, unlike the use of the term current here [in France], where "to tolerate" means to put up with what one cannot prevent. In the United States, tolerance has long rested on a genuine acceptance of diversity; the recognition, even from the ecclesiastical theology characteristic of certain denominations, of the fact that there can be other bearers of a share of the truth; at the founding of the political history of the United States, there is the idea that the public space is the place of cohabitation of several religious traditions. (CC, 64)

Read descriptively, this statement is not only controversial but perhaps also oversimplified. We must understand that Ricoeur's perspective is normative, that he responds to cultural and political ideals rather than to realities, and that these ideals constitute the foundation for his own conception of how to shape the public arena. At a descriptive level, Ricoeur has formulated pointed criticisms about social and political issues in the United States, particularly in respect to racial integration. The first part of his "full-time" period in America was marked by the civil liberties transformations associated with Martin Luther King Jr., to which Ricoeur paid attention without, however, seeing them as a true success. In his view, racial tensions and segregation can be traced to the fragmentation of the educational system, which does not afford equal opportunities for both black and white students. One would expect him, then, to endorse the policies of affirmative action. Yet Ricoeur is at best skeptical about affirmative action. With regard to the more general phenomenon in question, the birth of political correctness, he deems it a paradigm shift at the level of political and juridical philosophy, which seeks to modify the principles of legitimation inherited from the Founding Fathers (CC, 54–55). As long as the modification does not turn into a substitution or undermining of the "classical foundations of life in society," Ricoeur believes that political correctness can play an important role in rectifying social wrongs. But he seems rather worried about the transformation of political correctness—particularly at the level of language becoming inclusive at a superficial level and thus functioning as a kind of code that would only mask remaining biases—into an anti-individualist social philosophy: "one may fear that this preferential policy may come to explicitly contradict the principle of equal opportunity that is effectively based upon tests of qualifications for which individuals strive, as individuals, being judged in terms of their current performances" (CC, 55).

Such skepticism vis-à-vis political correctness can be explained as a theoretical stance grounded in his philosophical belief that throughout history societies articulate self-governing principles centered around a core set of immutable values. Individualism is such a value at the very center of the Founding Fathers' vision, and by this account social policies that contradict it are viewed as somehow alien and destructive. Conversely, it is the theoretical position that can be viewed as a response to what he perceived as the failure of affirmative action in America. I emphasize this distinction in how intellectual arguments are produced, as prescriptions or as suggested explanations, because the latter is socially more relevant and hence more rhetorically salient, and because it defines Ricoeur's approach. Much like Arendt, whose philosophical career was devoted to wrestling with some of the most troubled events of the twentieth century, Ricoeur has fashioned his work as a structured set of responses to real problems. His philosophical method—which I will describe in more detail later in this chapter—involves a social and political responsiveness most probably shaped by his personal experiences, but is quite unique as philosophies go.

Ricoeur's intellectual profile has also been observed in a series of important encounters he has had over the years. In one of his later books, *Oneself as Another*, Ricoeur reinforces Aristotle's belief that "the friend . . . has the role of providing what one is incapable of procuring by oneself" (OA, 185). Friendship, in Ricoeur's view, works toward establishing the conditions for the realization of life . . . and of consciousness" (OA, 186).

It is no surprise that a man who has had his intellectual career and personal life deeply impacted by friends like the existentialist philosopher Marcel, the historian of religions Mircea Eliade, and the moralist Jean Nabert, should put such a premium on *philia*. His relationships to these and to other individuals have played a formative role that goes well beyond what is commonly understood as mentoring. Indeed, Ricoeur flatly states that he "never submitted to the intellectual constraints of being their disciple" (CC, 25). Their role was much more important: "these men made me free" (CC, 25).

Marcel was the first person—outside his family—that Ricoeur looked up when he came back from the war. They saw each other regularly until shortly before Marcel's death, and nothing expresses better Ricoeur's gratitude to him than the following acknowledgment: "I believe that this is what I fundamentally owe to him—to have dared to try to do philosophy and to [do] it in a situation assumed polemically" (CC, 23). He also owes to Marcel an interest in Sartre, even though a very critical one, as the atheism and nihilism of the author of *The Devil and the Good Lord*—scandalized both Ricoeur and his mentor. The relationship with Marcel was formative beyond admiration or emulation. From Marcel, Ricoeur also learned what *not* to do:

> If I have moved away from his philosophy, it is not because of his deep convictions, but because of a certain lack, in him, of conceptual structure. His is fundamentally an exploratory thinking that slips from one concept to another, an idea playing the role of a melodic frame for a series of variations; thinking by conceptual affinity where one idea is specified by a neighboring idea. I would not go so far as to call it associationist thinking, but it does proceed by means of assonances and dissonances. (CC, 24)

Eliade and Ricoeur were introduced by Georges Dumézil when they were both living in Paris. A Romanian immigrant with a dubious Fascist past that would only later be uncovered, Eliade impressed Ricoeur with his erudition, and struck him as a "sort of Pic de la Mirandole" (CC, 30). Eliade left Paris for a position at the University of Chicago, as Ricoeur would later do. In Chicago, the two became close friends, so close that Ricoeur suffered a double stroke when Eliade died within weeks after his own son, Olivier, committed suicide. The intellectual connection between the two men was also what often separated them: a common interest in religion. Eliade's lifelong preoccupation with *religions* around the world (rather than religion as a spiritual activity) shaped his intellectual approach as an anthropological one. He had a deep insider's knowledge of Hinduism, which he had acquired in the two years spent in a Tibetan monastery, but in Ricoeur's view, Eliade embraced religion intellectually rather than experientially, as a topic of academic inquiry rather than as a spiritual exploration. For Ricoeur, on the other hand, religion has always played a central role in shaping him both as a person and as a philosopher. He regularly read the Bible, a practice he inherited from his grandmother and continued throughout his life, emphasizing its pneumatological dimension, was a source of inspiration for the leading of everyday life. He recounts that his grandmother's undogmatic approach to religion "gave preference to the private practice of reading, of prayer, and the examination of conscience" (CC, 6).

Raised as a Protestant by his grandparents, Ricoeur spent his adolescence in predominantly Catholic environments, where he often felt not just like an outsider but like "a heretic" (CC, 8). As a student in the predominantly Catholic town of Rennes, he spent most of his time reading rather than socializing, and preferred—on his own admission—secular circles to the Catholic ones. To this early marginality he attributes the relative lack of influence that environments have on him (CC, 8), but perhaps the most important intellectual consequence of these circumstances has been exerted on Ricoeur's ability to maintain his religious beliefs as a separate sphere. Although religion occupies a key position in his thought, he has gone to great pains to navigate the sometimes narrow course between what he calls "conviction and critique"—one religious and private, the other political and public, and even more specifically, grounded in democratic life (CC, 139). Prompted by Azouvi and de Launay to elaborate on the distinction between religion and philosophy in connection to the famous passage from *Exodus*—"I am who I am"—Ricoeur contrasts the biblical language as a synthetic expression that fuses existence and reflection to the language of philosophy, which maintains thinking and being as noncoincidental (CC, 149). "It is indeed another manner of thinking," according to Ricoeur, "a nonphilosophical manner, that is transmitted by the prophets, the collectors of Mosaic and other traditions, and that shines forth in what is said by the sages of this Orient of which the Hebrews are a part" (CC, 149).

In our age, it might seem superfluous to emphasize the autonomy of philosophy from religion if we did not recognize significant broader intellectual consequences, such as Ricoeur's reticence with regard to what he calls "ontotheological speculations" (CC, 150) that can be in part seen in Martin Heidegger's work. Ricoeur first met Heidegger in France in 1955, and was seduced by his "magnificent comments" and particularly by his way of infusing philosophy with poetry (CC, 21). But despite such admiration, further illustrated in the frequent references to Heidegger that can be found in his texts, Ricoeur has always shown a preference for an analytic approach over poetic revelations, which places him closer to another German philosopher, Hans-Georg Gadamer. In 1965, when Gadamer's *Truth and Method* was attacked by Jürgen Habermas, Ricoeur became involved in the debate from what he thought represented a third position, neither Gadamerian, nor Habermasian. Apparently, however, Gadamer viewed the intervention as an endorsement of the criticism against him, and his attitude to Ricoeur became reserved if not altogether hostile. In 1986 in Munich, where Ricoeur delivered a series of lectures, this hostility came to surface as Gadamer challenged his ideas in a pronounced polemical vein.

Yet Ricoeur's intellectual temperament leaned more toward cooperation than confrontation, toward useful compromise rather than sterile intransigence. In the series of conversations with Azouvi and De Launay, he admits to having an obsession with reconciliation, but that has not always protected him from skirmishes and fallouts. His encounters with three writers often seen as the French connection in the United States—Jacques Lacan, Michel Foucault, and Jacques Derrida—are paradigmatic in this sense. Ricoeur's study on Freud, which proposes a methodologically ambitious combination of phenomenology and psychoanalysis, was attacked by Lacan upon its publication in France in 1965. Indeed, Lacan spearheaded the rejection of the book in French intellectual circles. The disagreement was not amiable, and not even academic: Lacan accused Ricoeur of stealing the ideas he had presented in a seminar. The charge was surprising in light of the two men's previously collegial relationship. Ricoeur did in fact attend Lacan's seminar, but in his turn, Lacan attended a lecture in which Ricoeur outlined his hermeneutical approach to Freud. Ricoeur has explained that his volume on Freud had been largely composed by the time he was introduced to Lacan. But Lacan's reputation in France superseded Ricoeur's, and his attacks were not only intimidating—as Ricoeur admits—but also effective in the damage they were trying to produce: marginalization. But on an intellectual level, the incident had a long-term positive effect insofar as it pushed Ricoeur further into pursuing the links between phenomenology and other domains, including hermeneutics and philosophy of language. The latter would be at the center of *The Rule of Metaphor*, a book Ricoeur published in 1975, his first major study after the Nanterre episode. As Reagan observes, "its reception was a sign of the nearly total eclipse of this once-famous philosopher in his native land"

(44). Most of the few reviews were negative, and the French readership responded negatively to Ricoeur's emphasis on Anglo-Saxon sources and criticism of Derrida. Ricoeur repproached Derrida with the latter's argumentational poverty, excess of assertions, and too much self-reliance translating as mere dismissal of other theories, particularly the opposing ones. In his view, Derrida's success in the United States was to some extent based on the philosophical ignorance of literary scholars (Reagan, *Paul Ricoeur*, 62). Conceivably, Ricoeur did not have such reservations when after resigning from Nanterre he recommended Derrida as a successor of his chair. Derrida applied for the position, but he was not elected.

Ricoeur never had a direct confrontation with Foucault, and for the most part, their philosophies follow different routes. An implicit encounter took place in 1980, when both were candidates for one opening in the Collège de France, which went to Foucault.

An Intellectual Journey

As a student of Marcel, Ricoeur entered the philosophical arena through the door of phenomenology. After the translation of Husserl's *Ideen I*, his first original work was published in 1950 under the title *Freedom and Nature*. A decade later, *Fallible Man* and its companion *Symbolism of Evil* followed, completing a trilogy that establishes Ricoeur as a phenomenologist in his own right, while also opening the way for his later forays into hermeneutics, moral philosophy, and philosophy of action. The aim of this trilogy was to describe the experience of being in the world, approached from complementary angles designed to map its complexity. While summarizing these works is beyond the scope of my investigation, the method they employ deserves some consideration insofar as it announces Ricoeur's way of thinking, still recognizable in later texts. In these early works, Ricoeur advances a conception of life dialectically shaped by freedom and constraint: on the one hand, individuals decide on what courses of action to embark, but on the other hand their will is shaped by the larger environment in which existence unfolds. In one critic's words, "how we negotiate our lives between the freedom accorded us and the constraints that are imposed upon us by the fact of being humans living in the world is, then, the point of departure for Ricoeur's philosophy" (Simms, 9). The premises of *Fallible Man* are that "the possibility of evil appears inscribed in the innermost structure of human reality"(4), as a consequence of the freedom of choice, and that the human experience is agonistic insofar as the choices we make may sometimes contradict one another, acting as foundations for conflictual identities. *Symbolism of Evil* describes the transition from fallibility to fallenness as occurring when the possibility of evil is internalized in the form of guilt for which there is no redemption, when the very experience of being in the world is framed by a tragic vision crystallized in the Adamic myth.

From a methodological perspective, the contribution of *Freedom and Nature* lies in its mixture of traditional Husserlian phenomenology and empirical science: from such cross-fertilization, Ricoeur derives an original conception that does not mark a departure from the phenomenological project but takes it to a different level. Ricoeur has always been interested in science, and was eager to compare his arguments to empirically grounded findings. In 1996, he engaged in a series of conversations with the neuroscientist Jean-Pierre Changeux on the topic of cognition. This discussion was published in the volume titled *What Makes Us Think* whose goal was, as described by Ricoeur, not to resolve the disciplinary and conceptual differences between science and philosophy, but "to raise them to a level of argumentation permitting the reasons of one to be regarded as plausible by the other" (WMUT, 4). And while there are not many points of agreement between the scientist and the philosopher in this book, they both draw attention to the very need for interdisciplinary scholarship, not just for intellectual reasons but also as an exercise in bridging differences and in overcoming rivalries.

This seems to have been Ricoeur's professional stance throughout his career. Between 1960 and 1970, from *The Symbolism of Evil* to *Freud and Philosophy*, Ricoeur wrote dozens of essays on topics spanning a wide range of interests, from structuralism and linguistics, hermeneutics and phenomenology, psychoanalysis, and to religion. As Don Ihde explains, "the guiding thread which unites these diverse interests and which holds the clue for the direction of Ricoeur's thought is the question of *hermeneutics*, interpretation (x). In the early stages of his career, Ricoeur viewed hermeneutics as the interpretation of symbols, but he gradually moved to a broader conception that emphasizes the interpretive process over the objects of interpretation, extending the hermeneutical projects to discourse. The inquiry becomes one of discovering meaning, as Ricoeur's hermeneutics tries to uncover the intentional attitude that makes discourse meaningful. Many of the essays written in this period were collected in *The Conflict of Interpretations*, a book that revolves around the central theme of *suspicion* as a premise of the interpretive endeavor. Drawing on Freud and Hegel, whose "functional similarity . . . lies in their respective strategies of the dispossession of immediacy" (Ihde, xvi), Ricoeur advances a hermeneutical conception that underscores the gap between the inquiring subject and the object of interpretation. This gap will be bridged—by historical consciousness, morality, or narrative configuration—at different stages in Ricoeur's philosophical work, but it represents one of his most important contributions. Ricoeur advances a phenomenological conception of hermeneutics, which "suspends judgment about what I can know about the world through direct perception, in order to explore the routes of understanding the world" (Simms, 42). One reads and makes sense of a text by discovering its *universe of reference* or *proposed world* and by inhabiting it as one's own. Thus, texts become the bridge between subjectivity and the surrounding environment, the very link between the self and the world.

The Conflict of Interpretations includes several essays on language theory, fashioned as a critique of structuralism. In these essays, Ricoeur's attempts to integrate a philosophy of language into hermeneutics mark a departure from a structuralist doctrine at pains to purge subjectivity from language. As François Dosse notes, "hermeneutics was criticized . . . as running counter to the critical and epistemological concerns of the period . . . presented as an antiscience, a kind of phrenology of symbols" (48). Ricoeur's relationship with the structuralist camp became particularly tense after the 1963 publication of his article on Lévi-Strauss in the journal *Esprit*. Ricoeur countered Lévi-Strauss's general theory of relationship at the basis of understanding language, and proposed instead that we view interpretation as the foundation of linguistic activity. Dosse sees the force of Ricoeur's criticism as coming from the scientific rigor of his approach: "Incarnating a hermeneutics with which structuralism, in its heyday, wanted to ensure a radical rupture, Ricoeur was an all the more disturbing adversary in that his philosophical perspective had assimilated and integrated all the advances of the social sciences" (285). The main point of disagreement between Ricoeur and the supporters of structuralism concerns Ferdinand de Saussure's distinction between language and speech—a differentiation that lies at the center of the structuralist enterprise.

While Saussure argued that speaking (*parole*) is only an ephemeral and imperfect reflection of the abstract and more systematic level constituted by language (*langue*), Ricoeur asserts the transcendence of language. Like Emile Benveniste, he sees language as inseparable from discourse, emphasizing that usage is what gives it substance, allowing words to have meaning. Along these lines, *The Rule of Metaphor* is a booklength critique of the Saussurian immanence of language, which draws heavily on analytic philosophy and Gestalt psychology. The main contribution of the study lies in proposing a holistic theory of metaphor that brings together rhetorical, semantic, and pragmatic perspectives. At the same time, though, Ricoeur describes this work as "essentially a plea for the plurality of modes of discourse" (RM, 7), as his theory remains sensitive to different metaphoric functions from poetic to philosophical and scientific texts. But across such differences, the book defines the metaphor as "the rhetorical process by which discourse unleashes the power that certain fictions have to redescribe reality (RM, 7). In the chapter titled "Metaphor and Reference," Ricoeur argues that poetic language is referential, insofar as metaphors have an ontological function of generating a new world: "poetic feeling itself also develops an experience of reality in which invention and discovery cease being opposed, and where creation and revelation coincide" (RM, 246). It is in this sense that figurative language, at the center at which he places metaphors, is living (*vivre*). In order words, language can reorganize reality, making "a breakthrough in experience" (CC, 83) by allowing us to perceive the world differently depending on the discursive rendition we choose.

If in *The Rule of Metaphor* Ricoeur's interest in poetic discourse is designed to scaffold his theory of metaphoric reference, poetics as productive activity becomes the major concern of his work *Time and Narrative.* Published in the mid-1980s, this trilogy consecrated Ricoeur as one of the most important thinkers of the twentieth century. Recognition came first in the United States, but the book was also well received in France. The key concepts featured in *Time and Narrative* are configuration and refiguration: one describes the emplotment strategies designed to structure raw experience into verbally recorded events, while the other refers to the transformation of one's own experience once that experience is analyzed in narrative terms. Volume 1 deals largely with the experience of time as problematized by Aristotle and St. Augustine, divergence or convergence, and then looks at emplotment from an Aristotelian perspective as the creation of "discordant concordance," testing its application in historical inquiry. Volume 2 is a somewhat unexpected homage paid to structuralism insofar as it explores semiotic theories of narrative, from Vladimir Propp to A. J. Greimas and Claude Bremond, and then illustrates them in interpretations of Virgina Woolf's *Mrs. Dalloway,* Thomas Mann's *Magic Mountain,* and Marcel Proust's *Remembrance of Things Past.* Finally, volume 3 discusses the connections between language and experience, proposing a theory of *mimesis* that stresses the transformative power of language. Ricoeur posits a dialectical relation between language and reality: "given that the sign is not the thing, that the sign is in retreat in relation to it, language is constituted marginally, in a sense, in relation to experience and becomes for itself a spoken universe" (CC, 86). The question then becomes, to the extent that time is a central aspect of experience: how does it become refigured by language? Furthermore, how does history, as a field whose object of inquiry is located in the past, shape its findings in language?

Unlike his study of Freud, which was vilified by the mainstream psychoanalytic community in France under the influence of Lacan, *Time and Narrative*, which features history so prominently, was well received by historians on both sides of the Atlantic Ocean. The book consolidated Ricoeur's American reputation, and marked his homecoming in France, but by the time the three volumes had been published Ricoeur was already at work on a new project, which would first become the Gifford Lectures delivered in Edinburgh in 1986, and would then be published as a book under the title *Oneself as Another* in 1992. All three volumes of *Time and Narrative* approached storytelling as action, and language as the realm in which such action is produced. *Oneself as Another* focuses on the agent committing actions, and refers to this agent as "the capable person." For Ricoeur, identity—knowing who one is—is modeled successively on determining who can speak, who can recount, who can act, and who can impute actions to oneself. The subject, then, is fundamentally a speaking and acting one, who can additionally hold herself responsible for her actions.

The circumstances in which Ricoeur wrote this book were marked by the suicide of his son Olivier, who had suffered from depression. This tragedy left the father wondering what happens when one's own life seems no longer meaningful, and how one can still make sense of one's experience in situations of risk or uncertainty, when epistemic, moral, and ethical foundations begin to crumble. Ricoeur saw a close analogy between personal crises and the epistemic and moral challenges facing the legal system when it deals with unprecedented, singular events or phenomena, such as the trial of criminals responsible for mass atrocities and human rights violations. His 1998 study, *The Just*, tackles this issue from the perspective of contemporary moral and political philosophy.

The one question that was missing from *Oneself as Another,* was, who remembers? This is the focus of Ricoeur's last book, *Memory, History, Forgetting*, published in 2000. This is perhaps Ricoeur's most comprehensive and erudite book—a foray into theories of memory from Plato and Aristotle to contemporary cognitive science, as well as into the philosophy of history from its German nineteenth-century intellectual origins to the French Annales school. The major goal of this study is to differentiate between memory and history, both dealing directly with the past, from the perspective of what makes forgiveness possible.

Ricoeur remained a productive author until shortly before his death, on May 20, 2005, at 92. His longevity—physical and spiritual—is the blazon of an intellectual family that includes more Germans than the French—an environment in which Ricoeur has always felt more comfortable. His work is vast and diverse, but also systematic and persistent in its diligent pursuit of several important themes. His articles and books have been translated into many languages, but unlike other intellectual works that travel across linguistic lines, his has been deeply entrenched in, and produced in response to, more than one culture. Ricoeur's *Frenchness*, as some would call his style as well as thematic preferences, is matched by his *Anglo-Saxonism*, and it is ultimately this cultural cross-fertilization that accounts for the unique blend of ideas, concepts, and expression that defines his work.

METHODOLOGICAL CHALLENGES

Four features of thought individualize Ricoeur's philosophical approach. The first is specificity: as the author emphasizes, each of his books approaches a specific problem, or a "well-circumscribed difficulty of thought" (CC, 81). Ricoeur has never asked big questions such as, "what is justice?" and hence has never offered broad theories or abstract models. This makes his ideas both relevant and manageable and easier to fit into a coherent system of thought. Second, from his early book, *Freedom and Nature* to the more recent ones like *The Just* or *Memory, History, Forgetting,* Ricoeur's works have developed cohesively, as all are interconnected in a way that reveals an intellectual system under permanent construction rather than a set of disparate, ever-changing, interests. Ricoeur explains: "After having completed a work, I find myself confronting something that has escaped it, something that flies outside its orbit, becoming an obsession for me, and forming the next subject to examine" (CC, 81). Third, the ideational gestation in many of Ricoeur's texts involves semantic and etymological examination—token of a linguistic sensitivity that links expressions to ideas in order to uncover connotations and to detect patterns that would otherwise remain unnoticed. For example, to differentiate between relationships among individuals that are shaped by group-defined expectations or that reflect individual preferences and responses, Ricoeur ponders the semantic distinction between the English word "neighbor" and the Latin word *socius*. To illustrate the paradoxical nature of personal identity, caught between sameness and change, he confronts the Latin roots of the word "identity": *idem* and *ipse*, one conveying the idea of constancy, the other signaling the inevitability of modification. But the author does not allow such linguistic speculation to substitute for demonstration or arguments, its strictly heuristic function not supplanting for further elaboration. Finally, fourth, Ricoeur makes his original contribution always after a detour in the history of philosophy on the topic in question—a strategy that affords him conceptual soundness, but not necessarily expository clarity.

These four features can also be seen as interpretive challenges, in both senses of the word, as affordances and obstacles. Approached through its emphases on particularity and on systematicity, Ricoeur's work becomes a valuable resource for intellectual coherence and precision, at a time when such characteristics are becoming rather rare. Similarly, Ricoeur's linguistic sensitivity is uniquely suited for the disciplinary aesthetics of our field. It is the author's impressive erudition that makes any critical engagement with his work so fraught with expository and explanatory difficulties, not to mention the more basic intelligibility one. Few can aspire to an engagement fashioned on a perfectly equal footing. For my part, I will frequently rely on Ricoeur's own specificity and systematicity to find my way through philosophical denseness—my ultimate rationale for the theoretical parsimony this study displays with its reliance on only four major concepts. But beyond these specific concepts, I hope to be able to define a conceptual foundation on which future inquiry can build additional analytic and theoretical models.

One of my goals in this book is to show that rhetoric can be legitimately added to the category of implications of Ricoeur's intellectual accomplishments. But my second, and more important, goal is to show how rhetorical theory changes once we look at it through Ricoeur's lens. Methodologically, this second objective takes precedence over the first, insofar as I have selected for presentation particular aspects of Ricoeur's vast body of work, those aspects that do not simply confirm that his writing are rhetorically salient, but that allow us to redefine the very notion of rhetorical salience. In other words, through focused investigations of four key rhetorical concepts squarely located in the classical tradition—*doxa*, *phronesis*, *polis*, and *epideictic*—and through analyses of provocative test cases, I hope to prove that a rhetorical enterprise refashioned with Ricoeur's help enables us to raise questions that are crucially relevant to our time, yet that are also grounded in the historical basis of the discipline.

Chapter Two

Doxa

Disciplines often profit when asked fundamental questions that force a radical reconsideration of the most taken for granted assumptions. One could fit in this category the query Paul Ricoeur wages at the very heart of the rhetorical enterprise: "what does it mean to persuade?" (RP, 326). And to explain what is at stake in raising this question, he adds:

> What distinguishes persuasion from flattery, from seduction, from threat, that is to say, from the subtlest forms of violence? What does it mean "to influence through discourse"? To pose these questions is to decide that one cannot transform the arts of discourse into techniques without submitting them to a radical philosophical reflection outlining the concept of "that which is persuasive" (*to pithanon*). (RP, 326)

For his part, we have seen that Ricoeur associates persuasion with the set of shared beliefs that bring together audiences and rhetors (see the introduction). To persuade, in his view, is to transfer "the agreement granted to premises onto conclusions" (RPH, 62). His conception of rhetoric, then, capitalizes on a particular aspect of rhetorical discourse, known in the terms of classical rhetorical theory as *doxa*, and described by Ricoeur as "the sedimented universe of conventional ideas" (RPH, 66). Traditionally, doxa has been defined as the domain of probable knowledge and contrasted to *episteme*, the realm of certainty. Ricoeur takes Aristotle's position on the distinction between probability and certainty, and like him, insists that "rather than denounce *doxa* (opinion) as inferior to *episteme* (science), philosophy can consider elaborating a theory of the probable, which would arm rhetoric against its characteristic abuses while separating it from sophistry and eristics" (RP, 326). Using Ricoeur's insights into what counts as persuasive, this chapter attempts to outline such a theory of the probable, and in so doing hopes to redefine the traditional concept of *doxa* from a perspective that does not attempt to separate epistemology from contingent factors. Drawing on Ricoeur, I discuss probability as a separate level of knowledge that is not on a par with certainty, but that has nevertheless an important cognitive as well as social function. I show that studying doxa from his perspective allows us to attend to the epistemic force of arguments by connecting it to the existence of a community-shared background against which arguments are formed before they get accepted or rejected.

In contemporary rhetorical theory we can distinguish two meanings of the classical term *doxa*. The first is more faithful to the classical heritage; it therefore stems from an epistemic perspective grounded in the contrast between certainty and probability. The second unfolds along a social and cultural dimension and is concerned with sets of beliefs widely espoused by particular audiences. These two meanings do not necessarily represent a shift from classical to modern theory. Aristotle distinguished doxa as opinion, from episteme as certainty. But in listing various beliefs with a high degree of probability—such as revenge being sweet, or rare objects as more valuable than those that exist in abundance—he also identified specific cultural, social (or what we would call ideological) assumptions based on which the premise of an argument can be seen as plausible and be agreed upon by the members of a particular community. This sense of the concept doxa can also be found in the writings of a modern critic like Thomas Farrell, who employs it in his *Norms of Rhetorical Culture* synonymously with "cultural premises" (Farrell, 231). Another critic, Michael Calvin McGee, makes the synonymy official by maintaining that doxa "is identical to the concept [of] *culture* that is so prominently featured in much contemporary discourse theory" (qtd. in Lucaites and Condit, 71). This second, broader sense of the term *doxa* is what interested Pierre Bourdieu, who also emphasized the element of concealment central to it. For Bourdieu, doxa was the "realm of the undiscussed," a set of such widely accepted beliefs that they are not thematized and can therefore become a source of manipulation. Drawing on Bourdieu, Robert Hariman has defined doxa as a "reservoir of potential meanings for epistemic claims," and as "'social knowledge' that grounds rhetorical practice and implies 'certain notions of preferable public behavior'" (qtd. in Lucaites and Condit, 47).

The English translation of Ricoeur's writings obscures the extent to which he might be interested in the epistemological aspect of doxa, or concerned with the broader cultural, social, and ideological dimension. But a careful inspection of his use of the term reveals that the distinction may no longer hold true at all in his case. In the English versions of his texts, "doxa" has been rendered mostly as, or at least in association with "opinion," but in the original French the author employs it in a qualified manner, as the "*right* opinion." To be persuaded, for Ricoeur, is to accept opinions one considers "right" against a background of assumptions, beliefs, and expectations that are part of one's social milieu. In an article devoted to doxa in the *Encyclopedia Universalis*, he summons the least expected ally, Plato, to defend probable knowledge as situated knowledge and as a form of contemplation concerned with various aspects of being in the world (qtd. in Mongin, 17). By such a view, an opinion should not be defined in terms of its content—probable knowledge rather than certainty—but as an aptitude, an ability to uncover what a community can accept as truthful where no formal procedures exist to guide the inquiry. Such an aptitude is molded on an awareness of what it means to exist in a particular world, community, or context for the specific purpose of knowing how to take advantage of its shared assumptions while also being able to challenge them strategically. Conceptualizations of doxa concerned with the social and cultural dimension tend to concentrate only on the influence of conventional practices on social knowledge, but ignore how or even whether going against shared beliefs might also be a source of knowledge. But a rhetorical theory focused on the conventional cannot explain the novel, and hence would not allow us to understand the discursive strategies used to implement change and to transform a community's view of itself. In this chapter I use Ricoeur to forge a connection between doxa and imagination to explore the way in which rhetorical agents can challenge and change the assumptions of their communities in order to allow new arguments and ideas to be heard. To build a bridge between doxa and imagination, I revisit the relationship posited by Ricoeur between rhetoric and poetics (discussed in more detail in the introduction), and argue that both disciplines have a mimetic component insofar as they use discourse to create visions or imaginative projections. But rhetoric and poetics rely on different mechanisms for stimulating their audience's imagination. Drawing on Ricoeur's twofold concept of imagination, as a mechanism that generates a social matrix as well as a cognitive breach in one's realm of experience, I describe specific processes through which rhetorical agents can use doxa to advance new, even subversive agendas. According to Ricoeur, these processes are ideological and utopian, one designed to create doxa by promoting commitment to a set of beliefs, the other intended to allow individuals to escape from the conventional and to propose alternative visions.

Imagination, ideology, and utopia are notoriously complex notions, hard to define, and fraught with assumptions and connotations reflecting a tortuous intellectual history. Fortunately, Ricoeur circumscribes them carefully through a series of strategic moves: (1) he defines imagination as a volitional act (rather than as a faculty) with social consequences, (2) he identifies specific *functions* of ideology rather than its broad spectrum, and (3) following Karl Mannheim, he links ideology to utopia in an attempt to explain them as centripetal and centrifugal forces that shape social life. Thus particularized, these concepts help us to revamp the classical concept of doxa, by providing new insight into its purview and mechanism of formation. To ground my theoretical observations, I draw on a well-known rhetorical speech, "I Have a Dream" by Dr. Martin Luther King Jr., and a less-known one by a famous author, Václav Havel's eulogy at the death of a Communist official. I chose these two cases because although produced in very different contexts (one at a time of social turmoil but nevertheless in a democratic society, while the other at the darkest hour of totalitarianism in Eastern Europe) they both reveal the ability that rhetorical agents have in order to intervene in doxa, unearthing and transforming its assumptions.

From the Probable to the Possible

For much of the difference between rhetoric and poetics (discussed in the introduction), the two also share an important component, in Ricoeur's view. Both "intersect in the region of what is probable" (RPH, 65). But, he argues, while the poetic act seeks verisimilitude by imitating life in art through the invention of plots and characters, rhetoric manages actual life with its concrete problems, through the elaboration of arguments that consolidate opinions into convictions. Ricoeur contrasts persuasion to *catharsis*, the goal of poetics, as the latter "consists in the imaginative reconstruction of the two basic emotions by which we participate in any great deed: fear and pity" (RPH, 10). Through an emotional participation in the plot, audiences gain access into an imaginary world and perceive the actions of fictive beings as relevant to their own experience. "Conversion of the *imaginary* is the central element of poetics," insists Ricoeur (RPH, 66). And because it centers on what is imagined, "poetics stirs up the sedimented universe of conventional ideas which are the premises of rhetorical argumentation" (RPH, 66). With this definition, the poetic act seeks to expand, challenge, or even explode the very basis of agreement on premises without which the rhetorical act cannot exist. Like the disciplines to which they belong, doxa and imagination would thus seem to be fundamentally different.

But it is easy to see that the distinction collapses when the rhetor's goal is no longer to settle a controversial issue, but to generate a radically new conviction. Ricoeur himself admits that the poetic "projective function" of imagination aids persuasion when the argumentation process must not only be launched and grounded in conventional ideas, but must also be capable of identifying and then unfolding in new avenues. Consider, for instance, King's speech given in 1963 on the steps at the Lincoln Memorial in Washington, D.C. The reverend advanced a view that was intended to "stir up" the conventional premises of the time, by according African-Americans the same rights as the white citizens of the United States. More than two centuries of racial discrimination had made King's dream of an emancipated future for black people appear to be indeed fanciful. But the impact of the speech relied precisely on the speaker's ability to operate an imaginary projection into a future when black and white Americans would live together as equal members of the same nation. The speech tapped into the imaginative resources of the audience, and encouraged the listeners to try out new ideas, values, and ways of being in the world. The availability of such imaginative resources cannot be explained poetically as recourse to a cathartic purging of fear or pity. In "I Have a Dream" the appeal to imagination works differently than in watching a play and in sympathizing with the hero's misfortune. The function of the imagination in the speech is argumentative, making it possible to conceive of a possible world and then to strive to attain it. As such, the imaginative projection into a better future directly challenges the doxa, and King's dream is designed precisely to "stir up the sedimented universe of conventional ideas" insofar as such ideas include the inequality of rights between races.

This argumentative function makes rhetorical imagination more similar to, than different from, its poetic counterpart. It prompts us to consider whether both poetic imagination and its rhetorical counterpart might have a mimetic component—a projective function or representational impulse—that can be judged in terms of verisimilitude rather than logical status. King's vision of an emancipated future outlines a possible world, a future America in which actions that might conflict with the conventions of the present (African-American people voting, attending the same schools as white people, etc.) become plausible, and where it is possible for actors previously separated precisely by a conventional way of understanding social life to interact. Understood as "the sedimented universe of conventional ideas," doxa renders such actions and interactions improbable, and diagnoses that a speech created to describe them cannot persuade. But a lot of Americans, black and white, agreed to follow King's dream and to contribute to the creation of a new America. To contemplate the future world envisioned by the reverend required a questioning of the conventions that define the present one, of the assumed status quo, of the existing idea of social normalcy. In this respect, King's speech makes similar demands from the audience as Homer when depicting the Trojan heroes dying in battle. These demands concern an effort to relate to something that is not actually happening in front of your eyes. In neither case is certainty a relevant issue, or an adequate standard for evaluating the kinds of claims advanced by King or Homer. Obviously, poetic imagination does not set out to require a follow-up action in any concrete or immediate sense, as we do not read *Hamlet* and decide to avenge his father ourselves, even though in some cases literature can be a powerful incentive for action. On the other hand, a rhetorical imagination represents a direct and intentional propeller to action, as it identifies a probable realm not to make it an object of contemplation but to urge us to actualize it. Seen in Ricoeur's terms, then, rhetorical imagination becomes the link between an existing and a preferred state of affairs.

The importance of such a link has already been recognized, and explained as an existential mission of rhetoric. "By voicing the possible," John Poulakos maintains,

> the rhetor discloses his vision of a new world to his listeners and invites them to join him there by honoring his disclosure and by adopting his suggestions. Essentially, he is asking them to abandon the shelter of their prudential heaven and opt for that which exists "by favor of human imagination and effort." Of course, the risk always exists that the audience may decline his invitation. But this is a risk he must face if he dares stand up and offer an alternative to the mundane, the mediocrity, or misery of those he wishes to address. (qtd. in Luicates and Condit, 31)

But what we still need to ask ourselves is: how can a rhetor prepare to face such a noble risk? How can we invite audiences to go beyond the known and the familiar and to imagine new things, while also recognizing that doxa, the "sedimented universe of conventional ideas" is the foundation of persuasion? In King's speech the ability to imagine another world is not conditioned, or even aided by emotions, even though in the end the speech is intended to trigger a feeling of exhilaration about a better future. If it doesn't rely on emotions to create verisimilitude, what does a rhetorical imagination require in order to be effective? An answer to this question would allow us to understand how it is possible to strike a balance between convention and novelty, and to see how doxa can facilitate persuasion without, however, impeding change. But to find such an answer requires a refining of the concept of imagination that is at stake here.

A Rhetorical Concept of Imagination

Ricoeur is hardly the first theorist to suggest that the imagination be allowed a place in the rhetorical vocabulary. The concept has long been part of the rhetorical tradition, even though its meaning and value have varied widely from one epoch to another or even within the same period. In the Enlightenment alone, for example, the imagination was seen as the main faculty of creativity and invention, but also as the source of manipulation and deceit. It was also in the Enlightenment that the connection between the imagination and cognition was articulated explicitly through the works of the Scottish commonsense philosophers, David Hume in particular, and enthusiastically adopted by rhetoricians like George Campbell. But even though Campbell was attracted to the idea that images give force to arguments because thought processes are grounded in operations that involve the imagination—resemblance, contiguity, and causality—he, along with most rhetoricians, was ultimately interested in the imagination as a stylistic feature (Walzer, 72). Campbell read Hume's notion of a "lively idea" that captures the imagination in Quintilian's terms, with an emphasis on "lively"—as vivacious, arresting language or somehow memorable style of communication—rather than on "idea," as a cognition or argumentation (Walzer, 74).

Perhaps Campbell's preference for grounding imagination in style had something to do with the obfuscation the concept is likely to produce when taken beyond the concreteness of particular expressions. From Aristotle's indictment of imagination as inferior to reason, to Immanuel Kant's concern that the imagination remains, in the final analysis, impenetrable, the concept has systematically proven to be recalcitrant and difficult to handle. This difficulty is in part a consequence of the concept's relational nature, its entanglements in a series of shifting dichotomies, such as present/absent, real/fictive, experienced/desired, and perceived/conceived. In a comprehensive study of the major conceptual transformations of "imagination," Wolfgang Iser has argued that the variation in the meaning of the noun reflects differences in how the adjective "imaginary" has been attributed to a product or to a process, in other words, to certain entities or to the ability to conceive them. In some meanings of the term, the focus has been on the things (e.g., Humpty-Dumpty or a unicorn) and their reunion into a set that is potentially well structured and thus, identifiable as a "world" paralleling the realm of experience or perception (Pavel, 234). At the same time, Iser points out, the ability to conceive of such a world can be defined in static or dynamic terms, as a mental faculty, or as an act committed consciously. Imagination, then, can be seen as an intentional act of consciousness, and "imaginary" as the attribute of process through which consciousness creates certain objects for particular purposes.

The existence of a group as a social entity, Ricoeur points out, requires such an act of imagination: the individuals in that group must explicitly and actively imagine themselves as a group, or else they are not. Ricoeur maintains that "perhaps there is no social group without this indirect relation to its own being through a representation of itself" (TA, 183). From Mannheim, he borrows the idea that a social sphere emerges from imaginative acts that reinforce each other dialectically, one by constantly reinstating a particular state of affairs, and the other by challenging it and suggesting alternatives. The first impulse connects actors to their communities, while the second forces communities to come undone and to become reconstituted differently.

Ricoeur is not the first to fashion a theory of imagination for rhetorical use, but his is both different from alternative offers and precisely for that reason relevant to an attempt to reconcile imagination with doxa. Specifically, as I will demonstrate, Ricoeur views imagination in the context of social life, as a conscious act that promotes integration in, as well as transformation of, a community. This conception of imagination marks a shift away from style in order to explain the emergence of common beliefs in a community and the ways in which shared assumptions can be challenged. As such, imagination constructs and deconstructs doxa, drawing on two compensatory mechanisms labeled by Ricoeur as "ideological" and "utopian."

Ideology and Social Life

In "I Have a Dream," the attempt at challenging conventional beliefs through an appeal to imagination belonged to a particular individual. Note, in this respect, that King used the singular first-person pronoun, speaking in his name rather than that of African-Americans. Yet his ultimate goal was to create a vision that would be shared by the community, both black and white. Such a goal is feasible because, as Ricoeur contends, imagination is the basis of intersubjectivity, and as such, the foundation for experience shared with others in the present and over time:

> There is a *historical* field of experience because *my* temporal field is related to another temporal field by what has been called a relation of "pairing" (*Paarung*). . . . These fields are analogous in the sense that each of us can, in principle, exercise the "I" function in the same way *as everyone else* and can impute to himself or herself his or her own experience. It is here that the imagination is implied. . . . The analogy implied in pairing . . . is a transcendental principle according to which the other is another self similar to myself, a self *like* myself. The analogy proceeds here through the direct transfer of the signification "I." *Like* me, my contemporaries, my predecessors, and my successors *can* say "I." It is in this way that I am historically bound to others. . . . The truth of our condition is that the analogical tie that makes every man my brother is accessible to us only through a certain number of *imaginative practices*. (TA, 180–82, Ricoeur's emphasis)

Ricoeur is not alone in associating imagination with the formation of a community. In his *Imaginary Institution of Society*, Cornelius Castoriadis maintained that "a social-historical world is created *ex nihilo* in a burst of imaginative praxis carried out not by conscious individuals or groups but by anonymous masses who constitute themselves as a people in that very act of founding. This world-forming and meaning-bestowing creative force is the social imaginary of the instituting society" (qtd. in Parameshwar, "Toward New Imaginaries," 7). By attributing the emergence of sociohistorical worlds to the imagination, Castoriadis defines the latter as a "generative matrix" that shapes the existence of people living together, without anyone in particular being responsible for the form that communal life takes. Imagination is thus described as a repertoire of beliefs that position people historically and socially through both covert and visible practices—both what we do and do not do, and say and do not say. In this sense, the imaginary is what differentiates "each historical period, its singular manner of living, of seeing and of conducting its own existence, its world, and its relations with this world" (Castoriadis, 145). Arguing from a similar position, Charles Taylor employs the phrase "social imaginary" to refer to the "ways in which people imagine their social existence, how they fit together with others, how things go on between them and their fellows, the expectations that are normally met, and the deeper normative notions and images that underlie these expectations" (Taylor, 106).

As understood by Castoriadis and Taylor, the social imaginary foregrounds collective agency but obscures individual control or intervention. This emphasis on collective imagining, as a repertoire of representations that take shape "through discursive engagement among interlocutors in contexts of varying structure, scope, and formality" (Asen, 349) can benefit studies seeking to uncover doxa, the set of assumptions, values, and beliefs that inform positions and claims. Robert Asen has studied the specific ways in which viewing welfare recipients in the United States as lazy or exploiting the system can inform important political decisions. In situations when the deliberative process is systematically distorted by preexisting beliefs, it is necessary to examine the social imaginary, to foreground background assumptions, and to submit them to critical scrutiny in order to be able to change or discard them. But to critique and question the assumption that "welfare recipients are lazy and do not want to work" is possible only insofar as the assumption is *not* shared by everybody. The social imaginary, on the other hand, especially in the sense defined by Castoriadis and Taylor, comprises ideas with broad coverage, pervasive social habits that spread throughout the entire community and that leave no one untouched. This raises a difficult analytic question: how can shared cultural premises be both broadly representative of a collective's imaginative resources (potentially a very large collective), and identifiable for scrutiny? How can a social group still rely on shared assumptions to entertain new values and beliefs, so that it can eventually shed problematic assumptions, like racial or sexual stereotypes and prejudices? Do we even admit the possibility of social change, or do we follow Castoriadis in his conviction that social-historical formations are incommensurable entities, and hence, when change has occurred we are in effect dealing with a completely different formation? Without leaving some room for individual agency and allowing it to have social impact, a rhetorical, intentional, and audience-oriented function of communication is either completely disabled or reduced to minor instrumentalism.

Ricoeur emphasizes the individual's conscious participation in imaginative practices that lead to the formation of a community, while Castoriadis and Taylor focus on collective and unconscious processes that generate social life. Rhetoricians are perhaps more familiar with the latter view from McGee's work on ideographs. According to McGee, the beliefs that bring together a community become reified in specific words and phrases—ideographs that anchor the circulation of social energy. Focusing on ideographs is supposed to draw attention to the way in which "everyone in society, even the 'freest' of us, seem predisposed to structured mass responses" (McGee, 444). But if all the members of a society are predisposed to "structured mass responses," can they step outside an ideology in order to scrutinize it? If not, who can obtain sufficient critical distance from seemingly inevitable tendencies, in order to be aware of the tendencies and study them? How did King and other like him involved in social and political reform over the years manage to find a vantage point from which to perceive and critique the assumptions they wanted to challenge?

Such dilemmas are the product of a particular understanding of ideology primarily shaped by Marxism, and the solution requires, in Ricoeur's view, a departure from the Marxist tradition. Ricoeur is concerned about the "intellectual baggage" of the term "ideology," impregnated as it is by Marxist assumptions, because they seem to push the notion of pervasiveness to a level at which one can no longer recognize individual freedom of action or intervention. Specifically, he thinks the Marxist definition of ideology limits unnecessarily its functions to the distortion and dissimulation of social reality. But these functions make sense if we think of ideology largely in terms of content. Stressing the influence of Ludwig Feuerbach on Marx's early development of the concept, Ricoeur claims that the ideology *par excellence* that interested Marx (and against which he reacted) was religion. The distorting mechanism of ideological representation, which "makes us take the image for the real, the reflection for the original," was, in Feuerbach's view, the very cornerstone of religious thought, "for it is religion that effects the inversion of heaven and earth" (in Kolakowski, 113–114). But according to Ricoeur, an ideological function can be identified in any system of thought, including science and technology, or even in a certain phase of a community's history, as long as that system of thought is predicated on "an interpretation, in images and representations, of the social bond itself" (TA, 255).

In addition to the familiar Marxist *domination* and *dissimulation*, Ricoeur emphasizes a third function of ideology, *integration*. He argues that all three functions are correlates of ideology's basic role, that of "reinforcing and repeating the social tie in situations that are after-the-fact" (TA, 182). Between our enmeshment and participation in events and our everyday experience on the one hand, and the interpretations that articulate an awareness of such participation and its meaning on the other hand, "simplification, schematization, stereotyping, and ritualization" are bound to arise (TA, 182). These are all interpretive moves that constitute ideology. But if ideology is by necessity interpretive, it need not always be dissimulative. In this respect, Ricoeur adopts a Weberian stance, anchoring ideology in a theory of social actions and relations (TA, 184). According to Max Weber, social action is preconditioned by a belief that general human behavior is meaningful to individual agents, and by the orientation of an individual's behavior toward others' actions and conduct. Ideology, on such an account, is what gives meaning to action from the perspective of specific individuals, in other words, what turns potentially random encounters between individuals or groups, into social relations.

Ricoeur views the signing of the Declaration of Independence as an instance of a specific, concrete action that is meaningful to a group of individuals who thereon recognize themselves as members of the same community, and as creatures defined by specific rights and privileges. Centuries after the signing of the document, that action performed in a distant past carries meaning and significance for actors who never participated directly in it. Ideology is made necessary by temporal distance, by the irreducible gap between the levels of experience and that of interpretation. Its role "is not only to diffuse the conviction beyond the circle of founding fathers, so as to make it the creed of (a completely different) group, but also to perpetuate the initial energy beyond the period of effervescence" (TA, 249). Ideology, then, is both mobilizing, and when needed, justificatory. Therefore, it is the equivalent at a collective level of an individual's motive to act or communicate in certain ways. As social motivation, its fundamental function is to integrate individuals in communities, in order to create and cement social bonds and to offer concretions of identity (TA, 250). It confers legitimacy upon collective action, but such legitimacy can further serve as a basis for *domination*, inasmuch as what ideology legitimizes is "above all, the relation to the system of authority," and "it is when the mediating role of ideology encounters the phenomenon of domination that the distorting and dissimulating character of ideology comes to the fore" (TA, 252). By stressing the connection between ideology and authority, Ricoeur seems to contradict his initial counter-Marxist position. At the very least the difference between the two approaches is reduced to a matter of nuance or degree, rather than to strong disagreement. But for Ricoeur ideological domination does not inevitably lead to false consciousness, as is the case with Marx, because he also allows for a corrective. He views imagination as driven by two seemingly opposed forces, a dispersing one in addition to the integrative force. While ideology integrates individuals into groups, utopian reflection allows individuals to reject or undo the integration.

Transforming Doxa

In addition to the social dimension, Ricoeur also develops his concept of imagination on a cognitive level, by exploring the meaning of the term *image*. He notes that the concept has more than one denotation, as it can be used to refer to absent things (the image of a departed friend), or to nonexistent things (e.g., images produced in a dream or in a literary text). Images, he points out, can also refer to illusions, in a mixed mode, if we understand illusions as "representations that to an external observer or to subsequent reflection are directed to absent or nonexistent things, but that to the subject and in the instant in which they appear are believable as to the reality of their object" (TA, 170). But what all these different usages have in common, according to Ricoeur, is the fact that the varying meanings of "image" reflect differences concerning "whether the subject . . . is or is not capable of assuming a critical consciousness of the difference between the imaginary and the real" (TA, 170). In the absence of critical consciousness, the image is confused with the real, and imagination hence becomes a source of deception. Conversely, at the highest level of perceiving a critical distance between images and real objects, imagination becomes a way of advancing a "critique of the real" (TA, 171). Imagination, in his view, is "the free play of possibilities in a state of noninvolvement with respect to the world of perception or of action. It is in this state of noninvolvement that we try out new ideas, new values, new ways of being in the world" (TA, 174).

In "Imagination in Discourse and in Action," Ricoeur further develops this conception of imagination using linguistic innovation of the sort afforded by metaphors as the prototype:

> Instead of approaching the problem [of imagination] through perception and asking if and how one passes [how the transition occurs] from perception to images, the theory of metaphor invites us to relate imagination to a certain use of language, more precisely, to see in it an aspect of *semantic innovation*, characteristic of the metaphorical use of language. The change in the line of attack is always considerable in itself, so many prejudices having been tied to the idea that the image is an appendix to perception, a shadow of perception. To say that our images are spoken before they are seen is to give up an initial false self-evidence, which holds the image to be first and foremost a "scene" unfolding in some mental "theater" before the gaze of an internal "spectator." But it also means giving up at the same time a second false self-evidence, holding

> that this mental entity is the cloth out of which we tailor our abstract ideas, our concepts, the basic ingredient of some sort of mental alchemy. However, if we do not derive the image from perception, how could we derive it from language? (TA, 171)

Metaphors, as defined by Ricoeur, are predicated on the sudden abolishment of the logical distance between often-incompatible semantic fields. In the same vein, to imagine is to catch a "sudden glimpse of a new predicative pertinence, namely, a way of constructing pertinence in impertinence," and above all, to restructure semantic fields (TA, 173). Recourse to imagination is designed to introduce a "note of suspension" in our general experience, "reviving former experiences, awakening dormant memories, irrigating adjacent sensorial fields" (TA, 175). By emphasizing its similarity to metaphors, Ricoeur views imagination as "a method rather than a content, . . . the very operation of grasping the similar, by performing the predicative assimilation answering to the initial semantic shock. Suddenly, we . . . see old age as the dusk of day, time as a beggar, nature as a temple with living pillars" (TA, 173).

Defined as conceptual innovation that can be assimilated into a common vocabulary, imagination fuels (after having first challenged) doxa. The mechanism that allows it to do so is similar to a linguistic phenomenon, but Ricoeur further explains it as a utopian mode. His understanding of utopia capitalizes on, but also goes beyond the common associations with, a specific genre or author. In the case of utopia, he starts out by exploiting the generic sense consecrated by its creator—that of a fictive idyllic world. "Utopia" was the lexical invention of Sir Thomas More in his 1516 rendition of a heavenly land, described in vivid contrast to a decayed and corrupt England. The word was the Latin translation of the English "nowhere," More's strategy of signaling that the heavenly realm described in the book was nonexistent, not part of a social order as commonly understood. In his understanding of the utopian mode as a compensatory mechanism for the ideological mode, Ricoeur capitalizes on this idea of extraterritoriality, emphasizing utopia's eccentricity to an existing order. "It is indeed starting from this strange spatial extraterritoriality—from this nonplace, in the literal sense of the word—that we are able to take a fresh look at our reality; hereafter, nothing about it can continue to be taken for granted" (TA, 184). The function of utopias, then, is to effect a separation from our everyday world and the things with which we are so familiar that we no longer look at them with a critical eye: "Utopia is the mode in which we radically rethink the nature of family, consumption, government, religion, and so on. From "nowhere" emerges the most formidable challenge to what-is" (TA, 184). Most importantly, utopia does not mean "never": the utopian mode projects one outside one's familiar universe of reference, but it is not tantamount with a never attainable fantasy world. For utopia to function as a form of imagination that challenges doxa, it must operate a rapprochement between the nonexistent and the possible.

But Ricoeur is reluctant to argue for a utopian mode of argumentation as the corrective to ideological domination. On his account, utopias can develop into pathologies, whenever the utopian mode is pursued for its own sake as escapism rather than as a prelude to action and as a source of critical distance and reflection enabling. Ricoeur perceives escapism as an attempt to "delineate self-contained schemas of perfection severed from the whole course of the human experience of value," and thus, as "the eclipse of praxis, the denial of the logic of action" (TA, 322). The relation between ideology and utopia is a dialectical one: integration, in Ricoeur's view, is not possible without an awareness of alternatives.

If utopias emancipate and distance us from our conventional practices, their function is obviously the reverse of that of ideology: while the latter integrates individuals into an existing social matrix, the former provides the possibility of social subversion, by creating a vantage point from which the seemingly "given" can be questioned and a replacement considered. If the effectiveness of ideology rests on a surplus value—that gap between legitimacy claims and beliefs—utopia serves as a way to uncover the surplus, and thus "to unmask the pretense common to all systems of legitimacy" (TA, 184). Hence, when an ideology becomes a form of domination, one way in which the domination can be exposed, possibly overthrown, is through utopian construction or reflection. We see precisely such reflection in King's depiction of a future in which all Americans, black and white, would be equal, and the utopian thrust of such reflection is signaled by the framing of the depiction in a dream. The projection is not utopian in the sense of being impossible to achieve or unrealistic, but in the sense of being radically distinct from the given state of affairs. The utopian mechanism allows King to separate himself and his audience from the present, in order to look critically at it. Through a utopian projection of an enlightened future, he seeks an alternative order in order to find a vantage from which to analyze the present and to challenge its conventions.

IMPLICATIONS FOR ANALYSIS

It is fair to ask whether Ricoeur's refining of the traditional concept of doxa has explanatory value, especially of a sort unavailable from competing models of analysis. His main contribution in this respect lies in facilitating an integrated analysis based on reading rhetorical interventions through the lenses of a concept of doxa redefined from Ricoeur's perspective. Take again the case of King's "I Have a Dream." While the overall suasive power of the speech has never ceased to impress audiences and critics, its discursive mechanisms have been explained very differently. Some critics focus on the biblical allusions and eschatological vision; others dissect the ideological assumptions at stake in King's understanding of "equality"; others yet focus on his construction of temporality as urgency; or, finally, others focus on the orator's delivery or verbal performance. Clearly, these are all valuable rhetorical features. Can they all be explained in one integrating approach?

The vast majority of accounts agree that "I Have a Dream" is structured according to the conventions of the epideictic genre, and that its force lies in the speaker's ability to move the audience and to stir up their imagination, rather than in being constructed in an argumentation mode per se. But what exactly enabled this imagination-based appeal and made it both opportune and lasting has been analyzed by many. In and of itself, the lack of a scholarly consensus on this matter is insignificant, and it might in fact attest to the complexity of the object of investigation. Yet at the same time, the divergence of opinions concerning the source of King's persuasiveness is in part based on the assumption that some concepts have more explanatory value than others, such as ideograph over temporality, or delivery over style. Ricoeur's elaboration of doxa provides a framework that makes such rivalries unnecessary. Reviewing briefly the rhetorical scholarship on this particular speech, I want to show that seemingly distinct explanatory concepts employed in rhetorical analysis can be integrated under the coherent overarching banner of doxa, as redefined with Ricoeur's help.

The emphasis on the ideological dimension of the speech is apparent in John Louis Lucaites and Celeste Michelle Condit's analysis, which argues that the public legacy of "I Have a Dream" concerns King's effort to define "equality." Lucaites and Condit view "equality" as an ideograph, in the sense established by McGee. According to them, in 1961, this ideograph had a meaning and significance that had been fundamentally shaped within the ideological discourse of the *white* Founding Fathers. King sought to redefine it as an inclusive notion, hospitable to the black citizens of America. King's rhetorical exigency, by such an account, seemed almost impossible to address at the time of its undertaking: caught in the "double-consciousness" of African-American rhetoric, the preacher was seeking recognition for black people while also trying to avoid "sacrificing the difference that made them inherently unique and individual" (Lucaites and Condit, 89). In other words, precisely because equality was one of the main tenets of an ideology whose function was at that point one of *domination*, to invoke it as a strategy of emancipation of the *dominated* might seem to be self-undermining. But King did not rely on some preexisting meaning of "equality" as an ideograph. Rather, his strategy was to articulate a definition in the speech itself, as the very foundation upon which a national American identity rested: "the commitment to 'equality' that he expressed presumed what he called the 'beloved community,' a world defined in terms of the total assimilation and integration of all races and creeds" (Lucaites and Condit, 93). Put differently, King exploited an ideological concept, that of equality, for its *integrative* function. Yes, equality defined the identity of the Founding Fathers, and because the black citizens of this country are Americans, too, they share the basic ideological beliefs, rights, and privileges, which shaped the very notion of an American identity. The logic of the argument, thus explained by Lucaites and Condit, can strike some readers as flawed: it relies on a historical fallacy that conflates chronologically distinct notions of citizenship and national identity, in Lincoln's time and those shaped by subsequent social and political developments. In Ricoeur's view, however, such conflation is precisely what allows ideology to function as integration, with its two-forked subfunction: mobilization and justification. What Ricoeur says about the "foremost task" of productive imagination turned oppressive or dissimulating, captures eloquently King's rhetorical task: "to keep alive all the types of mediations that constitute historical ties, and among these, the institutions [or ideas] that objectify social ties and ceaselessly transform the 'us' into the 'them'" (TA, 180).

King relies on the integrative function of ideology in generalizing the concept of "equality," and in rendering historical distance moot. But his recourse to an ideological function to challenge doxa cannot be reduced to the use of the word "equality," which is only mentioned a few times in the speech. Rather, King's conversion of ideology from domination to integration is grounded in a variety of specific discursive strategies—the theological rhetoric that allows him to invoke a generic person, created in God's image; the accumulation of the personal plural "we" in varying referential contexts: for black people, Americans in general, and our ancestors; and specific metaphors, particularly that of the promissory note, which links the past to the present. With these devices, King encourages his 1960s heterogeneous audience to see themselves as a historical community that includes people who lived in Lincoln's time and the speaker's contemporaries.

In addition to pleading for equality among all American citizens, including African-Americans, King advocated civil disobedience, a direct challenge to doxa, yet this was different from the use of force demanded by Malcolm X. The reverend encourages disobedience and conveys a sense of immediacy and urgency, but critics have tried to separate these two goals, or to foreground one over the other. J. Robert Cox, for example, insists that the main function of "I Have a Dream" was to define the present as "morally-charged, urgent" (Cox, 204) in order to fight the doctrine of gradualism, which promoted moderation in modifying the social order, over radical, immediate change. In response to Cox, Hariman wants to restore the analytic priority of ideological concerns, arguing that "King's rhetoric does aim to legitimize change, but that change only appears to require urgent action if it is set against the ideology of white resistance" (Hariman, 206). In fact, according to Hariman, King was reinforcing at least some of the main assumptions of gradualism by advocating nonviolence. Even worse, he may have ultimately fallen prey to the *dominating* function of ideology, by romanticizing history, both the one that was and the one to come, and thus "failing to accept that American racial conflict has not just a present, but a past, and that solutions to our problems lie not in divining the future, or even calling it to us, but in challenging the continuities of injustice of our time" (Hariman, 217). What Hariman does not tell us, is how such challenging might become possible, especially when the continuities of injustice in question have a debilitating effect on groups and individuals. Through visions of an idyllic past and a prophetic future, King invited the audience to engage in the kind of utopian reflection theorized by Ricoeur. Utopia functioned as a way of gaining perspective and of distancing them from a present informed by practices and conventions that encouraged racism. Only when such distancing was achieved could King make the present an object of reflection in order to charge it morally and to advocate change.

RECLAIMING THE INDIVIDUAL

King's vision of a better future was crucial in galvanizing social energies toward the achievement of specific ideals. In celebrating his legacy we recognize the power of individuals to envision and initiate change, and indeed much of rhetoric's history is staked on the idea of individual agency. In fact, individual agency is glorified in every enthusiastic reception of a famous speech, as the speaker is seen as its creator. This is a truism, of course, but one we choose to ignore when we opt with equal enthusiasm for theories predicated on the "demise" of individual authorship. Ricoeur never lets go entirely of the issue of individuals' assent and ability to see the available means of persuasion, in Aristotle's terms. He posits a correlation between ideology as a source of authority and individuals' willingness to acknowledge it:

> The relation between the claim issued by the authority and the belief that responds to it is essentially asymmetrical. I shall say that there is always more in the claim that comes from the authority than in the belief that is returned to it. I see therein an irreducible phenomenon of surplus value, if by that we understand the excess of the demand for legitimation in relation to the offer of belief. (TA, 252)

Leaving room for individual agency depends crucially on this "surplus." The extent to which a rhetor can challenge an existing ideology is conditioned by the asymmetry that Ricoeur posits. That there can be a disparity between the authority of a collective and individual belief or assent is a philosophical statement on Ricoeur's part, rather than an empirical observation. And as a philosophical statement, it is vulnerable to a skeptic's claim that such a gap does not really exist. One way to back up Ricoeur's view is to look more closely at historical circumstances that seem to support the very opposite perspective. It has been argued that in totalitarian societies, for example, the dominant (and dissimulating) ideology engulfs all sectors of public and even private life, and hence leaves no room for disbelief. Ricoeur has taken a sustained interest in the totalitarian regimes of Eastern Europe in his contributions to political philosophy, so it seems fitting to submit his theory to the analytic test of an intervention produced in communist Czechoslovakia.

Consider the eulogy presented by Václav Havel in 1988 at the funereal services for František Kriegel, a reputed physician, government official, and political leader in the Czech communist party. The epideictic conventions of the genre would have required it to focus on the features of the individual in question, evoking and praising him. But Havel did not enumerate the dead man's virtues, dwelling instead on what he deemed to be a fundamental contradiction: Kriegel's ideological commitment (as expressed by the membership in the Communist Party) and his personal moral values. Even though Havel does not assert explicitly that there is an insurmountable conflict between being a good man and being a communist, the dichotomy emerges clearly from his depiction of Kriegel's ideological convictions as incommensurable with his "profound respect for the pre-ideological ethical tenets held by those who truly live in the everyday world." Due to his unselfishness and dedication to his fellow-citizens Kriegel wanted to become involved in public life, to play a role in the decision-making process of his community. Yet by taking on a public position and by becoming a politician and later a government official, he also became a spokesperson for the dominating ideology. The eulogy describes the deceased's private moral standards as incompatible with "the ideology . . . of a movement that has managed to exalt—and hence readily manipulate—the imaginary world of so-called higher interests and universal ideals above that of ordinary human feelings and common sense" (Havel, 234). František Kriegel, Havel concludes, was the embodiment of a tragic paradox: a good man who served a bad regime.

Nowhere did Havel explicitly attack communism—in 1988 Czechoslovakia doxa, or dogma rather, made such public defiance liable to immediate and severe repression. But because his assertions were advanced in an epideictic context designed to valorize the *individual* features of the dead, their critical force emerged clearly and recognizably. Specifically, his criticism of communism stemmed from the very mention of the asymmetry between ideological claims to authority and individual responses to them. Kriegel responded to such claims and accepted the Communist ideology, but it was his option rather than a necessity: One could argue that such an asymmetry leads ultimately to a tragic paradox, and ask whether František and others like him living in totalitarian societies really did have an alternative to becoming a Communist, if they also wanted to act publicly, to "get involved," and to help people in a society where such involvement was mediated by the dominating ideology of communism. Was the option a necessity after all?

Havel did not respond directly in that eulogy, but his own dissident stance throughout the decades of communist ruling is an eloquent answer, and a negative one. Not only did he not take the same route as Kriegel and conveyed his anti-Communist beliefs directly, but even that eulogy was a form of participating in public discourse, and it provided him with a strategic medium of expression in which to challenge official (not just shared) assumptions. It is also indicative that one of Havel's most efficient forms of protest—which was widespread in Communist Eastern Europe—was literature: through the imaginative projections afforded by his literary characters, the playwright offered the audience ways in which to envision an alternative, better world, and ultimately the moral support they needed to overthrow communism. Along with Martin Luther King Jr., Havel illustrates Ricoeur's philosophical credo that individuals can uncover and challenge deep-seated, indeed concealed assumptions, "stir[ring] up the sedimented universe of conventional ideas" (RPH, 66) through acts of imagination comparable to a poetic experience, yet resolutely rhetorical in purpose and nature.

Conclusion

The classical tradition relegated rhetorical discourse to the province of probable knowledge, because such discourse rests on beliefs, customs, and values shared by a given community under specific circumstances. Yet in a Western intellectual tradition striving more and more arduously to achieve certainty, a discipline married to contingency and probability is forced to defend itself over and over again. Much effort has gone into such defenses, and significantly less has been spent on refining our understanding of how probable knowledge takes shape and then how it persuades, whether it can be systematically accounted for, emulated, or analyzed with any rigor. Ricoeur's treatment of imagination, as both social and cognitive in mechanism and purpose, furthers our understanding in this neglected yet important direction. The notion of doxa conceived through recourse to Ricoeur's notion of imagination as either an ideological and/or a utopian practice foregrounds individual agency, in contrast to approaches that obscure it. Both ideology and utopia are frequently associated with obliterations of concrete individual action, one because it insists on the bonds that form a social network rather than the nodes themselves, and the other because it propagates ideals of communal fusion in which the network functions so well that its nodes are basically reducible to the whole. By writing the individual back into the social imaginary, Ricoeur is true to one of the core values of the rhetorical tradition. At the same time, his commitment to individual agency encourages us try to find ways in which it is possible to think about large-scale phenomena, such as social or political change, in connection to specific actions or verbal interventions of the individuals involved.

Chapter Three

Practical Reasoning

> Nothing is more necessary today than to renounce the arrogance of critique and to carry out with patience the endless work of distancing and renewing our historical substance. (TA, 129)

The contingent nature of rhetorical discourse—its very hallmark by Ricoeur's and others' account—requires some form of epistemic compensation, if it is to have any pragmatic value. For how can it be possible, as Plato insisted we wonder, to produce valid responses to the problems of social life from the thickness of contingency, and with no recourse to any general principles? The importance of this question hardly needs to be emphasized: it is, after all, what has put the discipline of rhetoric in a state of perpetual defensiveness, especially in relationship to philosophy. One frequently offered answer, originating in Aristotle, tries to define a particular *rhetorical* form of rationality that would enable such interventions and make them effective. Thus, *rhetorical reason* "broadens the idea of what is reasonable well beyond the analytical, the demonstrative, and the calculable" (Gross and Dearin, 28); "its investigation bears upon discourse which allows a place to the non-conventional, to the implicit, to the indeterminate . . . which affects ideas and which is manifested when the meaning attributed to these latter finds itself contested either by a new truth or by a new situation" (Loreau, 457–58). But such definitions still leave the question in part unanswered: how is rhetorical reason achieved, what allows it to function efficiently and can it be taught or is it completely ad hoc and intuitive?

In Aristotle's design, rhetorical discourse required a special faculty called "practical reasoning" (or "wisdom"), *phronesis*, defined as experiential, moral judgment operating in lived situations by combining the generality of reflection on principles with the particularity of perception into concrete circumstances. Aristotle stressed the *nontheoretical* aspect of phronesis by contrast to the knowledge offered by scientific demonstrations. But does that mean that practical reasoning is entirely devoid of a reflection that could transcend the situation at hand? The contrastive element—between practical and scientific reasoning—that was introduced by Aristotle, has had the effect of obscuring the reflexivity specific to phronesis. My goal in this chapter is to enlist Ricoeur's help in recovering the reflective dimension of phronesis as knowledge that comes from history or from some set of rhetorical precedents that can be adopted to new situations. Thus approached, phronesis is essentially interpretive and adaptive—the first being the reason why rhetorical discourse cannot depend upon strict formulas, and the second a mark of prudence. Aristotle defined practical reasoning as a faculty of judgment that is needed in deliberative matters that require the ability to make the right choice with little or no recourse to any formal decision procedure (*Nichomachean Ethics*, 1144a23-8). Indeed, since Aristotle we commonly recognize that a rhetor needs practical reasoning when confronted with a choice among several possible courses of action, none more obviously necessary or useful than the others. From an Aristotelian perspective, to reason practically is to be able to discern the salient features of the task at hand, to see the connection between the particular occasion in, and a more general category of, similar instances, to understand chains of events that have led to the existence of such a category, and to be able to anticipate how the decision made will affect future actions. These features allow an agent endowed with practical reasoning to opt for a course of action, which she can also explain to others who are concerned about the fulfillment of a particular goal or intention. Practical reasoning, in other words, represents a combination of invention and proof, giving rhetors the ability to see solutions to particular problems and then to also convince others to adopt them.

The very existence of such a concept in our theoretical vocabulary reveals the practical dimension of rhetoric as a *techne*. In his reflections on the classical rhetorical legacy, Ricoeur defines techne as "something more refined than a routine or empirical practice, [which] in spite of its focus on production, . . . contains a speculative element, namely a theoretical inquiry into the means applied to production. It is a method; and this feature brings it closer to theoretical knowledge than to routine" (RP, 340). Similarly, practical reasoning—as recognized by Aristotle as well as by Ricoeur—is not merely inspired momentary intervention but rather a systematic investigation into the conditions that have led to a certain exigency and to the general criteria by which an intervention can be planned and assessed. The concept of practical reasoning I propose here draws on Ricoeur's work from two directions, his philosophy of action and his hermeneutical theory. In *From Text to Action* Ricoeur defines practical reasoning as the ability to identify a course of action in response to a particular problem and to account for the choice from the more general perspective that explains acts that are deemed comparable. The first aspect represents the "conditions of intelligibility," while the second refers to the "conditions of desirability." The abstractness of these terms, in part an effect of the translation from the original French, might easily obscure the direct link to the inventive and probative dimensions mentioned earlier. Take the case of a president who opts for military intervention as the course of action when his country has been attacked. The conditions of intelligibility refer to the identification of different actions (asking people in uniform to fire guns at others who are considered enemies, manufacturing weapons, overthrowing foreign governments, etc.) as steps in a concerted effort to address the exigency. The conditions of desirability identify that particular military intervention as a just, retaliatory war of the sort that has previously solved similar problems. The first category cannot be separated from the second, because it is only when intelligibility has been matched with desirability that we can even use the vocabulary I employed, and refer to some as "enemies" and "prisoners," and to others as "heroes" and "martyrs" even though in practice all may have engaged in the same practice. Practical reasoning is faulty when the match can be questioned, allowing the "war" to be called an "occupation," or the "liberators" "invaders."

In his philosophy of action Ricoeur views practical reasoning as what allows agents to move back and forth from the particular to the general and from empirical practice to theoretical reflection. His hermeneutical theory allows us to understand *how* such a shift occurs, and identifies history as the plane of the general and as the source of the theoretical speculation in question. Ricoeur describes the connection between the general and the particular as the result of an interpretive effort that matches conditions of intelligibility with the larger categories of desirability. Given the interpretive act at its core, practical reasoning faces one of the fundamental epistemic issues that have confronted hermeneutical theory over the ages: what makes a certain interpretation more reliable than, or preferable to, others? How to best go about matching intelligibility with desirability, and the particular with the general, making certain, for instance, that a war is perceived as just and emancipatory? The second direction I pursue in this chapter delves into Ricoeur's own hermeneutical theory, searching for clues for how to address the epistemic question of the fit between the two components of practical reasoning.

Throughout the chapter I use two cases of rhetorical discourse, relying on history to articulate the interpretive dimension of practical reasoning as established with Ricoeur's help: the 1858 debates between Abraham Lincoln and Stephen Douglas, and the speech delivered by President William Jefferson Clinton at a black Baptist church in Memphis in 1993.

WISDOM FROM THE PAST

To many Europeans—and Ricoeur is no exception—Americans often seem to be oblivious to the past, obsessed with the future, and impatient with the present. Yet when it comes to framing persuasive communication, the past seems no less important in America than in the Old World: "Nearly all twentieth-century presidents (in the United States) have turned to history," observes a critic, "to find justification for the policies they have wished to pursue" (Stampp, 17). This remark will surely not fail to remind the reader of some famous examples. I will stop at a familiar one: the debate between Lincoln and Douglas during the political campaign of the 1850s, and its heavy reliance on historical arguments. On more than one occasion, Lincoln invoked the famous phrase from the Declaration of Independence, "all men are created equal," whether his goal was to discuss the general principles based on which national identity was shaped (in the Gettysburg address), or to promote specific antislavery policies. His frequent appeals to history have been explained as a cultural habit characteristic of nineteenth-century America, rather than Lincoln's particular mark. Indeed, Douglas, his opponent in the presidential campaign of 1860, also used history but to the opposite end, in order to advance anti-abolitionist views. In Douglas's reading of the Declaration of Independence, the principle of equality referred strictly to white men of European descent, and was intended as a political statement announcing the emancipation from British tutelage.

The disagreement between Lincoln and Douglas can be explained as a failure to present a particular reading of the past and of a particular historic text as accurate and reliable over competing interpretations. Neither man succeeded in truly making history his ally, as neither managed to recommend a particular course of action that would resonate with the experience of the audience. In each case, the interpretation of the action in question—the abolition or preservation of slavery—failed to explain it uncontroversially as faithful to the principles inherited from the Founding Fathers. To be sure, there were segments of the American public that accepted both arguments, some Lincoln's and some Douglas's. That there was no consensus on the issue has been explained as an indication that nineteenth-century America was undergoing a crisis of its own cultural identity (which ultimately led to the war) that made many things contentious, including history. But history inevitably constitutes a plane of generality that is too inclusive for a domain—rhetorical discourse—fundamentally committed to the particularity, and must hence be submitted to a process of interpretation that would yield a particular scenario. This hermeneutical challenge, however, has not prevented history from continuously sponsoring important arguments in the public and political arena. We ought to ask, then: why such frequent appeal to a potentially problematic source of argumentation?

The debate between Lincoln and Douglas is commonly explained as a confrontation between historical perspectives, and the disagreement is usually seen as the consequence of the two men's conflicting beliefs. Each of them used a different historical argument to advance his political agenda, strategically drawing on the "filiopiety of the age" (Zarefsky, 143). History, then, had a culturally enforced *probative* value: if either party could convincingly have shown that his reading of the Declaration is correct, he would have proven the other wrong. But if Lincoln's and Douglas's different understandings of the Founding Fathers' philosophy shaped their different political positions, and if their conflicting beliefs truly ensued from conflicting interpretations, then history also had an *inventive* value. Such an inventive value is not accidental or limited to the Declaration of Independence: historical documents form traditions, and as a repository of "conceptions of symbolic relationships among problems, persons, interests, and actions, which imply (when accepted) certain notions of preferable public behavior" (Farrell, "Knowledge," 4), tradition is a concrete and perceptible presence in everyday life, as well as an abstract force that can give meaning to our experiences and practices. In Ricoeur's view, a tradition constitutes a community of interpretation without which "no transference, no translation [of meanings] is possible" (RPH, 68). Different generations might have widely distinct views, norms, and expectations, but as members of a historical community they nevertheless share an allegiance to crucial documents that continue to regulate their life. Studying the formation of tradition through texts constitutes the domain of hermeneutics. The original objects of hermeneutical study were religious, legal, and philological texts. What these texts have in common is that they define traditions, seen as higher grounds of meaning in accordance to which one could make sense of various experiences at a local, specific level. Hermeneutics situated the general in history, in previous experiences reified and crystallized in a practical knowledge that can inform present practice and provide guidance for dealing with contingent matters that do not readily lend themselves to abstraction or generalization. By seeking to provide an understanding of legal, scriptural, or philological texts, hermeneutics represents an effort to create points of access between such a level of general signification and particular applications.

Ricoeur is best known for creating a "hermeneutics of suspicion," which demands that the interpreter suspend any assumption about what a text might mean, as she continues nevertheless to believe that, and to act as though the meaning of a text is readily available and can be recovered. Such hermeneutics challenges the facility but not the accessibility of a point of contact between the world of a text and those who seek to enter it. Through this distinction, Ricoeur seeks to preserve the correlation posited by Gadamer between tradition and knowledge. According to Ricoeur,

> Gadamer's distinctive contribution concerns, first, the link he establishes, purely phenomenologically as it were, between prejudice, tradition, and authority; second, the ontological interpretation of this sequence in terms of the concept of *wirkungsgeschichtliches Bewusstsein*, which I shall translate as "consciousness exposed to the effects of history" or "consciousness of historical efficacy"; and third, the epistemological or "metacritical" consequence, as Gadamer calls it in his *Kleine Schriften*, that an exhaustive critique of prejudice—and hence of ideology—is impossible, since there is no zero point from which it could proceed. (TA, 278)

Gadamer had a Romantic conception of tradition, seeing it as a formative influence on behaviors and attitudes. As a set of beliefs inherited from the past, prejudice, for him, crucially informs understanding of everyday experiences and the world in which they take place. By contrast, Habermas, who, according to Ricoeur, subscribed to an Enlightenment view of tradition, discredited prejudice in favor of a rationalist view of understanding, which emphasized objectivity and detachment. Gadamer, however, ontologized tradition by describing it as an inescapable dimension of the human existence. He emphasized the interconnectedness of experience, while also pointing out that the disagreements often accompanying questions about the past reflect an awareness of cultural and temporal distance between *now* and *then*. Such an awareness defines the human condition, and Gadamer sees the realization that meaning-making is grounded in history as the fundamental characteristic of consciousness.

Gadamer elaborated on this idea in a crucial passage that draws Ricoeur's attention:

> We are always situated in history . . . I mean that our consciousness is determined by real historical becoming in such a way that it does not have the freedom to situate itself over against the past. In addition, I mean that for us it is always a matter of becoming conscious once again of the action exerted upon us in this way, so that every past that we have just experienced obliges us to take complete charge of it, to assume in a way its truth. (TA, 158)

On Ricoeur's reading, this passage articulates the idea that the meaning of the present is an effect of the past, and consciousness is an awareness of the "effectiveness" of history. On Gadamer's account, understanding is possible as the result of a fusion of the horizon of the present and that of the past (*Horizontverschmelzung*), which allows a calibration of perceptions and beliefs, providing a way in which we can step out of the immediate context in which a particular experience unfolds. At the same time, though, as Ricoeur points out, for Gadamer "there is no *overview* [or privileged standpoint] that would enable us to grasp in a single glance the totality of effects" (TA, 281). By this logic, then, to try to look objectively at history and to gain an uncontroversial understanding of the past is tantamount to trying to jump out of one's skin. Does such historical embeddedness, then, commit us to the inevitability of systematic distortions, as Habermas insisted in his criticism of Gadamer? Were Lincoln and Douglas, each differently but both inevitably, distorting the past in order to support their own agenda?

In response to such concerns, Ricoeur has maintained that "it is possible to place oneself in another point of view and in another culture" (TA, 282). Such a possibility crucially informs the decisions and actions that we make in the present, for "only insofar as I place myself in the other's point of view do I confront myself with my present horizon, with my prejudices (TA, 283). Historical reflection allowed Lincoln to step outside the framework of his time, and to discover alternative frameworks within which all individuals could be equal and slavery unacceptable. But if history is inevitably the subject of multiple interpretive reconstructions, how could it provide evidential support in a debate that needed to promote one particular viewpoint over another? Was the appeal to the Founding Fathers, inasmuch as it required interpretive mediation, bound to have no probative value, despite the historicist inclinations of the period?

The dilemma confronting us can be traced to an essential tension between the act of interpretation—as amenable to more than one end result—and the focus on controversy at the center of rhetorical discourse in general. It is such a tension that has led Ricoeur to insist on maintaining a separation between rhetoric and hermeneutics. His agonistic conception of rhetoric—as a confrontation of opinions of which one must win—clashes with his irenic definition of hermeneutics. Emphasizing the openness of the interpretive process, which does not set out to discard some accounts in favor of others, Ricoeur concludes that

> faced with this hermeneutical freedom, one could say that the task of an art of interpretation, compared to one of argumentation, is less to win acceptance for one opinion over another than to allow a text to signify as much as it *can*: not to signify one thing rather than another but to "signify more," and thus to make us "think more" according to Kant's expression in the *Critique of Judgment* (*mehr zu denken*). (RPH, 69)

In Ricoeur's view, the "surplus of signification" introduced by the interpretive process is a consequence of the fact that texts "travel" in time, always reaching newer audiences and extending beyond the circumstances of their production and the readership that first had access to them. If writing, as a medium, enables a message to be available to a reader who was not born when and where the message originated, interpretation is the intellectual process that conditions its understanding. In so doing, interpretation forces a text to constantly "signify more" than it did to its initial audience and than it was intended to by its author. Hermeneutical freedom is a consequence of the fact that a text continues to signify across audiences and generations, emancipated from its author's intention or from the cultural assumptions once embedded or reflected in it. Yet if cultural traditions can be formed and maintained through sharing the meaning and significance of fundamental texts, there must be a systematic way in which the interpretation of texts can be deemed reliable, and hermeneutical freedom restrained at key moments. At some point, we want the text to reflect its author's intention and the cultural world in which it was created. Ricoeur is willing to admit that this requirement makes it necessary for interpretive processes to have a rhetorical phase:

> compared to rhetoric, hermeneutics possesses argumentative phases, in that it must always explain more for the purpose of understanding better. . . . But its argumentative phases remain a subset of a more vast project, which is certainly not that of re-creating a situation of univocity by thus settling in favor of a privileged interpretation. (RPH, 68–69)

For Ricoeur, the connection between rhetoric and hermeneutics is one of partial inclusion. As an example of hermeneutics freed from the constraints of argumentation, he mentions the "wise decision of the early Christian church to allow the four Gospels, whose differences in intention and organization are obvious, to subsist side by side" (RPH, 69). The four Gospels tell a unique, yet multifaceted story, complementing rather than contradicting each other. Hermeneutical freedom, then, becomes the corollary of multiplicity defined not only in terms of multiple audiences, but also in connection to a rich ontology that resists one unified representation.

Thus redefined, the distinction between rhetoric and hermeneutics also seems to revolve around the nature of the conduct of inquiry in each discipline. In the case of rhetoric, whatever interpretive activity is involved, the inquiry is largely motivated by an ideal of definitiveness and singularity, while in hermeneutics, openness and multiplicity seem to be in order. By such an account, the rhetor's interpretive practice must end conclusively with one admissible interpretation. Even when several possibilities can be equally entertained, their number is ultimately going to be reduced to one in the process of adapting the interpretation to the specific needs of a present, clearly identifiable, audience. Hermeneutical freedom, on the other hand, as I mentioned before, is connected to the constant turnover of audiences, the indefinitely varying demands for adaptation making it impossible for the interpretation of the text in question to be other than a one-many correspondence.

Insofar as they gather around them national communities across centuries, historical documents such as the Declaration of Independence might be interpretively more stable than, for example, literary texts. But over time their reading, too, has supported different goals and has changed accordingly. Any text, regardless of the effort to stabilize its meaning, maintains a "surplus of signification" that encourages different interpretations. The shift from one accepted interpretation to another, or the adjudication of rival readings at any given time requires a constraining of hermeneutical freedom, and indeed marks the transition to the domain of rhetoric. At the same time, it is precisely the "surplus" that enables the rhetorical function, as each interpretation entering the competition finds a justification in the inexhaustibility of the text in question.

From Motive to Intention

As I mentioned earlier, framing arguments historically was common in nineteenth-century America, and it has continued to play an important role in contemporary presidential and political rhetoric. But beyond such specific cultural preferences or generic conventions, recourse to the authority of historical texts assumed to express shared beliefs and values exemplifies the importance of community-enhancing argumentation strategies. In his definition of practical reasoning, Ricoeur puts special emphasis on its communal dimension. He insists on the symmetry between the motive for a particular course of action, as understood by the agent, and the intention for that action, as identified by those who are asked to embark upon it. Through this requirement of symmetry, phronesis becomes a binding force, a way of thinking that promotes individuals' integration in groups. Indeed, for Aristotle, phronesis was a constitutive element of the *polis* insofar as part of an agent's acting rationally was the capacity to consider the consequences of his actions for himself as well as for others, by measuring personal benefits against the public good. From the agent's perspective, phronesis defines the ability to establish conditions of intelligibility for rational, meaningful action. This ability is reflected in how agents can identify correctly what they are doing, and then explain the action by linking it to a motive. But the conditions for intelligibility must be further connected to a category of general "desirability," which operates at a collective (rather than at an individual) as well as more abstract level, where particular cases can be seen as similar or different, and explained through recourse to a larger class to which they are assigned. Practical reason, then, consists in identifying motives for actions, and thus accounting for a particular action "in light of a class of motives capable of explaining other acts as well" (TA, 191). In other words, Ricoeur notes, "explaining an action is interpreting it as an example of a given class of dispositions . . . presenting a character of generality" (TA, 191).

As a shift from intelligibility to general desirability, and from the agent's perspective to a collective, social standpoint, practical reasoning represents an explanatory mechanism. Ricoeur clarifies, "to say that someone acted out of a spirit of vengeance is to say that this disposition brought him to, pushed him to, led him to, made him . . . act this way. This sort of causation invoked here, however, is not linear causation, moving from the antecedent toward the consequence, but teleological causation" (TA, 191). The concept of *teleological causation* was initially proposed by Charles Taylor, who defined it as an explanation "in which the global configuration of events is itself a factor in its own production. To say that an event occurs because it is intentionally aimed at is to say that the conditions that produced it are those which, as belonging to our repertoire of know-how, are called upon, required, and selected to produce the intended event" (Taylor, 191). Put differently, a teleological account assigns an intention, in addition to the motive, offering a specific awareness of how to go about achieving one's goals in a way that can make sense not just to oneself, but also to others. Indeed, by Taylor's and Ricoeur's account, the intention is closely connected to the level of general desirability insofar as to form it is to search through a repertoire of know-how and to select the appropriate item(s). At the same time, though, the intention is assigned *retrospectively* as the action supposed to be based on it is analyzed. The occurrence of a particular action is interpreted and assigned significance from the perspective of other actions, deemed comparable to, or different from, the one under consideration.

The concept of teleological explanation distinguishes motive from intention by associating one with the agent's perspective, and the other with the social order (the others' standpoint). The potential asymmetry between motive and intention is also the main challenge for practical reasoning: an actor might be able to identify a motive that led to a particular action, yet fail to articulate that global configuration within which the action will appear intentional. The correspondence between motive and intention, or intelligibility and desirability is often fraught with difficulty precisely because the alignment between them is not a hard science but an interpretive decision. And to question the compatibility between the two levels—individual and social—or to point to the asymmetry, is to contest the practical reasoning of the agent in question. The death of a person, for example, can be seen as revenge, necessary justice, or unjustified murder. Douglas accused his opponent of advancing unreasonable claims—the abolition of slavery—precisely because he saw Lincoln proposing actions that were incompatible with other actions committed by the Founding Fathers. Practical reasoning, then, depends crucially on the extent to which there is agreement on the interpretation that links motive and intention in a teleological explanation. To obtain such agreement is to constrain the freedom defining hermeneutical projects and to fashion interpretation as a purposeful and strategic activity, in other words, to give it a rhetorical dimension.

To describe this conflation, Steven Mailloux has coined the phrase "rhetorical hermeneutics," which he sees as "historical sets of topics, arguments, tropes, ideologies, and so forth which determine how texts are established as meaningful through rhetorical exchange" (Mailloux, 15). Such rhetorical hermeneutics allowed President Clinton in 1993 to make an effective plea for nonviolence in a black community used to paying heed to messages coming from their own. The president spoke in Memphis, at the same location where Martin Luther King Jr. delivered his last speech. As King did on many occasions, Clinton, too, condemned violence, specifically the violence of self-destruction in the African-American community. His audience was made up of five thousand African-American ministers, who surely knew already that violence is destructive. But what Clinton wanted was to present specific economic reforms and public policies that were part of his political program as a way of improving the lives of African-Americans. Only a few months earlier, another white democratic politician addressed an African-American audience on a similar issue, and he came across as condescending and smug. Clinton's challenge was to avoid such an appearance, and he met it successfully: his arguments were favorably received, and his political program became widely recognized as concerned with the welfare of the African-American population.

In his Memphis address, Clinton sought a commitment to nonviolence from his audience, beyond sheer acceptance of an abstract set of moral values. Practical reasoning allowed him to find an interpretive framework in which such a commitment could be first explained to, and then demanded of, the audience. Clinton proposed something simple and commonsensical enough: that violence must end in African-American communities. But he knew that such action would be embraced by his audience only if he could justify his proposal by locating it in a class of dispositions with a general character—King's philosophy of pacifism. What is most instructive about this approach is the specific way in which the speaker fused what made sense to him to what would also be seen as meaningful and desirable by his audience. Clinton invoked King's principles with such accuracy and poignancy that his speech did not seem to interpret but simply to voice them. As critics have pointed out, he *spoke in King's voice*, appropriating not only ideas but also a framework for presenting them, through a careful selection of stylistic and argumentation patterns that defined King's rhetoric. In Clinton's address, King became present in a manner that made history seem alive, its message loud and clear.

Early on in the speech, the president asked his audience to imagine that the reverend stood by his side ready to give a report card on the last twenty-five years. Encouraging them to think of what he would have to say, Clinton invited the audience to a dialogue not just with King as an individual, remarkable as he was, but with another era from which the present one seemed alienated. For Clinton, King's spirit was the key to an interpretive master code that equated community with love and peace, opposing it to violence. By relying on King's presence, Clinton couched his message in a political, moral, and aesthetic paradigm that placed his speech in what Thomas Farrell calls "an endless succession of discursive acts" defining a tradition (*Norms*, 44). Clinton's summoning of King's spirit to the site of violence in contemporary America was intended to establish a symmetry between what *he* regarded as a reasonable and necessary action—ending the violence—and what the African-American community was likely to see as desirable in that case. Clinton did not issue a personal antiviolence statement. In fact, he proceeded directly to identifying the categories of desirability based on which he could articulate the message for his particular audience. He defined such categories in the beliefs associated with the revered figure of King. Yet Clinton did not simply mention King's name (or any easily recognizable phrase from King's speeches, or a brief summary of King's philosophy). Neither did he try merely to confirm his own views by checking them against those of the minister. He did much more than that, orchestrating a complex revival of King's philosophy by interspersing specific quotes with his own language and ideas, and making stylistic and argumentation choices consonant with the pastor's own preferences (biblical allusions, certain lexical patterns, and specific tropes). Speaking as King was designed to allow Clinton, a white man, to enter a special relationship with his African-American audience, one that would establish a community of interpretation in which the interlocutors would all subscribe to the same values and beliefs, share a language—King's language—and would agree on what it means. This rhetorical strategy was intended to reduce the potential for alienation or misunderstanding, and the successful reception of the speech confirms that it worked well in Clinton's case.

The president could have advocated the ending of violence as an action meaningful in itself, and with a clear motive—if violence doesn't stop, the number of victims will continue to grow until the community is completely destroyed. Instead, he related both the meaning and the motive—the intelligibility criteria—to more general desirability categories, which in this case are represented by King's legacy. Note that it is only when King's legacy has been identified as the "desirability category," that the causal account explaining the connection between ending violence and fostering a sound community becomes teleological. In other words, the transition from the premise (stop the violence) to the conclusion (you'll have a better community) does not constitute a scientific prediction, unrelated to specific circumstances or actors. Rather, this transition marks an intention—to actively preserve King's values, and to recognize them as a legacy.

The practice reflected in the debate between Lincoln and Douglas, or in Clinton's Memphis speech prompts us to consider the epistemic status of the interpretive effort underlining historical reconstruction for communicative-strategic reasons. Should this effort be committed to accuracy, to recapturing the past as it happened? This seems to be the path chosen—although differently—by both Lincoln and Douglas. Or should the interpretive effort be more concerned about the context of the interpretation, and consequently focus on establishing a clear relevance for the present time and its exigencies? Clinton did not try to travel back in time, to King's era. Instead, he summoned King to our time, insisting on the link between past and present. The nature of the distinction between his approach and that illustrated by Douglas and Lincoln is contingent upon how we conceptualize a hermeneutical rhetoric, as a deciphering effort geared toward recovering authorial intentions, or as a strategy of re-creating the world captured by the author in a particular text.

TRUTH OR METHOD?

Lincoln and Douglas appealed to the authority of the Founding Fathers in order to justify their conflicting political positions on the issue of slavery. Both spoke in front of audiences around the country, explaining their political programs and the decisions involved as meaningful, indeed mandatory in accordance with the principles stipulated by the Founding Fathers. History in general, and the Declaration of Independence in particular, provided them with a frame of understanding within which they could present their own actions as reasonable and desirable. But Lincoln was interested in the ideas inherited from history, and read the Declaration as a document that established equality as a universal principle, while Douglas focused on the authors and tried to pin down their intentions by relying on the fact that many of the Founders were slave-owners and continued to own slaves after the Declaration was signed. If the claim that "all men were created equal" referred to people of both European and African descent, how could the Founders not have respected such principle in their own conduct? Lincoln would have to accept that "either the Fathers stood exposed of the basest hypocrisy—an inconceivable position in an age that venerated them so—or else [he] was simply incorrect" (Zarefsky, 150). Yet Lincoln's reading of the famous phrase was no more open to dispute than Douglas's. Some periodicals of the time agreed with Lincoln, others with

Douglas, but there was no overwhelming support for either one. Insofar as the two opponents based their interpretations of the Declaration on the intention of its authors, they were trying to reenact the past by gaining access directly to the mind of the Founding Fathers. The result was that there was no conclusive evidence on either side.

But what kind of evidence could have been deemed conclusive? The entire history of hermeneutics is defined by successive attempts at answering this question, which in more general terms illustrates an epistemic concern with criteria of validity and reliability. What makes some interpretations preferable to others? Or are all interpretations equally admissible? Friedrich Schleiermacher, one of the creators of the discipline, wanted to create a genuine method for providing true access, with no risk of misunderstanding, to scriptural and philological texts. Since the authors of these texts could not be interrogated with regards to their intention, Schleiermacher's work, as described by Ricoeur, aspired to systematicity, to becoming a *Kunstlehre* (methodology) for reaching "the subjectivity of the one who speaks, the language being forgotten" (TA, 57). Schleiermacher failed to develop such a method, but his concern remained a long-lasting one and was inherited by Wilhelm Dilthey. As Ricoeur explains, Dilthey connected the interpretation of texts to "a primordial capacity to transpose oneself in the mental life of others. . . . Man is not radically alien to man, because he offers signs of his own existence. To understand these signs is to understand man" (TA, 59). Thus, the goal of hermeneutics is to provide understanding, which to Dilthey involved empathic identification with, and transposition in, the mind of another human being. By his own maxim, we explain nature, and understand mental life.

Ricoeur reads Gadamer's hermeneutics mainly as an attempt at situating interpretive method between technique and revelation, and thus between Schleiermacher and Dilthey. Indeed, throughout *Truth and Method*, Gadamer wonders whether "truth may be coming to light not simply as the result of a technique—of something that the subject does—but as a result of a something that happens to us over and above our wanting and doing?" (in Howard, 123). Ricoeur doubts that Gadamer in the end managed to develop hermeneutics as a method, and even suggests that the conjunction in the title of his monumental work, *Truth and Method* would do more justice to the project if replaced with a disjunction, *Truth or Method.* Insofar as there is a method in his hermeneutics, it does not offer systematicity, as the veracity it affords cannot be rigorously pursued and is not guaranteed by the structure of the inquiry. For Gadamer, an interpretive method concerns the creation of a fusion of horizons, an interpenetration of two different realms of reference, an alien one recorded in the text, and that in which the interpreter is located.

Many of the arguments exchanged between Lincoln and Douglas reveal the assumption that to understand a text produced in the past is to re-create faithfully the world referenced in it. Douglas, in particular, insisted on recapturing "the realities of 1776." In a speech delivered at Alton, Illinois, Lincoln argued that equality was the Fathers' philosophical conviction, not an empirical description but an ideal principle established as a guide for the future. Signing the Declaration "meant to set up a standard maxim for [a] free society which should be familiar to all; constantly looked to, constantly labored for, and even though never perfectly attained, constantly approximated and thereby constantly spreading and deepening its influence" (qtd. in Zarefsky, 153). Interpreting equality as a statement for the future, rather than as a description of the Founders' present is the direct mark of what Gadamer calls a "consciousness of effective history." Lincoln shows, and attempts to create in his audience, an awareness of the legacy of the past. The Declaration of Independence, and the world in which this document was created, represents a cultural horizon distinct from that of nineteenth-century America. It is from such a historical vantage that Lincoln wants the audiences to consider both his and his opponent's political program. But at the same time, the historical perspective is shaped by the horizon of the present—a time that valued the past, and revered the memory of the Founding Fathers. The fusion of horizons helps explain how Lincoln framed his deliberation, and thus confirms the inventive value of history. But Lincoln won the confrontation using not a historical but a religious argument about slavery—claiming that no human being deserved to be enslaved, and promoting freedom for the slaves as an absolute value central to Christianity. In the end, history had no probative value in the debate, or at least not one we can explain using Gadamer's fusion of horizons.

As Ricoeur convincingly demonstrates, the concept of the fusion of horizons has no probative value because it is not based on, or linked in any explicit way to, criteria of reliability. Indeed, how can our knowledge of the past be considered reliable, as long as tradition and history frame our epistemic abilities, providing us with the interpretive context in which we make sense of everything? Can the past be both an object of knowledge, and what makes knowledge possible in the first place? Ricoeur phrases this question in deliberately paradoxical terms, to stress the dilemma left unanswered by Gadamer: "*how is it possible to introduce a critical distance into a consciousness of belonging that is expressly defined by the rejection of distantiation?*" (TA, 73)

History as Text

Ricoeur departs from the Gadamerian approach because he believes that distance from the past can become a critical vantage "only insofar as historical consciousness seeks not simply to repudiate distantiation but to assume it" (TA, 73). Ricoeur attempts to clarify it by drawing attention to a paradox:

> in spite of the general opposition between belonging and alienating distantiation, the consciousness of effective history contains within itself an element of *distance*. The history of effects is precisely what occurs under the condition of historical distance. It is the nearness of the remote; or to say the same thing in other words, it is efficacy at a distance. There is thus a paradox of otherness, a tension between proximity and distance, which is essential to historical consciousness. (TA, 73)

For Ricoeur, texts embody this paradox of otherness, and they constitute the model for understanding communication at a distance (TA, 74). How do we identify the meaning of a text like the Declaration of Independence? Ricoeur views the precedence of speech over writing as a sociological phenomenon, but in epistemic terms, much like Jacques Derrida, he puts writing and speech on a par. Writing can substitute for oral communication not by simply transcribing it, or by recording in a sustainable medium what would otherwise belong to "the fugitive manifestation of language" (TA, 130), but by "occurring at the very site where speech could have emerged . . . as a direct inscription [of an intention-to-say]" (TA, 107). To explain the way in which texts work, Ricoeur relies systematically on the contrast to speech. But he stresses that interpretive occasions arise "at the most elementary and banal level of conversation" (TA, 54). Even in oral exchanges, polysemy demands that interlocutors be able to select appropriate contexts in which to disambiguate the intended sense of a word. The speaker's presence crucially helps this process of disambiguation, enabling "an activity of discernment that is exercised in the concrete exchange of messages between interlocutors, and that is modeled on the interplay of question and answer" (TA, 55). Through questions and answers, interlocutors negotiate meaning, zooming in on the "relatively univocal message the speaker has constructed on the polysemic basis of the common lexicon" (TA, 55). Therefore, in speech the reliability of comprehension is guaranteed by the fact that the speaker can identify explicitly the intention. Yet even so, the polysemic nature of language indicates that the potential for misunderstanding, increased "when the dialogical situation ceases to exist, when the play of questions and answers no longer permits us to verify our interpretation as the dialogue unfolds" (TA, 128), is already nascent in spoken communication, in "the infinitesimal distance that infiltrates itself between the saying and what is said" (TA, 129).

Even though not committed to recapturing the intention behind texts as a means for comprehending them, Ricoeur links meaning to a speaker's intention to communicate something. With his usual penchant for etymological and lexical speculation, he points out that some languages—French and German—often employ synonymously "meaning" and "intention." In English, too, when a person asks, "What do you mean?" she is soliciting the intention of the speaker, rather than an abstract meaning that could have been communicated by anybody else. But although we cannot (always) interrogate the author of a text in a similar way, we count on our ability to read and comprehend texts. Such reliance is justified, Ricoeur contends, because texts have a *matter* that transcends the author's intention, while also constraining the interpretive idiosyncrasies of readers. The idea that texts have a kernel that travels in time and space plays a crucial role in allowing Ricoeur to redefine interpretation as a critical operation that involves explanatory moves—rather than as the result of a transposition into someone else's mind, or as a fusion of horizons. As an "independent" entity, irreducible to production or reception, this kernel permits and invites analysis, thus promising a reliable result. The "matter" of the text is a space of intersection between two realms of reference—of the author's and of the reader's. For the purpose of an analysis, this notion is difficult to pin down. As Ricoeur cautions, "matter" is not some hard core waiting to be discovered. It is also not the author's intention, and it cannot be uncovered from any particular linguistic patterns, as Schleiermacher's "grammatical" principles attempted to do. How to reach it, then? The rather infelicitous translation "matter" of the French original "*chose*," which does not have pronounced materialist connotations, makes it particularly tempting to think in positivist terms. The "matter of text" represents the potential of any text to be *about something in the world*, a potential that is actualized by a reader interpreting the text.

Thus defined, the concept reveals the influence of Emile Benveniste's philosophy of language on Ricoeur. According to Benveniste, language becomes realized in discourse when communication is situated, addressed, and intentional. As language *in use*, discourse is *about something in the world*, as seen by a speaker who tries to communicate this "aboutness" to the interlocutor. For Ricoeur, meaning and this "aboutness" are closely linked, as meaning is what remains beyond the ephemeral contact between interlocutors. As such, meaning involves both an "intention-to-say" and an awareness that such an intention exists. This intention also posits a connection between communication and an extralinguistic realm, as discourse, in Ricoeur's view, "intends things, applies itself to reality, expresses the world" (TA, 85). When discourse is realized in the copresence of two interlocutors who are both aware of the circumstantial context, meaning as a potential identification of the "world expressed" can become available through "ostensive designation where speech rejoins the gesture of pointing" (TA, 108). But when discourse is inscribed in writing, meaning is deferred, and that particular reality that would conceivably be more easily recognizable to two interlocutors, that reality to which a speaker and hearer could point their finger, is bracketed, or suspended.

Notably, though, Ricoeur uses the adjective *suspended*, not *suppressed*. What we seek to understand in a text is a "proposed" world, and our understanding depends on the extent to which we manage to see this world as a place "wherein [we] could project one of [our] utmost possibilities" (TA, 86). Through this self-projection the quasi world of the text is "appropriated," and its suspended meaning restored. To understand a text is to make it part of the interpreter's cultural and social horizon while also changing this horizon by virtue of providing a renewed perspective on it. By effecting such transformation, the text comes alive, or, to use Ricoeur's apt phrasing, "actualized." But isn't this account a revised version of Gadamer's "fusion of horizons"? Furthermore, doesn't the notion of self-projection in the "world" of a text sound like the old Diltheyean psychologism?

The distinctiveness of Ricoeur's concept of "self-projection" lies in the fact that it involves an analytic ability to grasp the text as "work," a "finite and closed totality . . . submitted to a form of codification . . . (as well as) given a unique configuration that likens it to an individual and that may be called its style" (TA, 80). To perceive a text as work requires an explanatory detour in the process of understanding, a concern with the relations among elements forming the text as a totality that is on one level distinctive from other texts and on another level structured similarly to them.

This philosophy of the text, as just briefly summarized, challenges us to reconsider how we understand and consequently incorporate texts and the traditions they create in discourse that seeks to persuade. Specifically, Ricoeur's notion of the "matter" of a text affords us some insights into the explanatory phase of interpretation, and thus allows us to see that it depends on interpretation to have probative in addition to inventive value. Indeed, the combination of these two aspects of interpretation used to form the very core of a rhetorical enterprise.

As Michael Leff points out, in the classical program for rhetorical education reading and interpreting texts played a crucial role. Given its weak theoretical basis, rhetoric had to be parsimonious with its practical accomplishments. The principle of *imitatio* required orators to be familiar with strategies already tested and proven in previous interventions, and to be able to recycle such strategies by incorporating them into a new speech. *Imitatio* is frequently and mistakenly defined as a mechanical reproduction of rhetorical patterns and strategies. Leff reminds us that *imitatio* was a process with two stages, an interpretive and an inventive one, as in classical oratory where interpretive judgment of an existing text was necessary in order to determine whether and how a set of strategies could be appropriated for future use. In *imitatio*, the relationship between interpretation and production of discourse changes into one of coextension, as "within this practice, the interplay between understanding and production creates an organic connection between the historical text and the new composition; the old text leaves its impression on the rhetor's product, but the rhetor's productive act has left its interpretative impression on the original" (Leff, "Hermeneutical Rhetoric," 202). Rita Copeland notes a similar fusion of interpretation and invention, and defines *imitatio* as a relationship of lineage:

> the model, or ancestor, discovers and posits the ground for future invention. Such an evolutionary pattern is enabled or sustained by the very interpretative community which it creates. Hence, to justify the imitative enterprise, the copy produces, not [a] conspicuous likeness of the original, but rather what is understood and revalued in the original. (Copeland, 27)

Both Leff and Copeland propose a concept of *imitatio* that can seem to be paradoxical, as it involves an "imitative invention." But the process thus described is well illustrated by Clinton's appropriation of King's particular style, topics, and arguments. Clinton's invocation of King relies on capturing the "matter" of the minister's texts—a reactualization of a realm of reference captured in the reverend's speeches. To this end, Clinton's interpretation required an explanatory dimension, which focuses on King's language and arguments as the "compositions" of an individual. A composition, for Ricoeur, refers to the internal structure of a text, which makes it recognizable within the larger context of a genre, and hence, in relation to other texts. But the text's unique, distinctive identity resides in its style, defined by Ricoeur as "labor that individuates, that is, that produces an individual, so it designates its author" (TA, 82). Style "individuates" by promoting a "particular standpoint . . . in response to a determinate situation" (TA, 81–82). By appropriating into his discourse some of the lexical patterns and tropes used by King in his speeches, Clinton establishes a generic format, while at the same time promoting his particular standpoint. Notice how this combination of the general and the particular is effected in one of the opening paragraphs:

> Proverb says, "A happy heart doeth good like medicine, but a broken spirit dryeth the bone." This is a happy place, and I'm happy to be here. I thank you for your spirit. By the grace of God and your help, last year I was elected President of this great country. I never dreamed that I would ever have a chance to come to this hallowed place where Martin Luther King Jr. gave his last sermon. I ask you to think today about the purpose for which I ran and the purpose for which so many of you worked to put me in this great office. I have worked hard to keep faith with our common efforts: . . . to reward work and family and community and to try to move us forward into the twenty-first century. I have tried to keep faith. (1982)

The passage begins with an explicit biblical reference, and it ends with a line that echoes the words of Apostle Paul in his Second Timothy Letter—"I have fought the good fight, I have finished the race, I have kept faith" (4:7). Clinton's mode of address follows the generic convention of the pastoral letter, a special communicative form whose role was to "provide instruction to church leaders for the preservation of the Christian community (Murphy, 80). The passage also contains an explicit reference to King, who in his turn used the religious epistle format in his "Letter from a Birmingham Jail" and "Paul's Letter to American Christians" to plead for nonviolence and racial reconciliation. Twice embedded in a generic format, Clinton's speech uses the original Pauline rhetoric with its emphasis on humility and diligence ("I have *tried* to keep faith") *and* King's appropriation to create a sense of continuity and to stress his own belonging to a moral and philosophical paradigm. The generic format, then, corresponds to a moral order, and by identifying this paradigm in King's rhetoric, and by subscribing to it himself, Clinton can ask his audience to reaffirm their belief in a set of values, and to reestablish a social order predicated on them. In another passage of the Memphis speech, particularity is obtained through deliberate deviation from the general pattern, specifically, through misquotation:

> If Martin Luther King, who said "Like Moses, I am on the mountaintop and I can see the promised land, but I'm not going to be able to get there with you, but we will get there,"—if he were to reappear by my side today and give us a report card on the last twenty-five years, what would he say? (1983)

Clinton misquotes King in an important manner, as the original speech ran

> I just want to do God's will, and He's allowed me to go up to the mountain, and I've looked over and I've seen the Promised Land. I may not get there with you, but I want you to know tonight that we as a people will get to the Promised Land. (King, 321)

In Clinton's adaptation, King no longer speaks as a visionary mortal, but as an immortal prophet. This modification restores the "pastness" of the past, and thus refocuses the attention on the present situation, the present speaker, and the task at hand: King is not physically present in 1993 America, but his legacy must be preserved. The conclusion of Clinton's speech recapitulates the transition from general desirability to particular intelligibility, and from a textual paradigm and moral order to a referential realm and social context. Notice the force of the commitment, marked by the conversion of the imperative, previously stated through modals like "must," "should," or "need"—into a declarative:

> We *will* honor the life and the work of Martin Luther King. We *will* honor the meaning of our church. We *will*, somehow, by God's grace, we will turn this around. We *will* give these children a future. We *will* take away their guns and give them books. We *will* take away their despair and give them hope. We *will* rebuild the families and the neighborhoods and the communities. We *won't* make all the work that has gone on here benefit just a few. We *will* do it together by the grace of God. (my emphasis, 1986)

At this point, Clinton speaks as someone who knows that the audience has decided to act.

Lincoln, and later King, invoked the Declaration of Independence. Clinton invoked King. Others will invoke Clinton. Such textual and historical continuum does not emerge accidentally: documents form traditions, and as a repository of "conceptions of symbolic relationships among problems, persons, interests, and actions, which imply (when accepted) certain notions of preferable public behavior," tradition can be deemed both tangible and "more refined than a routine or empirical practice" (Farrell, "Knowledge," 4). As Ricoeur reminds us, a tradition is first and foremost a community of interpretation, without which "no transference, no translation is possible" (RPH, 68). Different generations might have widely distinct views, norms, and expectations, but they nevertheless share an interest in some crucial documents that continue to regulate communal life. The original objects of hermeneutical study were religious, legal, and philological texts. What these texts have in common is that they define traditions, seen as higher grounds of meaning in accordance to which one could make sense of various experiences at a more local, specific level.

Edward Schiappa has proposed a distinction between historical reconstruction, which attempts to reconstruct the past "in the words and mindset" of its protagonists, and rational reconstruction, which reads the past from the perspective of present actors (193–94). With Ricoeur's help, I have tried to introduce a third possibility of historical reflection, one that seeks to capture the past from the perspective of the present, but that can also consolidate such a perspective as epistemologically reliable, shaped by systematic explanatory moves.

Conclusion

In a plea for a historical turn in rhetorical theory, David Zarefsky argued that "historical study aids in understanding the present by placing it in the context of the past. It counters a common presentist assumption that what happened had to happen—and it does so by directing attention to the roads not taken. And in an era concerned with cultural pluralism, history like the arts is valuable as an enlargement of human experience" (Zarefsky, 31). Zarefsky further invokes a long-held belief among historians, which views history as "a way of getting out of the boundaries of one's own life and culture and of seeing more of what human experience has been" (Lathem, 12). History, by such accounts, is a source of personal and collective enlightenment, a source of awareness of one's inevitably humble particularity on the grand scale of general temporality. But can we also maintain that history is a repository of advice for how to address particular problems, from the thickness of one's contingency? Before anyone can argue that history is a prime resource for elucidation and edification, we must first understand its function, its specific way of shaping practical reasoning. This has been the overarching goal of this chapter.

Under the banner of phronesis or practical wisdom, classical rhetoricians tried to provide rhetorical discourse with a conceptual foundation that would combine reflection on general principles with the observation of concrete circumstances. Ricoeur's hermeneutics allows us to see a methodological link between practical reasoning thus understood, and historical reflection. Drawing on Ricoeur's definition of practical reasoning as an alignment of intelligibility and desirability, and on his critical hermeneutics as an appropriation of "textual matter," I have argued that history becomes a source of wisdom when its interpretation is shared by the members of a community, and that such sharing depends on giving life to the past and incorporating it through recourse to key textual traces. The argument is couched in Ricoeur's conception of practical reasoning as interpretive activity, specifically in the distinctions he draws between hermeneutical freedom and the controversial fulcrum of argumentation, motive and intention, and speaking and writing. Historically, hermeneutics emerged as a discipline concerned with a general level of beliefs and principles that can also inform, govern, and explain particular instances. Insofar as it sought to provide an understanding of legal, scriptural, or philological texts, hermeneutics represents an effort to create points of access between such a level of general signification and particular applications. More importantly, hermeneutics locates general signification in history, in previous experiences reified and crystallized in a practical knowledge that can guide present practice from an epistemologically higher vantage that makes it seem, in its normative force, theoretical.

But this leaves us with another question: is history safe from becoming a source of manipulation?

Chapter Four

Epideictic

Chapter 3 analyzed the interpretive dimension of practical reasoning, as revealed by rhetorical discourse that draws on the past by searching through history as through a repository of master narratives, source of authority, and wisdom for the unanswered questions of the present. Invited to discuss the challenges posed for political leaders by the troubled climate of the last decade of the twentieth century, Ricoeur maintained that there is

> a fundamental problem in the world in which we live, particularly Europe—western, central, and eastern—the problem of a disabled memory: in some places there is an excess of memory, while in others a deficit. In some places, people are still obsessed with the memory of a golden age or the memory of humiliation. In other places, the past remains unspoken. This distinction is not only instantiated in countries, Germany, France, or others, but in moments in our own reflection vacillating between too much and too little; these two different mechanisms illustrate the same phenomenon—an inability to articulate an identity that is both intelligible and acceptable. Intelligible, in the sense that we can explain to ourselves and others on what grounds it was constructed. Acceptable, in the sense that if offers us a deeper, otherwise unavailable, understanding of ourselves. (PM, 28, my translation)

This problem of a "disabled memory" forces us to question more critically the availability of the past to decisions affecting life in the present. The challenge observed by Ricoeur is not unique to Europe—the reparations debate in the United States or the postapartheid efforts to recover evidence about the abuses committed in South Africa are two powerful examples outside the old continent. Nor is the problem limited to the last two decades. But the recent proliferation of debates in countries around the world demands a renewed reflection on the challenges posed by historical legacies that pin individuals, groups, and nations against each other. Dealing with such legacies often defies the separation of elucidatory efforts from moral responsibility, and of objective historical inquiry from commemorative celebrations. At the same time, the "problem of a disabled memory" described by Ricoeur concerns an erosion of the very foundation of rhetorical discourse, if "the first principles of all public argument appear to lie in the society's collective judgment of its past," as scholars have suggested (McGee, 34). The influence of the past in shaping the present is confirmed by its frequent invocation in political discourse around the world. In America, a critic writes,

> from the Fast-Day sermons of seventeenth-century New England to the battlefields of the Civil War, from speeches of inauguration to farewell address[es], leaders have availed themselves of a rhetorical form distinctively equipped to construct and promote public memory. However diffuse their particular style or semantic content, such discursive forms collectively enact vested visions of time present, past, and future. (Browne, 465)

The discursive form in question is, of course, epideictic, a remarkably underrepresented topic in the history of rhetorical studies. In an essay published in 1986, Celeste Condit observed that most theories of epideictic are restrictive per force, insofar as they explain the characteristics of only a few ceremonial speeches or situations privileged as representative exemplars. "In the face of the pervasiveness, variety, and significance of the genre," Condit complained, "our understandings of it are inadequately complex. Because students of epideictic have directed their efforts towards identifying a single, simple, and essential characteristic that might uniquely distinguish such discourse, each of the several existing explorations has been inadequately sensitive to the variety of functions epideictic serves for its speakers and audiences" (Condit, 485). In this regard, ten years later a new survey of the scholarship on the subject found some improvement, taking special notice of several attempts at defining epideictic in teleological terms as "a discourse that serves more exigent social and civic functions than simply celebrating, reinforcing, or reexamining values" (Sheard, 787). Methodological efforts to avoid the reification of epideictic—as we see in Condit's complaint—or its marginality in relation to the social and civic goals pivotal to any rhetorical discourse, bespeak the problematic nature of this concept, burdened as it is from its Greek beginning by suspicions of mere aestheticism, partiality, or manipulation. In his insistence on the tripartition of rhetorical discourse into the three well-known categories, Ricoeur himself hesitates whether to put epideictic on the same level with the other two. At fault might be the Procrustean nature of the tripartition itself. But throughout the history of rhetoric this division has often been seen as a major source of conceptual clarity (Garver, 52), even as historians of the field have also pointed out that such a neat differentiation could hardly have reflected the composite practice of Athenian public discourse. How could it reflect the practice of contemporary discourse without forcing more or less arbitrary boundaries among often hybrid forms of communicative interaction? Along with Dale Sullivan, we can further ask: "Given the present order of things, is it possible to modernize a concept like epideictic rhetoric? Does epideictic, which once functioned to uphold a monolithic culture, operate in the postmodern world?" (Sullivan, 339).

In this chapter I argue that we can answer Sullivan's question affirmatively, on the condition that we carefully qualify the traditional concept in question, paying heed to Ricoeur's concern about an internationally disabled public memory. Through the comments that open this chapter, Ricoeur prompts us to rethink the nature of the discursive efforts needed to gather a community around shared values and to convince it to subscribe to certain visions of the past, present, or future. His work, I will show, tells us specifically how to rethink the role and specific mechanism of epideictic on the contemporary political arena. To put Ricoeur's ideas in the appropriate context of our discipline, I start with a brief examination of some common assumptions about epideictic made by rhetorical scholars, drawing mainly on Aristotle and Perelman and Olbrechts-Tyteca. Tracing the intellectual trajectory of the concept, I suggest that epideictic discourse relies on a particular way of constructing the past rhetorically for the purpose of forming and maintaining national identities through an allegiance to values and beliefs grounded in a shared past. The nation, as often pointed out by historians, emerged first as an idea and was the brainchild of political elites before it could be embraced or recognized as a readily available basis of identification. And as an "imagined community," in Benedict Anderson's terms, nationhood has always relied on discursive strategies that can manipulate feelings of belonging and cultural intimacy. Epideictic discourse, often the purveyor for such feelings, lies on the verge of propaganda, from where it can invoke positive images from or about the past to enable manipulation, creating conveniently glorious and mythical accounts that can become justifications for condemnable actions committed in the past. In presenting

Ricoeur's views on the goals and standards for reconstructing the past in historical investigation, as well as the criteria for assigning responsibility for past action while also allowing for rehabilitation, my aim is to create a heuristic rather than provide definitive definitions for complex concepts like *history* or *morality*. I put forth this heuristic as a way of explaining the constraints and conditions for epideictic discourse delivered in response to some of the most challenging exigencies of our time.

The test case I have chosen for this chapter concerns the regeneration of national identity through epideictic—specifically through commemorative acts—in postwar Germany. I take to heart Condit's complaint that theoretical studies of epideictic often generalize findings valid only for particular (and often idiosyncratic) interventions, and look at Germany as a paradigmatic case for the challenges posed for epideictic by the "problem of a disabled memory," as Ricoeur puts it. Responsible for committing the worst atrocities in the history of humanity during World War II, the German nation has had to cope with a phenomenally difficult task: to carry on the record of a collective murderer and to still retain pride in its own identity; to teach its children culpability for their parents' actions, yet not condemn them to eternal shame for being German; and to never forget yet also to move on and become again (at least economically) one of the most powerful nations in the world. Postwar Germany is a litmus test for the effectiveness and dangers of epideictic discourse: if we can understand the mechanisms of epideictic in such a problematic setting, it means that we have a concept with both generalizable explanatory value and relevance for particular contemporary political problems, rather than just an idea detached from an intellectual tradition and lifted out of a cultural context. I focus on two interrelated sets of events: first, a 1980s debate among West German historians over the proper goals and methods for historical inquiry, which began in specialized forums but continued in the mass media and attracted both scholarly and political participants. In the context of West Germany's increased economic success, this debate had high political stakes, and important consequences for a much broader, public understanding of how to face the question of the country's past. To ground the theoretical contribution of this chapter in such a case study seemed especially apt in light of Ricoeur's own personal and scholarly interest in the historians' debate, recorded in his last book, *Memory, History, Forgetting.*

The second set of events refers to the commemoration of the war in public speeches given by political leaders in West Germany roughly during the same period as the historians' debate. In 1985, President Ronald Reagan was invited by the German chancellor Helmut Kohl to participate in the festivities organized for the fortieth anniversary of the end of the war. Since the relations between the two countries, and the personal bond between the two men were particularly strong at the time, he accepted. On the itinerary were included stops at Bergen-Belsen, the site of a former concentration camp, and at Bitburg cemetery where several American soldiers had been buried. While Reagan altered his first plan not to give a speech about the Holocaust (initially justified due to his concern for not renewing the pangs of German guilt), he remained undeterred in his decision to speak at the military cemetery. He did not change his mind even when informed that several SS officers had been buried there as well. The political, social, and broader cultural impact of this commemorative situation can hardly be overstated: the Bitburg affair marked a sea change in German-American relations; in the attitude of the Jewish population around the world toward America; in the dynamics of the cold war; and in the conceptualization of the link between history, law, and national identity. According to Saul Friendländer, "Bitburg came to symbolize all the dilemmas of forgetting and remembering, for Germany and its victims, for the victorious allies and the vanquished enemy, for those who lived through the war and those born after 1945: the second generation, and by now, the third" (27). I focus on two speeches delivered by the American president at the Bitburg Air Base and by the German President to the *Bundestag*, the West German Parliament. These two texts are related through the centrality of their epideictic concern: how to think about what has been called Germany's "unmasterable past" in a way that would allow for the assumption of responsibility without forever demonizing the German people, and in a way that would not create a breach in national identity but that would also not take historical continuity for granted and condemn all Germans to the status of Hitler's heirs.

I focus on two sets of events, rather than on only one particular speech, as a way of showing the pervasiveness and significance of epideictic in the life of a national community, and the ubiquity of a troublesome past, which although often the business of scholars or professional politicians, affects the conduct and self-esteem of average individuals by measuring their worth against the deeds of their ascendants.

"The Spell of an Ideality"

Epideictic was largely an Aristotelian conceptual innovation. It brought together distinct rhetorical practices and artifacts in "an original synthesis that offered a somewhat different understanding of the social and political functions of such [practices] than what can be detected from the available historical evidence" (Schiappa, 186). Under the newly created rubric of epideictic, Aristotle grouped the existing genres of encomium (*enkomion)*, panegyric (*panegyrikos*), and epitaph (*epitaphios*). The first in this series, best known to students of rhetoric from Gorgias's *Encomion to Helen,* was a primarily didactic type of discourse designed to praise historical or mythical characters. "The importance of the genre," explains Schiappa, was "to praise actions and qualities that the audience should emulate" (Schiappa, 189). Thus, the encomiastic discourse proceeded from a strong moral basis, which would commonly serve as a foundation for further deliberative interventions (Poulakos, 325). Panegyrics were delivered to large groups on festive occasions. Such discourse also extolled praise, but not so much of individuals (unless they were officials) as of institutions, cities, or activities (e.g., contests or games). Early panegyrics, Schiappa stresses, "were openly political in orientation and aimed at encouraging the audience to follow a course of action" (Schiappa, 190). Likewise, funeral orations celebrating the soldiers' sacrifice for their country were a genuine "political *institution*" in democratic Athena" (Schiappa, 193, my emphasis). "Particularly in a democracy where persuasion must replace force," Schiappa explains, "the *epitaphios* [Eng. epitaph] played an important persuasive function to maintain the will of the citizenry to meet the ongoing institutional needs of Athens (e.g., finances, soldiers, unity), reinforce commitment to Athenian style democracy, support the current military policies (whether imperialistic or defensive) and, in short, to assure the continued existence of Athens as a political institution" (Schiappa, 195). By establishing criteria according to which individuals would be glorified and remembered, and honored and set up as role models, epideictic practices had the function of "socializing citizens as to what it meant to be Athenian" (Schiappa, 196).

The overarching function of epideictic discourse was to create a shared space for persuasive interactions. Importantly, however, that space was not a concrete location, not Athens the city, but "something like an ideality, well beyond the sum of concrete experiences that made up [the Athenians'] political life" (Loraux, 328). The setting of the *epitaphios* in a period of increased military conflict and political stress in Athens reveals that the celebration responded to a need for discursive mediation in a time of confusion and crisis. Epideictic provided a framework in which citizens would read events and experiences that could otherwise be hard to understand or accept. In order to do so, pre-Aristotelian epideictic discourse relied heavily on a revival of the past—evoking previous successful military campaigns, the exemplary deeds of past heroes, and the reputed traditions of social practices or institutions. The epideictic rhetor, then, was what Tzvetan Todorov would call an "activist of memory," his task not simply to record but rather to draw on lessons from a glorious past. Such discourse dealt in representations of a *heroic* past, a veritable age of origins (Le Goff, 64), its domain not memory but anamnesis. Especially in times of uncertainty or crisis, epideictic discourse played a crucial role in redirecting attention to a period deemed not just safer but emblematic, to dispel any potential doubts that better times will come again. The past, by such an account, is not a term of comparison so much as a point of reference. Epideictic was not equivalent to a historical reconstruction proper even though an important function assigned by the Greeks to funeral orations was as "one of the models in relation to which historical inquiry must situate itself" (Loraux, 290).

But in Aristotle's reconfiguration of existing rhetorical practices under the new rubric of epideictic, political, social, and cultural dimensions became largely subsumed to an aesthetic goal that emphasizes form over function, and style over argument. Although the new aesthetic orientation was not entirely without deliberative overtones (see *On Rhetoric* 1367b37–1368aI), Aristotle's conceptual innovation had the long-term effect—noticeable in Ricoeur's own treatment—of placing epideictic discourse on a different level than judicial and deliberative and several degrees removed from the teleological, action-oriented nature of rhetorical discourse (Loraux, 224). Because it relied so heavily on stylistic display, the genre teetered on the brink between rhetoric and literature, more often than not falling into the latter category (Walker, 45). The word itself *epideiktike* means "art of display" and it had been originally coined by Plato to describe a sophistic show-off (Schiappa, 198). More than an aesthetic value, epideictic discourse had the quality of a performance and was intended for an audience of spectators rather than judges, as in the case of judicial and deliberative. The spectators of an encomium or panegyric were not asked to make decisions or pass judgment. "Much like the audience for a poetry performance or the theater," as Schiappa suggests, the listeners were asked to offer aesthetic rather than political evaluations, making decisions about the performance and not its content or implications (Schiappa, 199).

Despite making major changes, Aristotle maintained the function of the earlier epideictic practices by assigning to the newly created genre the end of "the honorable"—a placeholder for specific virtues ranging widely from courage to self-control, and from magnificence to magnanimity. As key ingredients of moral codes and models, the virtues listed by Aristotle were designed to regulate behaviors and attitudes, not so much in the service of a particular persuasion task as to stabilize public conduct—a crucial function in times of uncertainty or crisis. The virtues embodied in the praised hero were to be embraced and admired by the audience—an objective that resembles the principle of identification underlying the cathartic experience furnished by tragic spectacles. That Aristotle himself recognized such a function as strategic becomes clear when he switches from description to prescription, and advises speakers "to stretch the truth where necessary" (Schiappa, 201). But can the strategic not become distorting, or the normative manipulative?

If we deem the function of epideictic as one of integrating individuals in historical communities, the fulcrum of epideictic discourse becomes ideological in the sense defined by Ricoeur (cf. chapter 2). This also seems to be the main premise in Perelman and Olbrechts-Tyteca's study, insofar as they try to locate epideictic at the center of rhetorical discourse in general, broadening its base beyond that of a particular genre. In their view,

> the argumentation in epideictic discourse sets out to increase the intensity of adherence to certain values, which might not be contested when considered on their own but may nevertheless not prevail against other values that might come into conflict with them. The speaker tries to establish a sense of communion centered around particular values recognized by the audience, and to this end he uses the whole range of means available to the rhetorician for the purposes of amplification and enhancement. (51)

Notably, though, for Perelman and Olbrechts-Tyteca the role of epideictic seems to be that of an add-on, important as it might be, an increase of what already exists, namely, a shared ethical and moral space in which interlocutors are more likely to exchange ideas and adopt each other's beliefs and convictions. "The epideictic speech has an important part to play," maintain the two, "for without such common values upon what foundation could deliberative and legal speeches rest?" (Perelman and Olbrechts-Tyteca, 52–53). Perelman and Olbrechts-Tyteca do not explain where such common values originated, what generated them in the first place, and how a speaker could successfully identify and draw on them. The authors of *The New Rhetoric* maintain that "epideictic discourse, as well as education, is less directed toward changing beliefs than to strengthening the adherence to what is already accepted" (Perelman and Olbrechts-Tyteca, 54). But why was it accepted in the first place? Although the two Belgians do not explicitly link epideictic to a particular way of managing and marketing the past, the association looms large in their account. For them, epideictic is the instrument of conservatism. And it is not hard to see that in a conservative social setting in which moral values are fixed and explicit because they are preserved, the purpose and challenge of epideictic discourse is to give expression to a symbolic space inherited from the past and recognized as familiar by its inhabitants. But in a heterogeneous and pluralistic community that does not share an uncontroversial perspective on the past, epideictic must constantly justify its selection rather than count on being able to express existing values. That a particular set of values can be deemed more representative of a community than rival proposals constitutes the very strategic mechanism at the center of the epideictic function. As a tacit admission that epideictic fashions rather than reflects values, we have Perelman and Olbrechts-Tyteca's concern with the possibility of misusing a community's adherence to a particular set of values, of turning epideictic into propaganda. The distinction they posit between education and propaganda is tenuous in actual practice, as too many instances of efficient propagandistic persuasion masquerading as emancipation and enlightenment clearly attest. The propagandist manages to persuade by acting as an educator and pretending to speak from a moral platform acceptable to the community. But from what vantage can one tell the difference between genuine education and its manipulation or parody?

It is not easy to answer such a question in an era that questions the universality of moral standards, as well as the possibility of a privileged epistemic standpoint. The more general concern we can raise after reviewing Perelman and Olbrechts-Tyteca is: insofar as epideictic discourse shapes an ideality, how does it chart the narrow course between enlightenment and manipulation in making sure that it does not deal in convenient fictions? As an ideality, the shared space created through epideictic rhetoric is irreducible to historical reconstruction. Because the Athens of epideictic discourse was not an empirical location, it was not subject to historical or mnemonic verification. Yet on the other hand, in order for this familiar ideality to work its "spell," it had to have the appearance of an empirical order, to be recognizable to those who by subscribing to it would also adopt a set of values, and ultimately a set of behavioral and moral regulations for their own lives and identities. But while grounding in some verifiable data through history might enable detection of propagandistic manipulation, the "realism" of such an epistemic operation could put a dent in the ideal configuration it tries to protect. The challenge for epideictic thus appears to be one of striking the right balance between empirical validity and inspiring ideality.

Finding such balance does not profit, prima facie, from an understanding of the mechanism of epideictic still largely influenced by the style-based approaches initiated by Aristotle. What we need instead is a concept of epideictic elaborated politically and socially. Such a task is not impossible, for upon closer scrutiny of the social and political roles played by epideictic practices, we find one key issue that they tried to address: the creation of a shared ideality with which individuals were encouraged to identify in order to find meaning in their own lives. Subsumed to this issue are two other important concerns: how to create a mythical, glorious dimension in articulating such a shared ideality, and how to make it feel concrete and real. Epideictic, I will argue, must have an epistemic foundation that allows it to pursue the moral agenda of providing celebratory or condemnatory perspectives based on an ideal set of values, strategically located in the past. Drawing on Ricoeur, I will show that epideictic discourse can pay attention to questions of accuracy and legitimacy in order to avoid the charge of propaganda, and that such an epistemic foundation does not necessarily undermine its ability to create an ideality. Since when it comes to the past such epistemic foundation represents the goal and standard in historical inquiry, I proceed by looking deeper into the connections between epideictic and history.

THE GRAVEYARD OF HISTORY

As the first section of this chapter showed, the Greeks entrusted their rhapsodes with the preservation of the past. In more epistemologically circumspect times such as ours, historians step up to the task. In his trilogy on narrative published in the mid-1980s, Ricoeur described the historian's task as one of plausible storytelling, and stressed the constructed nature of emplotted representations while also being careful not to debunk the aspiration to truthfulness that should guide historical writing. In a similar vein and in the same epoch, Michel de Certeau argued that the function of history is to create a vantage "suited for marking the past so as to re-distribute the space of possibilities in the present" (Dosse, 268). But for Ricoeur writing in the late 1990s, history is a "funeral rite" (MHF, 605). At the same time, however, historiography, by his account, is not a kind of cemetery, "simply a place where to dump bones" (MHF, 605). It is more accurately described, in his opinion, as a reburial, a renewed effort to bring the past back to life, only followed by the realization that such a thing is not possible. "Doesn't every historian hope," Ricoeur asks, "to reach behind the mortuary mask and rediscover the true face of those who were once alive, acting and suffering, making promises that they did not live to keep? This is perhaps the secret desire that animates historical knowledge" (MHF, 605).

The association of history and death is a common trope among philosophers of history, who believe that "the historian's writing plays the role of a funeral rite. An instrument of exorcising death, it introduces death into the very heart of its discourse and enables a society to situate itself symbolically by endowing itself with a language on the past" (Dosse, 286). We perceive a similar emphasis on loss and absence in Maurice Halbwachs's argument that historical investigation becomes necessary when a community's image of its past is "fading or breaking up" (Halbwachs, 78). Halbwachs has influenced Ricoeur's thinking in *Memory, History, Forgetting*, feeding him arguments for the need to address history as a form of mourning. "The need to write the history of a period, a society, or even a person," maintained Halbwachs, "is only aroused when the subject is already too distant in the past to allow for the testimony of those who preserve some remembrance of it"(Halbwachs, 78). In a similar vein, Pierre Nora, another major interlocutor for Ricoeur, has claimed that the "age of history" begins when communal solidarity around values inherited from the past began to falter. When tradition no longer grounds the members of a community in a shared understanding of their past, "the equilibrium between the present and the past is disrupted," Nora maintains, and thus "things tumble with increasing rapidity into an irretrievable past" (Nora, 19). Deprived of a shared past, groups become transient associations of individuals who may temporarily have some common interests but who lack a systematic common vocabulary. What is lost in this process is the "memory nation," a cross-generational, transhistorical community irreducible to a sum of its members (Fritzsche, 90).

Nora's account of the dissolution of traditional communities appoints a professional category, historians, as custodians of the past, and hence, of national consciousness. This puts historians in a privileged, and by some accounts, dangerous position. Some historians admittedly play the role of ideologues, shaping political agendas and movements by fostering or maintaining strategic images of a country's past. Ricoeur warns that history has a "tendency to render official a *certain* state of memory. . . . being in the service of national grandeur, in the service of a certain collective memory which it support[s] without exercising its function of critical vigilance" (CC, 124). But he also argues that historical inquiry can provide points of reference for individual recollection, calibrating personal memories in a shared understanding of the past (MHF, 445, my translation). What lends historical representations ideological power is precisely their ability to resonate with individuals' perceptions, to mesh with memorial accounts and to provide confirmation for individual and private understandings of the past. History, then, has a public use value. Even while seemingly enrolled in an epistemic effort "to understand without exculpating," the historian can develop an ideological apparatus so much more effective since it is unnoticeable (MHF, 402, my translation).

It is precisely for this reason, Ricoeur urges, that we should resist accepting too easily the assumption that historical inquiry has unquestionable epistemic value. The most problematic aspect of historical inquiry, Ricoeur explains, is also its fundamental one—the very assumption that a historical event reflects in an ontological sense that something has actually happened and can therefore be known as such. Historical inquiry, according to Ricoeur, is guided by a series of premises:

> First, we admit that the property of having already occurred differs radically from that of not yet having occurred. In this sense, the pastness of what has happened is taken as an absolute property, independent of our constructions and reconstructions. This first feature is common to physical events and to historical ones. A second feature delimits the field of the historical event. Of all the things that have happened, certain ones are the work of agents similar to ourselves. Historical events therefore are what these active beings happen to undergo. The ordinary definition of history as knowledge of the actions of past human beings proceeds from this restricting of our interest to the sphere of events assignable to human agents. A third feature results from the delimitation within the practical field of the sphere of possible communication. To the notion of the human past is added, as a constitutive obstacle, the idea of otherness or an absolute difference affecting our capacity for communication. . . . To this threefold ontological presupposition—absolute having been, absolutely past human action, and absolute otherness—corresponds a threefold epistemological one. First, we oppose the unrepeatable singularity of a physical or human event to the universality of a law. Whether it be a question of statistical frequency, causal connection, or functional relation, an event is what happens only once. Next, we oppose practical contingency to logical or physical necessity. An event is what could have been done differently. Finally, otherness has its epistemological counterpart in the notion of the gap between the event and any constructed model or any invariant. (TN, 96–97)

The assumptions identified by Ricoeur make a series of crucial points about the connection between history and epideictic. If a historical event is singular, the present cannot aspire to repeat it, and hence epideictic discourse that draws on the past must accord it a significance that goes beyond urging imitation or repetition. Furthermore, to evaluate historical occurrences by the criteria of practical contingency rather than by logical necessity is to admit that the past cannot be justified, and therefore it should not allow epideictic discourse to function as exculpation. And finally, to acknowledge that there is a gap between an event and its reconstruction amounts to taking on an interpretive task in epideictic, and thus leaving it inevitably open to contestation. These critical consequences all played a major part in the historians' debate (*Historikerstreit*) that caused such a stir in political and intellectual circles in Germany in the 1980s. In his commentary on the debate, Ricoeur has focused primarily on the contributions made by Ernst Nolte and Jürgen Habermas, but it is useful to understand the broader context of the exchange first.

The Burden of the Past

At the end of the war, defeated Germany went into a large-scale program of reeducation that was designed to allow its people to dissociate from National Socialism and to become able to look upon the destruction it had created with the indignation of its victims. While the trials of the major political and military Nazi leaders provided some sense of justice, the epideictic question of blame—in Karl Jaspers's famous formulation, the German guilt (*die deutsche Schuld*)—was a collective not just individual culpability. This question continued to lurk in the background for decades after May 1945. But by the mid-1970s, and even more so in the 1980s, West Germany had impressed the world with its "economic miracle," and was increasingly becoming a pivotal political player in the coalition against the Soviet Union. To some, in a present shining so bright, the past, too, began to look less somber. There were increasingly voices from the conservative right, saying that the past must be put behind them so that the new generations who were not directly responsible for the horrors of the war would not feel burdened by such a dark history. Such attempts did not remain unsanctioned. Writing after his recent return from the North American exile, Theodor Adorno made the stakes clear: "Should we consider it pathological to burden oneself with the past, while the healthy and realistic person is absorbed in the present and its practical concerns? . . . In this forgetting of what is scarcely past, one senses the fury of the one who has to talk himself out of what everyone else knows, before he can talk them out of it" (Adorno, 117–18).

The West German historians' debate about the Nazi period is a telling example of the challenges involved in the relationship between historical awareness and the understanding of the present. The moral stake of the controversy concerned the responsibility of Germany in the 1980s for the crimes committed by Hitler's Third Reich. Under the rubric of the question, "how to interpret the past reliably," several professional historians also associated with the neoconservative political party proposed a reading of Germany's role in World War II that actively de-emphasized the magnitude of the destruction, its uniqueness, and the German people's culpability. The protagonists of the debate were Michael Sturmer, Andreas Hillgrüber, and Nolte on one side, and Habermas on the other. Sturmer explicitly defined history as creator of meaning based on which a country defines its future. Presenting his argument in the negative—"in a country without history, he who fills the memory, defines the concepts, and interprets the past, wins the future" (qtd. in Habermas, "Apologetic Tendencies," 213)—he invoked a sense of urgency and danger facing postwar Germany in the context of the Cold War and of the defensive alliance of North America and Western Europe. In this context, the Federal Republic of Germany must be, and had become, according to Sturmer, the very centerpiece of the European defense arc. Hillgrüber explained this centrality as a historical continuation of Germany's Eastern front during the war, thus shifting the inquiry from a perspective of blame to one of praise.

Nolte's conception of history was based on the distinction between inquiry leading to the attribution of moral verdicts (blame or praise) for certain actions, and accounts that locate chains of events that allow actions to take place in the first place. For him, this distinction translates into a separation of culpability from responsibility. As Ricoeur reads him, Nolte recognizes that "a negative judgment [of the Third Reich] is simply a vital necessity" (qtd. in MHF, 429, my translation). As a historian, though, he is bothered by accounts that recount the story of the Third Reich as a negative *myth,* letting the moral evaluation lead the inquiry to the point where the epistemic dimension—identifying factual information and making sense of it—becomes subsumed to that goal. Nolte admits that on a moral scale the war was tantamount to a series of horrific actions, but he wants to know why such atrocities took place, and in the interest of explanatory power he opts for modifying the frame in which the historical events are narrated, broadening the perspective and "letting in a multitude of extermination precedents, the closest one being Bolshevism" (MHF, 402, my translation). "The refusal to reinsert the extermination of Jews under

Hitler in this context has perhaps very noble reasons, but it falsifies history," argues Nolte (in MHF, 429, my translation).

Ricoeur identifies three techniques at work in this revisionist interpretation: expanding the temporal setting, finding analogous occurrences, and, most importantly, establishing a causal, rather than only a chronological link between historical events. The first two techniques go against Ricoeur's provisos regarding the uniqueness of historical events, while the third one contradicts the premise that past occurrences be viewed as practical contingencies. But the key move in Nolte's project, as seen by Ricoeur, is the description of the horrors committed by the Nazi as an imitation of (posited) preceding events, a particularly grotesque one, but still distinct from the original act. Through the use of comparisons, the historian denies the singularity of the Nazi past, thus refuting its status as a point of (negative) reference. An understanding of the present, or of what it means to be German in the present, then, cannot rely on the historical legacy of the Third Reich.

Nolte's revisionism drove a wedge between the epistemic goals of historical reconstruction and moral judgment. His controversial project received the support of some professional historians (among whom at least one of significant caliber, the French scholar François Furet) and neoconservative politicians. But other German intellectuals, most notably Habermas, attacked Nolte's revisionism, charging it with "apologetic tendencies," the criticism thus issued specifically on a moral rather than on an epistemic plane. Habermas was concerned that Nolte's historical interpretation would fuel conservative political agendas, and that it would license a dismissal of the crimes committed by Germany during the war, and an acquittal of Nazism. Yet according to Ricoeur, by formulating the problem as "the *public* use of history," Habermas simply reinforced the distinction between moral and historical judgment. By this logic, an indictment of the "apologetic tendencies" manifested in the revisionism of Nolte would be inappropriate if the historian had made known his theses in a scholarly venue, and not in the widely read newspaper *Frankfurter Allgemeine Zeitung*. Habermas fails, then, in Ricoeur's view, to offer a *historical* correction to Nolte's approach. The reason could be Habermas's more general allergic reaction to historical investigation, particularly when it is predicated on the assumption of continuity between past and present (cf. his debate with Gadamer, discussed in chapter 1). But Ricoeur is concerned with the very alignment of moral and historical judgment that both Nolte and Habermas oppose, though in different contexts. For him, this alignment rests crucially on the status attributed to historical events.

Nolte's treatment of history does not deny the singular nature of historical events, yet by inserting the emergence of Nazism in a causal sequence, the author accords it logical rather than contingent necessity. The Third Reich *could not* have taken a different historical trajectory—is the premise of Nolte's explanatory model. By itself, the premise does not commit its author to a moral position, as Habermas protested. Indeed, in Ricoeur's view, the explanatory model enables various moral options, "either endless lamentation and melancholic wallowing, or the awakening of civic consciousness—'what can be done so that such things [chains of events] never happen again?'" (MHF, 433, my translation). It is when the explanation tries to claim "the universality of a law" that history turns into an implacable impersonal force, unassailable and unpredictable, while historical actors, in their turn, lose their agency and become mere conduits of an abstract, transcending order.

Habermas's own position vis-à-vis Germany's past has been described as attempting to emulate what Walter Benjamin called "anamnestic solidarity" (Müller, 96)—remembering the war from the perspective of the victims. But such solidarity demands separation from the German nation, if the nation is defined historically, because one cannot identify at the same time with the victim and the aggressor. In Habermas's view, there is a link between the very concept of nationhood and the destruction of wars, and Nazi Germany represents the iconization of such a link. This link can only be undone once we shift away from our conventional understanding of the nation as grounded in a shared past, and move toward a postnational identity based in the law and on the universalist value orientations of the Constitution. Remembering the past, then, becomes the foundation for a democratic consciousness that deems group affiliation a kind of "political-*cum*-moral regression" (Müller, 95). In a society defined by the commitment to *not* renew its links to the past, the bond holding individuals together is that of constitutional patriotism. Collective identity thus becomes "postconventional," chosen rather than inherited, and postnational, grounded not in history but in the atemporal, abstract values underlying constitutional patriotism.

Notice the significant departure from the Greek vision of the epideictic role of evoking the past in order to guide a national community through a crisis or an impasse in the present. For Habermas, the past has therapeutic value only insofar as it can sponsor cautionary tales, providing a negative point of reference rather than an ideal to be cultivated and emulated. To be German, for Habermas, is to assume a historical burden for the sake of recognizing that it is simply too heavy. But at the same time, his plea for including national identities in a larger, transnational European configuration reifies the very notion of a national identity, particularly the German one. Paradoxically, Habermas wants Germans to stop being German *because* they are German. Not surprisingly, he sees postwar Germany as merely a "collective life context" (Habermas, 214), rather than as the repository of a collective identity. In his view, historical consciousness amounts to ideological manipulation, and is a twentieth century replacement for earlier periods' recourse to religion in the effort to mobilize and manipulate large groups of individuals to adhere to one cause. Like Nora, he conceives of historical consciousness as overtly associated with the rise of the professional historian, but he disparagingly describes historians as having as their sole purpose to support the state (Habermas, 226). The job of such "mandarin" historians, as Habermas deems them, is to establish causal links between the past and the present, and to invent legacies in order to manipulate commitments and allegiances. Historical inquiry is "guided by the functional imperatives of predictability, of securing consensus, of social integration through the creation of meaning" (Habermas, 225). Such an endeavor becomes particularly condemnable in a society characterized by

> ambivalence toward the burden of reconciliation imposed upon the griefwork of succeeding generations. In such a case would not the compulsory posthumous integration of those who in their lifetime were oppressed or ostracized into an undifferentiated remembrance be only a continuation of the usurpation—an extorted reconciliation? . . . Someone who nevertheless persists in mourning collective fates without distinguishing between perpetrators and victims must be up to something else. (Habermas, 214)

Suspicions such as Habermas's—that historical inquiry can have dangerous moral repercussions as they strive for epistemic value—discourage a hasty designation of history as the modern form or venue for epideictic discourse. To be able to identify the locus and fulcrum of epideictic discourse in contemporary context we would have to identify potential points of alignment between an epistemic and a moral dimension. In Ricoeur's view, this alignment is created when the past is not just approached epistemologically through explanatory moves but specifically reconstructed for the purpose of being deemed *exemplary*. As he construes it, the dimension of exemplarity is neither solely moral, nor solely epistemic. Instead, Ricoeur places exemplarity at the level of the reception. The past, he argues, must be recaptured by historians engaged in an epistemic effort, but the moral value it acquires for a particular community lies outside the domain of history as a discipline. "The assumed sense of history does not depend on historians, but on the citizen who defines the *consequences* for the events of the past" (MHF, 435, my translation). Thus, historical reconstruction of a morally reprehensible past must be addressed to "an enlightened public opinion, which converts the retrospective judgment concerning an instance of wrongdoing into the pledge to avoid repeating it in the future." (MHF, 436, my translation).

Yet the problem of the role played by epideictic is far from being resolved, as we still have to reckon with two methodological difficulties. First, what is involved in shaping an enlightened public opinion? Second, is it possible to continue to ground national identity in the past, while also qualifying the past as condemnable, or does vigilance over not repeating the past require a dismissal of the very notion of national identity? The issue at stake in both of these questions concerns the meaning and creation of what Ricoeur calls exemplarity. According to him, the paradigmatic setting for the creation of exemplarity is the law, which reinforces, by sanctioning infringements, a set of values that define the ideal normative space of a community.

We, The People

The entanglement of legal and epideictic efforts is well illustrated in the famous trials of war criminals and Nazi collaborators like Klaus Barbie, Paul Touvier, or Maurice Papon. As their goal was not just to prosecute individuals, but more importantly, to set up examples, these trials have been described as "psychotherapy on a nationwide scale" (Rousso, 210). Their significance exceeded the limits of a particular judicial situation, flowing into the public arena where the law represents a symbolic attempt to mend a deeply torn social fabric by re-creating solidarity around rules and norms and around the shared values on which these are supposed to rely. Exemplarity, thus viewed, is a normative mechanism enforced collectively in a court of law, which identifies particular events and individuals and focuses on them to make more general points that reflect the organizing principles and values of the community. Note, in this sense, that trials brought by the state against groups or individuals are carried in the name of "the people." "In reproaching those whose acts violate our most sacred beliefs and sentiments," writes a legal scholar, "we ensure that we remember what these are" (Osiel, *Mass Atrocity*, 31). As Ricoeur points out, the verdict issued by a court of law restores symbolically "the body of moral conventions that assures the minimal consensus of the political body, a consensus summed up in the idea of order" (TJ, 137). How does this process of reinforcement and remembering work?

Ricoeur defines judging as an act that "consists in separating spheres of activity, in delimiting the claims of the one from those of the other, and finally in correcting unjust distributions, when the activity of one party encroaches on the field of exercises of other parties" (TJ, 129–30). An injustice, according to him, creates uncertainty by temporarily suspending—through infringement—a community's norms and values, interrupting the usual order of things and making it possible to question. If the short-term aim of judging is to end the uncertainty by passing an authoritative decision that restores the order by enacting it, the more important long-term goal is to promote social peace by reintegrating the opposing parties into the same community. This long-term end is accomplished when the actors themselves are willing to go beyond the initial confrontation in order to discuss it at a level where they can reach an understanding as not merely opponents but as equal subjects of right. That does not mean that the conflict automatically disappears when the court has reached a decision, or that the law reconciles accuser with defendant:

> Let us not say reconciliation; even less ought we to speak of love and pardon, which are not juridical categories. Let us speak instead of recognition. But in what sense? I think that the act of judging reaches its goal when someone who has, as we say, won his case still feels able to say: my adversary, the one who lost, remains like me a subject of right, his cause should have been heard, he made plausible arguments and these were heard. However, such recognition will not be complete unless the same thing can be also said by the loser, the one who did wrong, who has been condemned. He should be able to declare that the sentence that condemns him was not an act of violence but rather one of recognition. (TJ, 131–32)

Ricoeur's understanding of how the law works is predicated on the assumption that legal decisions create consensus—even if it is by demanding equal submission to the verdict. He sees the enforcement of the law as a means for expressing symbolically the common will, and thus reinforcing the frame of the community in which individuals are linked to one another, even though the connection is oppositional, as between innocent and wrongdoer, helper and opponent, and perpetrator and victim. What two individuals locked in this relational conflict are ultimately recognizing and deferring to is not the other's claims or demands, but a collective persona engendered by the norms of the community transcending any of its members. Put differently, they recognize an ideality, and the recognition functions as a way of remedying the conflict and re-creating a condition of agreement.

Ricoeur is aware of alternative perspectives on the idea that a community manifests itself through consensual commitment to core values and beliefs. Specifically, the legal scholar Mark Osiel has questioned whether consensus allows a group "not to disintegrate into a heap of mutually antagonistic and self-seeking individuals" (in Osiel, "Making Public Memory," 217). Osiel is particularly wary of a conception that deems legal systems responsible for the creation of social cohesion. Concerned with how the law in various countries has been used to influence the collective memory of massacres and atrocities in a way that would allow the community to heal and move on, he discovers a number of recurring problems, some of which "suggest the task's impossibility, others, its undesirability" (Osiel, *Mass Atrocity*, 7). Among such problems are the sacrifice of individual rights "on the altar of social solidarity"; distorted historical understandings of the past, faulty analogies between the past and the present designed to maintain "delusions of purity and grandeur"; a demand for more repentance than most people can undertake; and, perhaps most disturbingly, a systematic dishonesty on the part of the law that meddles with collective memory while "concealing its deliberateness [in shaping memory] from the intended audience" (Osiel, *Mass Atrocity*, 7–8). Notice that the problems identified by Osiel echo the propagandistic dimension of epideictic discourse, as defined by Perelman and Olbrechts-Tyteca. As a remedy to these pitfalls, Osiel advocates disagreement as the leading force in creating "flexible, sophisticated liberalism [that] can absorb the insights and exhortations of both [accusatory and exculpatory] camps" (Osiel, "Making Public Memory," 238). In order to promote such liberalism, the legal proceedings "ought to be self-disruptive, periodically reminding readers that the persuasive coherence they seamlessly present is an illusion, secured only by compliance with disciplinary conventions that must themselves be made transparent and subject to critical scrutiny" (Osiel, "Making Public Memory," 222).

Osiel directly targets Ricoeur in questioning the argument that narratives of the past become "incorporated into a community which it gathers together" (*Mass Atrocity*, 75). He is particularly dissatisfied with what he sees as Ricoeur's emphasis on the singularity of the narrative that recaptures the past. Responding to Osiel's criticism, Ricoeur agrees that collective memory can be based on manipulation and distortion, and that those who shape memory must be aware of such pitfalls and be prepared to avoid them (MHF, 424, my translation). But at the same time he cautions that the educative function of dissent advocated by Osiel is contingent upon a notion of conflict, which oddly enough, ignores precisely the antagonism. Disagreement, as Ricoeur understands it, could not lead to genuine emancipation if it did not also pay heed to the possibility that some of the voiced opinions might seek out manipulation and distortion, and must therefore be exposed and eliminated. In other words, the disagreement cannot accord equal status to all positions. By allowing all opinions to be conveyed, Osiel's approach lets in potential justifications and exculpations, while at the same time running the risk of hiding them and other pernicious positions under the innocuous banner of equality and pluralism (MHF, 425, my translation). The connection between exculpation and explanation, Ricoeur points out, "is always part of a controversy, as one party's suspicion leads to the self-justification of the other, in a perpetual game of incrimination and exculpation" (MHF, 433, my translation). This game can only end in the name of a higher authority that can be seen as justified in intervening and ultimately adjudicating. This authority is, for Ricoeur, the law.

We have seen that at the center of judicial systems lies, in Ricoeur's rendition, a communitarian ideal founded on symbolic sharing. But, as he points out, the meaning of this sharing ambiguously connotes both commonality and separation: "In sharing there are shares, that is, those things that separate us. My share is not yours. But sharing is also what makes us share, that is, in the strong sense of the term, share in. . . ." (TJ, 132). The act of judging, then, "has as its horizon a fragile equilibrium of these two elements of sharing: that which separates my share or part from yours and that which, on the other hand, means that each of us shares in, takes part in society" (TJ, 132.). In order to create a communitarian framework that brings individuals together, the second dimension of sharing must outweigh the first by conferring public recognition upon particular acts of infringement. The law consecrates a public recognition of the offense, which Ricoeur sees as equivalent to the cathartic experience made possible by the Greek tragic spectacles (TJ, 138). Aesthetic appreciation resembles, in his view, political judgment, both being doubly constrained by collective relevance and individual affirmation (TJ, 104). The comparison between the public admission of the offense and cathartic experiences serves as a basis upon which Ricoeur can argue that, by assigning culpability and sanctions, the law also creates a purging of guilt at the community level, thus making forgiveness possible.

It is this constantly reinforced ideality that allows legal sanctions to be followed by rehabilitation and pardons, in Ricoeur's view. But while the sanctions treat the victim and the aggressor as equal subjects of right subsumed to the community, the pardon confronts the subject with the ideality, empirical persons with symbolic personae, in an asymmetrical relation that does not conform to what Ricoeur calls the "logic of equivalence." Rather, the ideality works according to the "logic of superabundance": the members of a community do not irredeemably compromise the community through their condemnable actions, because the community does not merely amount to a sum of its members. The law functions according to the logic of equivalence, treating every individual equally harshly for their acts. Without punishment, pardons would not be possible either.

A pardon, Ricoeur contends, "is a kind of healing of memory, the end of mourning. Delivered from the weight of debt, memory is freed for great projects. Pardon gives memory a future" (TJ, 144). The logic of superabundance allows communities to survive wrongdoings sanctioned in court, and to move beyond the actions of their members. The ideality that Ricoeur sees recognized in the act of judging is an abstract configuration irreducible to anything in particular, and hence immune to deterioration. The superabundance consists in the fact that the ideality has a permanent reservoir of moral values, which guarantees that redemption remain possible. No concrete dishonor can exhaust the potential realm of the "honorable."

This perspective on wrongdoing is not exculpatory, because it does not excuse individual, specific actions and their actors. It also does not promote generalized amnesia for the wrong that has happened in the name of the good that could happen. In this vein, it is indicative that Ricoeur is adamantly against amnesty as a form of rehabilitation. Indeed, he sees amnesty as the opposite of pardons, which, he insists, require remembrance. His view comes close to Benjamin's and Habermas's concept of "anamnestic solidarity." It is possible to forgive, he believes, insofar as we detach the agent from the action, and to continue to condemn the latter while we permit the former to repent and change (MHF, 456, my translation). This separation comes after an initial phase of imputation in which agents are held responsible for their actions.

To conceive of the epideictic function as defined by this logic of superabundance allows us to see national identity as an ideal configuration, and hence not only irreducible to history and to specific agents or their actions, but also and more importantly as the very vantage point from which the people of a nation can reflect upon actions committed by their fellow-citizens and by themselves. Such a vantage creates responsibility without permanent or generalized guilt, and as such it provides communities with a means of self-reparation not predicated on ignoring the wrong, or covering it up in propagandistic self-justifications.

"The Result of Sin Is Division"

A war memorial erected in Bonn in the 1980s bore the elliptical inscription, "To the victims of war." In response, Habermas protested what he saw as the demand of "a prodigious act of abstraction" on the part of viewers. In his opinion, by asking the observers to remember the victims without mentioning the perpetrators, the memorial distinguishes political responsibility from moral accountability, glosses over the singularity of wrongdoing, and collapses all instances into a generic category of evil. But then, he insisted, "one cannot simultaneously undertake a moral abstraction and insist on historical concreteness" (Habermas, 234).

One could describe Ronald Reagan's interventions at Bitburg in Habermas's terms, as an attempt at rewriting history in the name of a moral abstraction. President Reagan's address was broadly criticized as an embarrassing exoneration of Germany, arguably offered as a strategy for rallying German support for the American cold war agenda. Critics charged that Reagan had no right to offer absolution for the sins of the past, and that he promised it in exchange for collaboration in the present. But we must size up, nevertheless, the tremendous difficulty of the president's epideictic task: to speak on behalf of the victors, but not in order to condemn the defeated; to mourn the "German war dead," but not to absolve them of the "German guilt"; and to reverse roles by making friends out of former enemies (Germany), and enemies out of former friends (the former Soviet Union). He began with an acknowledgment of Germany's Nazi past, symbolized in his view by the very presence of the 48 SS officers in the Bitburg cemetery. Yet this admission is meant to get the problem out of the way so that Reagan can focus on the rest of the graves and those lying in them, "simply soldiers in the German army," not the "fanatic followers of a dictator . . . willfully [carrying] out his cruel order," but "conscripts, forced into service during the death throes of the Nazi war machine" (Levkov, 169). Reagan dissociates in Germany's troubled past between National Socialism and the German people, re-creating the dichotomy victim-aggressor within the German population. Insofar as there is a link between the past and the present, the Germans who are to become America's ally in the fight against communism are encouraged to recognize themselves in the victim, and are allowed to dissociate from the aggressor. To defend the legitimacy of such a breaking of links, Reagan had to make it seem natural rather than constructed, inevitable rather than preferable. His strategy for achieving such an effect relies heavily on how the agents are represented, as official participants in the events or as anonymous individuals. In this respect, the contrast between the indeterminate number and imprecise identity of the conscripts on the one hand, and the definite (as well as small) number of SS members (whose identity precisely as SS officers is very specific) fulfills an important function. If guilt can be assigned to the SS officers (or more generically to "the Nazi war machine"), it can also be safely contained. The others will be seen as innocent, indeed victims, in their own right. The purpose of Reagan's epideictic is to draw sympathy to these indistinct actors without making them heroes—they did fight after all against the American troops, whether obeying or also freely subscribing to Hitler's order. Notice how Reagan strives to navigate the difficult course between praise and blame, and sympathy and enmity:

> Many, . . . we know from the dates on their tombstones, were only teenagers at the time. There is one boy buried there who died a week before his 16th birthday. There were thousands of such soldiers to whom Nazism meant no more than a brutal end to a short life. . . . Our duty is to mourn the human wreckage of totalitarianism, and today, in Bitburg cemetery, we commemorated the potential good and humanity that was consumed back then, 40 years ago. (Levkov, 169)

At stake here is not an empirical issue—Germany conscripted very young men toward the end of the war—but a strategy of "childing" the individual to remove his agency. The removal of agency is also revealed by the use of the passive voice ("was consumed") and by impersonal constructions like "war machine" and "wreckage of totalitarianism." The focus on individual biographies as incomplete stories promotes exculpation by creating a "future past" that removes the German soldiers from the context of the war in order to present them simply as human beings. Reagan then hypothesizes about how the narratives of the lives ended at Bitburg could have gone on:

> Perhaps if that 15-year old soldier had lived, he would have joined his fellow countrymen in building the new democratic Federal Republic of Germany devoted to human dignity and the defense of freedom that we celebrate today. Or perhaps his children and grandchildren might be among you here today at Bitburg Air Base, where new generations

> of Germans and Americans join together in friendship and common cause. . . . (Levkov, 169)

Like the historian who reaches behind the mortuary mask to retrieve the past, Reagan brings back to life the adolescent soldier. The boy is resurrected in order "to join Americans in friendship and common cause" and to contribute to "building the new democratic Federal Republic of Germany." By representing Nazism through metonymy, as nothing but "a brutal end to a short life," Reagan individualizes the tragedy of the war and excludes any commitment or conviction on the part of the soldiers. By contrast, he envisions this life after death in social terms, as dedicated to a communal, indeed global good.

In Reagan's view, the lesson of the past is "that freedom must always be stronger than totalitarianism, that good must always be stronger than evil" (Levkov, 171). For Reagan, the exemplary role of the past—World War II—was to bring in a particular conjuncture values and agents, consecrating the allies as representatives of the good, and the others (whoever they happen to be) as forces of evil. The category "allies" has only one specific referent in Reagan's speech: the United States. Other potential referents, such as Germany, emerge through identification with the United States. We can see the mechanism of this identification at work, in reverse, in the President's famous invitation to the "freedom-loving people around the world" to say:

> I am a Berliner, I am a Jew, . . . I am an Afghan, and I am a prisoner of the Gulag. I am a refugee in a crowded boat foundering off the coast of Vietnam, I am a Laotian, a Cambodian, a Cuban, and a Miskito Indian in Nicaragua. I, too, am a potential victim of totalitarianism (Levkov, 172).

This transnationalism detaches totalitarianism from the connection to any particular countries, thus implicitly challenging the iconicization of Nazi Germany in relation to the evils of war. The past, with the war and the position of powers in its aftermath, becomes the basis for ratifying a distribution of roles, in which positions can shift (former allies are now enemies, and former enemies have become allies) as long as one remains fixed. Indeed, reifying this position becomes the exemplary function of the past, as illustrated in the chant of identification—I am a Berliner, I am a Jew, . . . I am a Laotian, and so forth—which changes predicate but not subject. The repeated element is what gives the changing objects a common basis that allows them to be seen as parts of a whole, identical and interchangeable. They are instances of totalitarianism creating victims, just as the speaker and his country are illustrations of freedom.

Reagan incorporating German identity into a broader configuration largely associated with America, was defined by an epideictic that engages in what Karlyn Kohrs Campbell calls

> the rhetoric of mythical America, whose business is the defense of freedom, whose strength has resulted from facing crises and rejecting the easy way, whose greatness has been the capacity to do what had to be done when it was known to be right. This mythical America is the last hope for the survival of peace and freedom in the world; this most powerful nation will not allow the forces of totalitarianism to suffocate the hopes of the peoples of the earth. This is a nation of destiny. (Campbell, 202)

The pitfalls of this rhetoric became clear that same year when a member of the Christian Democratic Union, named Alfred Dregger, sent a letter to U.S. Senator Howard Morton Metzenbaum, in which he claimed that the memory of his brother who had died on the eastern front deserves to be honored by the victorious West, i.e., America. "Didn't the Senate understand that his brother had died fighting Soviet Communism?" (Brockmann, 169). Indeed, if Germany's enemy at the eastern front was Soviet totalitarianism, which in the meantime had also become the enemy of the United States, wasn't Germany fighting a right cause even during the war? Of course, to American war veterans and to the American public, this would never be a tenable position. At bottom, this is an argument that does not define nations through their history but through reified yet contingent political positions. It is an argument that leads to paradoxes and inconsistencies—such as the fact that Germany fought both a heroic war (on the eastern front, against the Soviet Union) and an unjust one (against the other countries). As one commentator astutely observed, at Bitburg Reagan attempted an erasure of agents and a writing of history in which the protagonists are placeholders—forces of freedom against those of totalitarianism, allies against a common enemy (Brockmann, 172).

By contrast, among the German themselves there were people who urged that the burden of the past be assumed and carried with remorse and dignity. As we have seen in Habermas's case, proponents of historical lucidity faced the difficult task of defining German identity beyond history. After the war, to be German was tantamount with being trapped in a painful dilemma that demanded "reconciling in a single word the indelible stigma of earlier murder and genocide with later recovery and rehabilitation . . . the seams of destruction on the one hand and a good life [after the war] on the other" (Jarausch and Geyer, 11). To redefine the word "German" required a profound rediscovery if not reconstitution of national identity. On the same day as Reagan's speech, May 8, 1985, President Richard von Weizsäcker spoke in the Plenary Room of the German Bundestag:

> We Germans are one people and one nation. We feel that we belong together because we have lived through the same past. We also experienced the 8th of May 1945 as part of the common fate of our nation that unites us. We feel bound together in our desire for peace. . . . The people of Germany are united in desiring a peace than encompasses justice and human rights for all peoples, including our own. . . . We are confident that the 8th of May is not the last date in the common history of all Germans. (Levkov, 206)

But even though Germans were one nation, there were two Germanies after the war. By 1985, the destiny of this nation had been following the two different paths that were opened for Germany at the end of the war. For the Germans, then, commemorating the end of the war amounted to an acceptance of the sanction, the partition of the country: "The pathetic result of sin is always division," lamented Weizsäcker, quoting these words from the sermon delivered by Cardinal Joachim Meissner in East Berlin at the same commemorations. But to see Germany's partition as punishment requires an acknowledgment of the German nation as an ideal space or abstraction that does not disappear by political fiat. It is the space in which the shift from sanction to rehabilitation is possible according to the logic of superabundance. Weizsäcker believes not in a "zero-hour"—a symbolic cleaning of slates that would allow postwar Germany to shed its burdened legacy—but in "the opportunity to make a fresh start" (Levkov, 204). In the West German president's view, this new beginning requires full responsibility for the past, indeed the recognition of its negative exemplarity, not an erasure.

Such recognition comes through the very identification of May 8, 1945 as "a day of liberation," and its meaning for the German people as a time of mourning the victims of the war. But while the mention of "liberation" could suggest that the Germans themselves were victims of the war—in the sense defined by Reagan—Weizsäcker enumerates the victims made *by* Germany: the six million Jews in concentration camps, the Soviet and Polish soldiers, the Sinti and Romany gypsies, homosexuals and the mentally ill, hostages, and those who died resisting National Socialism, actively or not. This comprehensive list reads as a dark roster that seeks to avoid any justification that might come from operating selections. As Friedländer commented, the President

> does not avoid a detailed enumeration of Nazi crimes, and he stresses, with great sincerity and courage, the central place of the destruction of the Jewish people in Nazi ideology and practice. For the Western reader and certainly for the Jewish reader, Weizsäcker's address is an exemplary admission of the utter criminality of the Nazi state. (Friedländer, 32)

But the role of this admission is not to increase vigilance against a new raising threat—the Soviet Union. Unlike Reagan, who puts memory in the service of an emerging political alliance, Weizsäcker forges (and through specific policies puts into practice) the "anamnestic solidarity" invoked by Benjamin and Habermas. He explicitly adopts the victims' frame of reference:

> The Jewish nation remembers and will always remember. We seek reconciliation. Precisely for this reason we must understand that there can be no reconciliation without remembrance. The experience of millionfold death is part of the being of every Jew in the world, not only because people cannot forget such atrocities, but also because remembrance is part of the Jewish faith. . . . If we for our part sought to forget what has occurred, instead of remembering it, this would not only be inhuman. We would also impinge upon the faith of the Jews who survived and destroy the basis for reconciliation. We must erect a memorial to thought and feelings in our own hearts. (Levkov, 201)

The president does not try to separate the victims from the perpetrators, as to forget the perpetration is to also ignore the sacrifice. He does not remove the agency of those who committed the wrong. Those who suffered and those who caused the suffering are linked in a communitarian frame of significance, but within this frame, identities are specific and not subsumed to such generic hypostases as allies and enemies, victors and losers, and deceased and survivors.

Weizsäcker's emphasis on agency is revealed in his emphasis on individual culpability—"everyone who directly experienced that era should today quietly ask himself about his involvement then" (Levkov, 206). For the president, the issue of personal responsibility had particular acuity, as his own father had served in the infamous SS service. When it comes to the responsibility of the German nation, the exemplarity of the past resides in its function as a "guideline for [our] future behavior" (Levkov, 207). Insofar as the "the memory of [German] history" (Levkov, 205) shapes future behaviors and attitudes, and policies and decisions, it becomes the starting point for the renewal of a German identity that admits guilt, but that can also become rehabilitated through repentance and through the undoing of the wrong. Engaged in this act of self-transformation, German identity is rescued from the actions of Germans during the war and through a commitment to reparations: In memory of the mentally sick who were murdered, this nation "will seek [the] care of people with psychiatric disorders as our own responsibility." In memory of those persecuted for their political and religious beliefs, or because of their race, and then rejected by the countries where they sought refuge, the German nation "will not close the door today on those who are genuinely persecuted and seek protection" (Levkov, 205). The exemplarity of the past affords a critical vantage from which self-reform becomes possible. But such critical reflection and the repentance it affords are only possible according to the logic of superabundance that allows a community to survive as an ideality.

In Habermas's conception of a postnational identity epideictic has no role at all. This actually confirms the direct relationship between epideictic and national identity. In Reagan's notion of a U.S.-centered international political alliance in which national specificity does not matter and where identities become subsumed under the overarching equation of freedom with the United States, epideictic functions as propaganda. If we follow Ricoeur's reasoning, the force of epideictic lies elsewhere: not in an exculpatory glorification of even the most dubious of pasts—supreme proof of propagandistic manipulation—but in finding a vantage from which to assess and process the past in order to learn from it, to critically evaluate individual accountability, and to understand how to rescue collective agency without shedding responsibility for specific actions. As used by Weizsäcker, epideictic makes pardon possible, in part because it explicitly asks for it while also accepting the sanction. The ideality that such epideictic creates does not act as a screen behind which epistemic and moral issues can be manipulated conveniently, but as a resource for individual and collective rehabilitation. It allows nations to redeem themselves. Weizsäcker's plea relies on the premise that as an ideality, the German nation is capable of surviving by indicting and repairing actions committed in the past. The premise, however, is not taken for granted. The president issues specific requirements: to take responsibility for the past or "to look history in the eye," through symbolic gestures such as Willy Brandt's kneeling at a war memorial in Warsaw; as well as through political, social, and economic plans and policies initiated by the German nation itself, rather than required by a self-appointed guardian of world peace.

CONCLUSION

In chapter 4 I looked at history as a source of practical wisdom. Ricoeur's hermeneutical reflections guided an inquiry into how historical consciousness can inform rhetorical discourse by addressing stringent and challenging problems in the present. Because it has such epistemic and moral value, history becomes a basis for self-identification, a shared past forging strong social bonds by providing individual agents with a frame of reference and a reservoir of meanings. Traditionally, the rhetorical practice of epideictic relied on the past and on history as a means for acculturation into a community. The challenge confronting such a practice comes from focusing on the acculturation to the point that history becomes merely a stepping stone, and as such, subject to manipulation. Hence, epideictic rhetoric has to navigate a narrow course between practical wisdom and manipulation, and education and propaganda. The Aristotelian treatment, with its emphasis on the aesthetic aspect of epideictic, merely ignores this challenge by trying to domesticate epideictic through its alignment with literature—a way of dismissing its social and political function. Perelman and Olbrechts-Tyteca acknowledge such a function, but they make it contingent on a rigid and hence somewhat simplistic dichotomy between education and propaganda. Ricoeur's reflections on the exemplary nature of the past and on the ideal nature of a community inspire a revised conception of epideictic, one informed by both epistemic and moral goals. His notion of morality is derived from an ideal communitarian space that takes shape in the legal act of judging. To think of the epideictic function as forging that ideal communitarian space through historical accounts that deem the past enlightening allows us to avoid the propagandistic pitfall. It allows us to be hopeful that communities and nations can understand and accept themselves while understanding and accepting their past. Finally, it gives us an entry into what leaders and citizens need to do so that the crisis of public memory bemoaned by Ricoeur does not become permanent.

Chapter Five

The Polis

In chapter 4, I explained how Ricoeur allows us to understand the role of epideictic discourse in shaping national identity, and in order to focus on the diachronic level of history I assumed the synchronic uniformity of the community in question. To engage this assumption more critically, in this chapter I turn my attention to the synchronic level. I am prompted to scrutinize this premise by much interdisciplinary work that questions from various directions the homogeneity of national communities and describes the formation of nation-states as based on a purposeful exclusion of various internal constituencies. The idea of a prior civil solidarity giving rise to homogeneous states can be traced back to the rhetorical concept of the *polis*, a political configuration in which participation was conditioned both by social status and ethnicity. But in more recent studies the collective sentiment assumed to reflect a preexisting solidary basis of ethnicity (in the polis and in other political structures) has been identified as a powerful construction strategically manipulated by elites rather than a genuine expression of the situation on the ground. Rhetorical scholars have seized upon this discovery and made a significant contribution to the study of community formation by carefully analyzing the discursive acts that create the illusion of inclusion, and mask or justify exclusion. The works of Stephen Browne, Barbara Biesecker, Gregory Clarke, Michael Halloran, Marouf Hassian, and Barbie Zeidel allow us to understand how a sense of community cohesion and equal political representation can be artificially orchestrated through presidential rhetoric, commemorative practices, historical evocations, preservationist policies, and even particular landscapes. At the same time, under the conceptual banner of the public sphere much attention has been paid to the efforts of particular constituencies to be actively and effectively represented in a polity and to be recognized as a legitimate component of the communities to which they belong. The works of Gerard Hauser, Robert Asen, Michael Calvin McGee, Barbara Couture, and Thomas Kent—among others—have marked important contributions to the development of a rhetorical concept of the public sphere. As developed in these works, the concept of the public sphere "recognizes that we engage in civic conversation on particular issues with specific interlocutors and audiences," and is primarily concerned with "how the dialogue within any given public sphere mounts appeals that lead participants to understand their interests and make prudent judgments" (Hauser, *Vernacular Voices*, 56). Hauser even questions the use in the singular of the term *public sphere,* and focuses on developing a pluralized rhetorical polis that has a reticulate structure and that is shaped around "vernacular rhetorics."

This chapter situates Ricoeur's contribution to understanding the nature of the rhetorical polis at the intersection of work on the rhetoric of nation-states and public sphere studies. This is a critical conceptual intersection, and one that is unfortunately insufficiently articulated, even though, as Nancy Fraser explains, much of the discussion on the concept of a public sphere presupposes a Westphalian/national frame. In her words, "a public sphere is supposed to be a vehicle for mobilizing public opinion as a political force. It should empower the citizenry vis-à-vis private powers and permit it to exercise influence over the state. Thus, a public sphere is supposed to correlate with a sovereign power, to which its communications are ultimately addressed" (Fraser, 1). The literature on nation-state formation and maintenance explains well the challenges faced by the public sphere and the difficulty of empowering citizens to deal with institutional power. To preserve itself, the institutional authority on which states are based employs various tactics designed to solidify loyalty to the core-nation (Marx, 107), and such strategies presume a selective allocation of citizenship rights (Hechter, 167). With his emphasis on the ideal dimension of national identity, preserved and revealed in highly normative institutional settings like the law, Ricoeur himself acknowledges the asymmetry between individuals and the community to which they belong—the political life of the community being based not on particular individuals but on an abstract, reified notion that holds them all together. The key task of a theory of democracy, as Ricoeur sees it, consists in making sure that the requirements of political life, centered on institutions like the state, do not trump individual freedom of choice and decision. The challenge facing proponents of democracy, in his view, is knowing "how to educate citizens in critical adherence when as citizens they are never in the position of engendering the political sphere from themselves" (CC, 102).

Such a concern comes in the context of a broader intellectual trend that has led scholars on both sides of the Atlantic to be increasingly critical of the communitarian premise—expressed in the focus on a "common good"—in most theories of democracy, and to look for models of social and political interaction that center on individual actors. In *Inclusion and Democracy*, Iris Marion Young has proposed a model of deliberative democracy that uses strategies of direct engagement—such as personal narratives, situated appeals, and greetings that identify citizens in their particularity—in order to increase political participation and promote inclusion. In France, this shift toward the individual has coincided with the revival of liberalism, a philosophical and political doctrine that moves agents to the fore, and assigns them a vital role in the formation and maintenance of social and political systems. Among the political theorists who have most significantly impacted Ricoeur's thinking in this regard are Luc Boltanski and Claude Lefort, whose theoretical explorations are based on empirical research on the social and political ties that connect individuals. According to Lefort, liberalism sees in every individual an "irreducible element" that should not be confused with any of the characteristics of the social group in which the individual is a member. Influenced by Alexis de Tocqueville's *Democracy in America*, Lefort espouses the former's belief that "humanity . . . emerges from the coming together of multiple individual perspectives (Lefort, 178). Both Lefort and Boltanski resist the notion of a "collective soul," and the imposition of likeness as the precondition for communitarian life. But they also stress the need for reconciling individual autonomy with collective affiliation: "The most remarkable feature of critiques of democracy," Lefort notes, "is the durability of the representation of *the man lost in the crowd.* It fuels both a horror of anonymity and a longing for an imaginary community whose members experience the joy of being together" (Lefort, 181).

Over the years, Ricoeur has consistently located individual autonomy at the center of "an ethical life in community with other rational beings" (Anderson, 15). His political beliefs have been described by Bernard Dauenhauer as constituting a form of "liberal communitarianism," a third way between political atomism and political holism" (Dauenhauer, 238). This sui generis political philosophy recognizes the autonomy of individuals (and hence their agency above that of groups or institutions) while also positing an interdependence among them. At the center of such a conception is a model of interaction similar to Emile Durkheim's notion of organic solidarity, defined as the bond that links different individuals, beyond transitory exchanges, in a cohesive group whose survival requires the participation of all members even as their actions within it can unfold unimpeded by the others around. Since Durkheim, most sociological theories of solidarity identify it as a labor relation, but they also stress the importance of a sense of reciprocity if not sameness among the actors involved, which can prompt mutual support and assistance. At the same time, the term *solidarity* has a distinct oppositional flavor that counterpoints it to institutional power and authority. For this reason, it "is much more frequently invoked by militants in collective struggles of a progressive character than by the Right or by politicians executing normal administrative operations" (Levine, 70). The paradigmatic case study for such an understanding of solidarity is the dissident organization that emerged under this name in Communist Poland. At the beginning of the 1980s, as the living conditions of millions of people behind the Iron Curtain worsened, Polish workers began to organize a series of strikes, at the Gdansk and Szczecin shipyards, in the Warsaw city transport, at the Lublin railways, and in the coal mines in Silesia. "For the first time in the history of the Polish People's Republic," a historian comments, "[the workers] formed a representation of interests on a class basis and against the institutionalized representation—the communist party" (Staniszkis, 40). From a labor union, Solidarity quickly grew into a broad-based political organization that cut across class, age, gender, or education. Its broad-based appeal and effectiveness stunned political commentators abroad, and exhilarated Eastern Europeans. How was the Solidarity miracle possible in a country ruled by a totalitarian party, if even democratic regimes find it difficult to achieve such inclusiveness and widespread political participation?

This is the question I want to tackle in this chapter, by way of addressing the theoretical concerns just discussed. Polish Solidarity has inspired rhetoricians like Hauser, who are seeking to develop a model of polity that supports broad participation and that makes no normative requirements. But Ricoeur aids significantly to the development of a heuristic based on which we can understand the creation of public spheres through broad solidarity in the context of a nation-state inclined to maintain its authority through exclusionary mechanisms. At the center of this heuristic is "a cluster of critical questions about how one ought to engage in politics" (cf. Dauenhauer, 246). The first question concerns the possibility of challenging the political institutions that organize a nation-state in an emancipatory rather than a reactionary fashion. The second question scrutinizes the conditions based on which individuals with different interests, backgrounds, and agendas can nevertheless find a common space of direct engagement. Third, Ricoeur challenges prescriptive models that assess participation in a community's political existence from the perspective of commitment to a moral norm, and suggests instead a descriptive account focused on how individual agents define collaboratively the parameters of the "common good" and commit to it as an ethical aim. The heuristic these questions devise reflects the philosopher's effort to establish a space of interaction in which mutual recognition leads to solidarity, as individuals consent to the pursuit of a set of goals and strategies that defines their ideal of a good life.

To ground the theoretical discussion of this chapter, I analyze a text written in prison by a prominent member of the Solidarity movement, the historian Adam Michnik. My choice of this particular object of analysis is motivated by its centrality in the history of the Solidarity movement. But I also took into account the fact that Hauser has discussed it in his essay, "Prisoners of Conscience and the Counterpublic Sphere of Prison Writing," thus providing a basis for comparison. Reading Michnik's rhetoric from a Ricoeurian perspective and measuring the results against those yielded by another analysis will reveal the explanatory value of his conceptual apparatus, its ability to tease out additional important ideas that we might otherwise miss.

Updating the Polis

In his *History of the Peloponnesian War,* Thucydides recounts an episode in which the Athenians force the Melians to join their side in the war against Sparta, thus illustrating the futility of rhetoric when one party has power over the other. To some ears, the historian's conclusion might still ring true today: "the powerful do whatever they want, while the weak yield" (qtd. in Conley, 2). Writing in the twentieth century, Perelman and Olbrechts-Tyteca explicitly oppose violence to rhetoric in their contention that

> the use of argumentation implies that one has renounced resorting to force alone, that value is attached to gaining the adherence of one's interlocutor by means of reasoned persuasion, and that one is not regarding him as an object, but appealing to his free judgment. Recourse to argumentation assumes the establishment of a community of minds, which, while it lasts, excludes the use of violence. (Perelman and Olbrechts-Tyteca, 55)

In this account, a community fostered through rhetorical speech transcends social, economic, and political determinations. This community emerges discursively as a space of communicative transactions in which participants are equally endowed with will and judgment. The emergence of the ancient Greek polis was an early attempt at shaping just such a community, by submitting political claims made on its behalf to public scrutiny, and indeed by defining the norms of reason within the parameters of the public domain. The polis relied on the authority of Logos insofar as "all questions of general concern that the sovereign had to settle, . . . had to be formulated as a discourse, poured into the mold of antithetical demonstrations and opposing arguments" (Vernant, 50). Yet the polis was a community in which interactions took place among individuals who were likely to agree with one another because they often shared a worldview. Issues of public concern were openly discussed among the members of the polis, but the agreement was aided significantly by the fact that the community was defined first and foremost by *isomorphism* among members. Likeness "laid the foundation for the unity of the *polis*, since for the Greeks only those who were alike could be mutually united by *philia*, joined in the same community" (Vernant, 60).

Despite such a prerequisite of likeness, the Greek polis did not completely ignore potential discrepancies between an individual and the collective. Protagoras, Thucydides, and Democritus—among others—devoted much effort to finding a "dynamic reconciliation of man's particularity and autonomy with the requirements of communal life" (Farrar, 2). But whether such reconciliation was indeed found in antiquity remains a contentious issue among scholars. In Hauser's opinion, because the polis lacked a "buffer between the individual and the state" ("Civil Society," 24), the Greek political system of organization enabled the subjugation of "the private self to the public realm" ("Civil Society," 25). Such a relationship still informs, according to Hauser, many rhetorical theories that privilege a macrodiscursive level assumed to be also relevant to the microphenomena characteristic of the level of individual actors. Hauser wishes to counteract this implicit monolithic communitarianism defining rhetorical theory, on the grounds that it is "inconsistent with the realities of contemporary public life" ("Civil Society," 25). In his view, contemporary public life occurs in a pluralized sphere consisting of a "montage of discursive arenas . . . themselves . . . situated in the larger and not always coterminous arena of *civil society*" ("Civil Society," 25). Accordingly, civil society represents a historical formation markedly different from the polis, one that replaces isomorphism with modularity, being "composed of nested arenas with a reticulate structure" (Hauser, "Civil Society," 21), "a network of associations independent of the state whose members, through social interactions that balance conflict and consensus, seek to regulate themselves in ways consistent with a valuation of difference" (Hauser, "Civil Society," 26).

As many others have, Hauser rejects Jürgen Habermas's conception of a bourgeois community as the model for a public sphere, because his model "excludes many arenas in which public dialogue occurs and, moreover, establishes criteria for communication that are insensitive to its essential rhetoricality" (Hauser, *Vernacular Voices*, 39). But the most often voiced objection to Habermas's model, formulated among others by Geoff Eley, concerns its exclusive reliance on one social class, and the dismissal of the activities of other groups. Efforts at modifying this conception have often proceeded by expanding its empirical foundation, limited by Habermas to the bourgeoisie. Thus, based on the nineteenth-century voluntary associations of elite American women, Mary Ryan has proposed an alternative model, which replaces a unitary concept of the public sphere with "a variegated, decentered, and democratic *array* of public spaces" (Ryan, 264, my emphasis). The shift from the Greek polis to the civil society emerging in the Enlightenment, and later to the creation of voluntary associations in nineteenth-century America occurred in the context of a long series of social transformations in Western civilization. These transformations gradually decentralized and diffused political power, creating a web of authorities that enabled and constrained one another, each forging different social roles and challenging the very notion of an all-inclusive polis. In the eighteenth century, civil society arose in response to the need to mediate between newly created social roles, to reconcile group interests, and to create a political, moral, and economical basis for dealing with diversity. At its core, civil society was not concerned with shared practices but with sites of contention. As such, it had to be equipped for managing dissent rather than simply counting on agreement. And in the philosophical conception advanced by the Enlightenment thinkers, especially the Scottish moralists, this foundation rested on the equation of private values with the public ideal. If the civic tradition reversed the subordination of the individual and society, it did so insofar as it adopted an important proviso that stipulated, in Adam Smith's terms, a natural ability to sympathize and empathize with other fellow beings. Smith claimed that there is a *disinterested perspective*, internalized in each individual as a supervising authority that legitimates one's beliefs and conduct:

> We endeavor to examine our own conduct as we imagine any other fair and impartial spectator would examine it. If upon placing ourselves in his situation, we thoroughly enter into all the passions and motives

> which influenced it, we approve of it, by sympathy with the approbation of this supposed equitable judge. (Smith, 110)

Smith's impartial spectator assumes a self-distancing ability based on the availability of a neutral perspective, invariably applicable from one individual case to another. From such an equidistant perspective, individuals can both assess their beliefs and understand others', the impartial spectator acting as a plane of encounter among different yet compatible viewpoints. This conception defines a public order that confirms itself through instantiations in private moralities. Yet we can press further: can a public sphere created through identification with an imaginary moral arbiter reflect a particular perspective that tries to pass for general and representative, and in the name of such a perspective exclude or flatten individual variation? Does civil society use the guise of private moralities to reinforce a particular perspective and impose isomorphism?

Such concerns are a good reason to depart from a conception based on universal moral values, and to seek, along with Hauser, a model of civil society in which differences are resolved "not by exemplary manifestations of a superordinate cultural ideal, but through accommodations developed through a discourse conducted outside of authority and regulative of it" ("Civil Society," 31). Instead of a cultural ideal unifying the space of encounters (as in the case of the polis), Hauser wants to see a superordinate public sphere containing multiple subdomains as the context for such discourse. But the challenge facing any account that wants to preserve the very notion of a public sphere in the singular is that of reification, and consequently, of carrying over some of the same homogenizing function accomplished by the Greek polis. This is perhaps the conceptual difficulty most often bemoaned by critics of civil society.

Hauser's solution to the perpetuated problem of homogeneity lies in his notion of "vernacular conversations," which focuses on the recognition of difference among various discursive arenas within civil society. In his view, such recognition becomes possible if individuals agree not to project their own beliefs and representations onto others, and not to accord universality to their own particular standards and norms. In its turn, this self-relativizing requires a critical separation between an individual and her position, the opening of a gap between individuals and "what was formerly fused with the subject as unconscious presupposition" ("Civil Society," 19). Hauser does not feel that individuals must fuse with one another in a self-effacing effort, but he expects them to be willing to recognize multiple available meanings, and to entertain those "producing solutions interdependent partners regard as acceptable *for their own reasons*" ("Civil Society," 36, my emphasis). On this account, empathy replaces similarity, and cooperation becomes possible without the requirement of homogeneity.

Perhaps the greatest intellectual merit of this work lies in its emancipatory mission, its potential for opening the realm of rhetorical interactions to actors of various backgrounds. But critics have raised concerns about its methodological strengths, and Hauser has been repeatedly reproached for a lack of explicit heuristic criteria. Most seriously, he has been accused of advocating an approach that "cannot distinguish between democratizing or emancipatory discourses on the one hand and the reactionary discourses that run against democratic interests on the other hand" and for supporting "an uncritical populism [in which] there can be no differential treatment of authentic utterances as opposed to instances in which people are spoken through and by the systems they inhabit" (Cloud, 210). Such objections reveal the assumption commonly made by theorists of the public sphere who, as Fraser puts it, are concerned with political validity: how to make sure that increased political participation does indeed yield positive results for the community, and not chaos or disorientation. In response to his critics, Hauser has maintained that his goal was to change the set of questions we ask about the public sphere, a change necessary but also preliminary to revising existing models of social and political interaction. Hauser's goal was to define the conditions for *participatory* discourse, for which the standard of evaluation is broad representation of interests and agendas, not validity.

But Hauser can also be taken to task on another, even more basic, issue. Participatory discourse is emancipatory insofar as it draws on the interests and beliefs of groups that are commonly not represented. But the very idea of participation presupposes a common arena. Implicit in Hauser's conception is the unchallenged possibility and opportunity for discourse across boundaries, and for solidarity among individuals who might belong to different discursive arenas but who can nonetheless reach out beyond the confines of their own sphere. Based on his amendments to Habermas, Hauser concludes that solidarity is more effective than rational consensus as a foundation for a reticulate public sphere, and turns to the Polish case as confirmation. Oddly enough, though, his analysis of Solidarity's mission and constitution identifies the sources of its success in precisely the categories that Hauser discards in his theoretical discussion as inadequate for an understanding of a pluralistic civil society. He stresses, for instance, the importance of the moral dimension in Solidarity's rhetoric, after having dismissed the possibility of shaping a community around moral values (*Vernacular Voices*, 38). Poland's Catholic church and the pope's interventions in particular are also credited by Hauser as having played a critical role in encouraging emancipation from the Communist state. But religion is a highly problematic factor, and difficult to consider as the engine of civil society, especially when reified, according to Hauser, to represent an entire nation. While it is clear that many Solidarity leaders drew on religion in their public interventions, and that John Paul II was personally involved and invested in the movement, the actual religious beliefs of the participants probably varied, in kind and intensity. The role of the Catholic Church, then, must be carefully qualified. Hauser tries to be prudent, and argues that Solidarity's religious discourse had a secular dimension that tried to recapture the history of Poland and the inspiring example of its heroes (*Vernacular Voices*, 124). But his emphasis on history goes against what experts in the Solidarity case have identified as the profoundly "ahistorical" dimension of the movement, its anchorage in the present and appeal to the average Pole rather than recourse to the example of national heroes (Garton Ash, 44). Indeed, historians and political scientists have gone as far as to argue that Solidarity was successful precisely because, unlike previous attempts at organized resistance, it did not draw on Poland's past but capitalized on the needs so acutely perceived in the present. The spark that ignited the revolt was the price of meat, not a sense of heroic national calling.

The civil society shaped in Poland by the Solidarity movement appears remarkably monolithic, in Hauser's analysis. Reified through morality, religion, and history—all three dimensions normative through and through—such a public sphere seems to have no need for dealing with difference, since it reveals none. How can Solidarity, thus described, be the very model for a reticulate public sphere? One way to avoid such a disparity between theoretical observations and analytic insights is by elaborating a framework that is not simply based on amending an existing concept designed in a different historical setting, but that starts with a series of general questions about the condition for, and constraints on, political participation in the context of a nation-state. The framework proposed by Ricoeur, while indebted to several theorists, is more coherent and has more explanatory value because it is centered in a systematic investigation of the communication between the state and its citizens, which constitutes, by Fraser's account, the conceptual foundation of the public sphere.

"The Political Paradox"

The key elements of Ricoeur's conception of political organization can be traced to a major influence in twentieth-century political philosophy, that of Hannah Arendt. In *The Human Condition*, Arendt described political activity as taking place along a horizontal and a vertical dimension. On the horizontal plane political activity is the effort of people wishing to live together in the present, whose behaviors and convictions must be calibrated and coordinated for this reason. The horizontal level is that of particular individuals who participate together in everyday practices, but such practices define them as a *community* only insofar as they extend beyond the present moment and the particular actors involved at any given time. Political activity, then, also unfolds along a vertical dimension, which connects the present to the past and establishes a hierarchy of positions and roles to be occupied by different individuals over time. In Ricoeur's view, the horizontal plane is that of a "silent, generally unnoticed" wish to live with others, a wish that becomes manifest when people are faced with the distinct possibility of it not being realized. At such a point in the history of a community, the ties that keep individuals together have already "come undone," and the vertical dimension, too, is in question (CC, 99). The goal of politics is to maintain a community, and it can only do so by simultaneously engaging both the horizontal and the vertical axes. The peculiar nature of political intervention, according to Ricoeur, is that the two dimensions are inseparable yet also asymmetrical. This peculiarity is unavoidable insofar as it

> comes from this imbalance in structure; we undoubtedly feel it to be desirable that all power should emanate from the wish to live together, that the vertical relation be entirely absorbed within the horizontal relation—this is in a sense a desire for self-management—but perhaps this would also be the end of politics, including the end of its benefits in the sphere of linking the generations together and of reconciling traditions and projects. It is possible, in the final analysis, that this corrective function of politics can be exerted only if a compromise is found and worked out between the hierarchical relation and the consensual relation. (CC, 99)

This "corrective" function of politics must be understood in the context of Ricoeur's broader conception of the *polis,* also influenced by two landmark texts in the Western tradition, Aristotle's *Politics* and Jean-Jacques

Rousseau's *Social Contract.* Ricoeur relies on Aristotle's separation between the sphere of politics (*polis*) and the socioeconomic structure of a society to contend that sociopolitical organizations cannot be reduced to class conflicts, or to economic relations. Instead, he suggests, the polis must be seen as an autonomous plane characterized by a specific rationality, a system of rules and principles that enable individuals to make decisions together "and achieve a historical efficacy that would otherwise not be possible (Dauenhauer, 67). In Aristotelian terms, the polis is a space in which speech and action are oriented toward a public good and where individuals come together in a "sort of partnership" (*Politics* I, 5). Thus, for Aristotle the criterion for citizenship and that for humanity overlap: the person "who by nature and not by mere accident can exist without a state would be a despicable individual." As Ricoeur comments, ""henceforth, man cannot evade politics under penalty of evading his humanity" (HT, 261).

To problematize this conflation of communal and political life, Ricoeur turns to Rousseau, who was particularly sensitive to the constructed rather than natural or spontaneous nature of a "general will" reflected in sociopolitical organizations. In the *Social Contract,* Rousseau contends that political organizations are seen *retrospectively* as configurations that have always existed within communities. As critics have noted, "[w]hile the Greek conception is more objective and naturalistic, Rousseau's is more subject centered; but the latter's 'general will' occupies an objective status just as Aristotle's naturalism harbors a human or humanistic telos" (Dallmayr, 181).

Ricoeur finds both theories concerned with "manifesting the coincidence of an individual or desiring will with the objective political will, in short, . . . making man's humanity pass through law and civil restraint" (HT, 251–53). But he pays heed to Rousseau's idea that

> the body politic is born of a virtual act, of a consent which is not an historical event, but one which comes out in reflection. This act is a pact: not a pact of one with another, not a pact of abstention in favor of a non-contracting third party, the sovereign, who by not being part of the contract would be absolute. No—it is a pact of each individual with all, a pact which constitutes the people as a people by constituting it as a State. (HT, 251–52)

In that case, Ricoeur comments, even if all individuals had a penchant for congregating in communities, the "social contract" never requires each single member's explicit and voluntary adherence to the group. As the product of a virtual act, political organization can become a "ready-made fiction to clothe the hypocrisy of a ruling class, . . . ignore particular cases, real differences of power, and the real conditions of persons" (HT, 253). The virtual agreement laid at the foundation of the polis becomes a legitimizing basis for the exercise of power against those who might want to challenge specific aspects of the political sphere in question. From the perspective of a presumed original agreement—repeatedly confirmed under the banner of the "public good"—individuals can never be on a par with the collective abstraction to which they are subsumed. What keeps the community together, then

> appears to us all across history as a living contradiction. On the one hand, its greatness is to transform a historical community into a unique will, able to make decisions, to survive danger, and to organize itself in tranquillity. No historical community can exist without a power that surpasses the play of individual interests, without a State. But on the other hand, power can only appear as a force which does violence, as a constraint that limits interests, limits even the vocation of individuals. The State . . . is a force of unconditional constraint. It is legitimate violence in history. (qtd. in Dauenhauer, 77)

This paragraph reveals two convictions that play an important role in Ricoeur's understanding of the polis. First, he defines political organizations in the context of the state, clearly operating in the tradition of Aristotle. Second, he assumes that founding acts behind political organizations are implacably violent, such inaugural violence later converted into a symbolic capital that legitimizes the exclusion of those who threaten or challenge the hierarchy defining the vertical dimension. Political violence, as Ricoeur sees it, is not limited to coup d'états or revolutions, but is more generally created "by harmonizing . . . private languages in a common fable of glory" (PSE, 94). While claiming to represent the general interest, the state can in fact only legitimize the interests of some and systematically eliminate or repress those of others.

The political paradox is the consequence of the disparity between the illegitimacy of action directed against the state at the microlevel of individuals, where it is seen as reactionary because it can be accused of breaking the rational concord, and its legitimacy at the macrolevel of the community, where it can be defended as not repression but simply as reinforcing the social bond. Such disparity is inevitable insofar as it "emerges by virtue of the fact that concord is always crisscrossed by particular strategies and the need for concretely binding, though necessarily partisan, policies" (Dallmayr, 183). This discrepancy becomes an "occasion for abuse" insofar as a system designed to regulate life in common can turn against (some of) those who live it by speculating the symbolic capital of the initial violence absorbed in the legitimacy of political action. We can now understand why the distinction between emancipatory and reactionary politics, as formulated by Dana Cloud in response to Hauser, is difficult to draw. Political validity, then, by Ricoeur's account, tends to be associated with the vertical level. But Ricoeur has repeatedly insisted that his recognition of the political evil should not be misconstrued as a generalized criticism of political intervention. "Politics," he contends, "can be the seat of the greatest evil only because of its prominent place in human existence" (HT, 264). Furthermore, "the enormity of political evil is commensurate with man's political vocation" (HT, 264). The question then becomes: if exclusion is the consequence of the two-dimensional nature of the polis, how exactly can "man's political vocation" prevent it? How to adjust or transform the polis in order to guarantee participation and decrease the hierarchical relation while maximizing the consensual one?

Perhaps we can understand Ricoeur's ideas even better if we place them in the context in which they first appeared. The year 1956, when "The Political Paradox" came out, was marked by the Soviet invasion of Hungary, which indeed inspired the essay. The Hungarian uprising against the Soviet Union that was trying to seize control over the country with the cooperation of the local Communist officials, brought to fore the tension between the horizontal level of the polis—that of people wishing to live together—and the vertical dimension, that of the socialist state. The socialist regime claimed to act on behalf of the many, while violently suppressing them when its legitimacy was questioned.

The bloody events of 1956 took many in the West by surprise, particularly the leftist intellectuals who had regarded communism as a form of democracy. The violence erupting when Soviet tanks marched on the streets of Budapest called into question many of the political beliefs widely shared particularly among the French liberal intelligentsia. The "flames of Budapest," as the event came to be known, made headlines in the Western media and became the topic of special issues in academic journals, demanding the reexamination of what constitutes political intervention. Much of "The Political Paradox" was concerned with the assumptions and consequences of Marxism—the doctrine itself had come under trial—and as such it argued for a conceptual shift in the understanding of democracy broadly defined. Ricoeur maintained that leftist thought had failed to recognize the distinctiveness of political action. As he later explained, "by underscoring to excess the role of the economico-social dimension, Marx had behaved as though there were but a single source of evil: the oppression of the workers by money—money which had been reified by capitalism and had thereby lost its proper link with living labor" (CC, 96). After the Hungarian Revolution, it became imperative to understand "the specificity of the political with respect to the economic and social" (CC, 96).

But in 1956 France was experiencing its own political upheaval, and Ricoeur faced a difficult choice concerning his personal political stance: how to protest the French military intervention against the Algerian uprising. Some tried to boycott the war by either engaging in or publicly encouraging draft-dodging and desertion from the French army. Though decidedly against the war, Ricoeur opted not to give his public support to such forms of resistance, because he questioned their effectiveness. This stance can be easily mistaken for a form of political abstinence, especially if we ignore the fact that Ricoeur specifically argued for the possibility of an effective political intervention, as I mentioned earlier. He refused to condone draft-dodging because he believed that within a system whose legitimacy is predicated on the "common will" instantiated in state mechanisms of control, any form of resistance that explicitly identifies itself as protest and as contestation of the "pact" cementing the mechanisms is doomed to be rendered illegitimate and hence easily eliminable. Instead, he advocated a generalized social transformation and dissemination of values and beliefs that would become reflective of not only a limited group, the protesters, but of society at large. Rather than political change understood as a break, a sort of leap from one form of organization to another, Ricoeur espoused a broader ethical and moral reform that would enable different understandings of the same problems. In his view, only then would change be possible. Insofar as "power contests are also struggles for recognition presupposing a shared public space," as Dallmayr observes, that space "cannot simply coincide with radical dissent or hostility" (192). Rather, such a shift is possible when politics exercises a "corrective function," which capitalizes on the horizontal level of consensual relations. In other words, the behavioral change advocated by Ricoeur as the prerequisite for political transformation began on the horizontal level. The question that remains, then, is: how to effect such a modification.

In "The Political Paradox," Ricoeur maintained that the specific rationality of the polis uniquely recommends it as a space for deliberation and reflection, and thus makes it into a repository for specific strategies of intervention. He identifies these strategies in judicial due process and in the freedom of speech—the "two lungs" of any sound public sphere—as well as the right of free associations (in labor unions specifically). The first strategy refers to the attributes of the judge, in his view someone placed "by the *consent of all* on the fringes of the fundamental conflicts of society" (HT, 267, my emphasis). Unlike Smith's notion of an impartial spectator, which posits absolute moral values as a normative common ground, Ricoeur's judge is a social position designated and agreed upon by the members of a community. This position is still an abstraction, but one fashioned within a particular society. The judge represents a privileged vantage, yet one located above, rather than in, every individual. The judge's perspective is unavailable to others (cf. chapter 4). Ricoeur explains:

> The independence of the judge, it will be objected, is an abstraction. Quite so. Society requires for its human respiration an "ideal" function, a deliberate, concerted abstraction in which it projects the ideal of legality that legitimates the reality of power. Without this projection, in which the State represents itself as legitimate, the individual is at the mercy of the State . . . without protection against its arbitrariness. It stands to reason that the proceedings of Moscow, of Budapest, of Prague, and elsewhere, were possible because the independence of the judge was not technically assured nor ideologically founded in a theory of the judge as a man above class, as an abstraction of human proportions, as the embodiment of law. Stalin was possible because there were always judges to judge in accordance with his decree. (HT, 267–68)

A second strategy refers to the ability of the individual members of the polis to listen to arguments and to form opinions "*by themselves*," based on free access to "sources of information, knowledge, and science, independent of those of the State" (HT, 268). Agents, then, must evade the specific rationality of the polis insofar as that rationality acts as an interpretive framework that informs their judgment and perception. Notice that Ricoeur's emphasis is unmistakably on agents—both the judge located outside societal conflicts and citizens formulating personal views are placeholders for individual agency—deemed capable of resisting and challenging social structures. This emphasis on individuals assumes that they can articulate a political intervention without the mediation of the state or any other abstract form of coordination. Does such an assumption contradict the nature of the polis? The assumption seems all the more problematic in light of Ricoeur's profoundly agonistic view of the human condition, which he defines as an "interminable confrontation of man and woman, old age and youth, society and the individual, the living and the dead, humans and gods" (OA, 243). Where to locate the horizontal plane of commonality, avoiding the reification offered by the vertical plane of institutions?

The Common Good

Many political philosophers locate the horizontal level within civil society, but continue to rely on highly normative models that stipulate rationality as the main criterion. Similarly, Ricoeur's conception of civil society was influenced by sociological models, which define it not just as a social-political space but also as the repository of a set of specific validity criteria, or a "grammar of worth." In particular, the research on conflict resolution conducted by Laurent Thevenot in collaboration with Boltanski shows that the arguments exchanged in various public litigious situations, while belonging to different fields, tend to follow one of several patterns that allow the actors to find a common ground. The sociologists identify several "grammars of worth" to which actors have recourse in order to defend their positions. In Ricoeur's reading, these "grammars of worth" function as ways of explaining an individual's actions based on criteria that also explain the actions of others. By matching in turn each individual's actions with that of others, a grammar of worth becomes the basis for shared meanings, defined by transitivity: your actions represent to me what mine represent to you, and what a third party's actions represent to me also represent to you. And while the notion of a necessary correspondence between the level of an individual and that of the collective was already important to Ricoeur, as we saw in his reflections on practical wisdom, Thevenot and Boltanski drew his attention to the *plurality* of desirability criteria, or as Ricoeur calls them in a 2000 study, "regimes of justified action" (TJ, 83).

The two sociologists locate the source of the grammars of worth in domains of social activity. Thus, one grammar of worth is that of "market performance," whose source is the domain of commerce; industry issues norms of success and rightness based on "technical competence and long-term planning"; civil society is governed around equality and solidarity; the private realm is focused on "trust," which is entrenched in local and personal ties; the intellectual domain deals with "inspiration," expressed in creativity, emotion, or religious grace; and the realm of "renown" is based on public opinion and fame" (Lamont and Thevenot, 5). Ricoeur views these domains of evaluation as symbolic "cities," which "give some sufficient coherence to an order of human transactions. But they are 'worlds' insofar as some things—objects or arrangements—serve as established referents, something like a 'common world,' for tests that occur within a given city" (TJ, 83). The distinction he posits between a "city" and a "world" is designed to flag the possibility of domination: when one order of evaluation is seen as a "world" rather than as a "city," the others are ignored or excluded. Thus, for instance, to try to evaluate all actions and individuals solely by the criterion of reputation is to focus on the inspired city as if it included the entire domain of human experience.

The idea of multiple orders of evaluation acts allows the partitioning of the public sphere and the increase of participation by rendering irrelevant the requirement of similarity. Importantly, though, as adopted by Ricoeur, the concept of a grammar of worth does not invalidate the idea that there is one public *sphere* (rather than *spheres*). In this reticulate public sphere, individuals can transfer from one city to another, borrow arguments from different orders of evaluation, and become critical of the city they usually inhabit by looking at it from the perspective of another city. Ricoeur claims that "this capacity for mutual challenges is structural and not accidental. The common good of one city is vulnerable to the critique provided by the vision of another city" (TJ, 91). The cities are open to each other, allowing free transit, but at the same time no city can be so radically transformed by a critique furnished from the perspective of another city that it would lose its distinctiveness or validity. Ricoeur points out that to presume that some people are "capable of changing worlds, and therefore of transporting with them the internal vision of the world from which they come" implies that the individual "who goes over the wall, so to speak, [is] moved by the vision of a common good that is not just that of one city, of one world" (TJ, 91). Furthermore, if such individuals exist, then the very idea of a "common good" transcending or subtending the modules becomes plausible. And yet, by what grammar of worth can such common good be evaluated, if, as Thevenot and Boltanski insist, "there exists no overarching position, external to and above each of these worlds, from which the plurality of justices could be considered from on high, like a range of equally possible choices" (qtd. in TJ, 90)?

Ricoeur departs from Thevenot and Boltanski in considering the civic city as an overarching vantage on all the other ones. For him, the civic city is "placed in the uncomfortable situation of an entity called upon to behave at the same time as the whole and as the part, as the container and the contained, as an inclusive agency and an included region" (TJ, 91). By approaching civil society as the locus of solidarity and communal life, Ricoeur establishes a conceptual ground for the intersections of the other spheres—a vital element for their own maintenance as well as for making sure that they do not develop into atomistic configurations, indifferent at best and hostile at worst to one another. The question of how solidarity is created is still on the table, but at least now we have an understanding of what might constitute the plane of commonality that allows individuals to come together and deliberate on issues involving the common good. Specifically, Ricoeur offers a notion of civil society as an evaluative perspective that can borrow criteria arguments from various sectors of public life. He himself borrows critical arguments when he modifies Arendt's two-axis political model through recourse to concepts from theology. Although convinced that "the theologico-political regime is outmoded," he turns to theology as a source of heuristic inspiration for the conceptualization of the horizontal dimension:

> If something still remains [from the theological model], it is in the direction of wishing to live together that one must look, rather than toward the vertical structure. I mean very precisely in the direction of wishing to live together as the practice of fraternity. I am convinced that there are in this regard, in the notion of the "people of God" and in its composition of perfect ecclesial reciprocity, genuine resources for conceptualizing a political model. (CC, 105)

Ricoeur's understanding of "ecclesial reciprocity" and a "practice of fraternity" must be traced back to his reading of the parable of the Good Samaritan, particularly of the concluding question: "which of these three men [the priest, the Levite, and the Samaritan] . . . was neighbor to him that fell among the thieves?" Ricoeur interprets the term *neighbor* as describing "the *personal* way in which I encounter another, *over and above social mediation*" (HT, 101). The two travelers who refuse to help the victim acknowledge his misfortune, but do not see him as belonging to their world and hence do not see themselves as required to assist him. In fact, social mediation prohibits such help, as both "occupy the summit of the religious hierarchy and it is precisely in order to avoid the ritual pollution involved in touching a body, and therefore in obedience to the law, that they pass on by" (Boltanski, 9–10). For them, the victim is a *socius*, someone they see in a mediated fashion, "in this or that capacity. . . ." It is only for the third traveler, the Good Samaritan, that

> the event of the encounter makes one person present to another. . . . In [the priest and the Levite], the institution (ecclesiastical institution, to be precise) bars their access to the event. In a way the Samaritan is also a category; but here he is a category for the others. For the pious Jew he is the category of the Stranger; he does not form part of a group. He is the man without a past or authentic traditions; impure in race and in piety; less than a gentile; a relapse. He is the category of the non-category. He is

> neither occupied nor preoccupied by dint of being occupied: he is travelling and is not encumbered by social responsibility, ready to change his itinerary and invent an unforeseen behavior, available for encounter and the presence of others. The conduct that he invents is the direct relationship of "man to man." Just as the Samaritan is a person through his capacity for encounter, all his "compassion" is a gesture over and above roles, personages, and functions. It innovates a hypersociological mutuality between one person and another. (HT, 99–100)

The point of making a distinction between "neighbor" and "*socius*" is to suggest that even institutions designed to protect life in common, such as those represented by the priest and the Levite, can foster indifference if not hostility toward problems that might occur in different regions of the sociopolitical sphere. As proposed by Ricoeur, a capacity for encountering others as "neighbors" constitutes "primarily an appeal to the awakening of consciousness" beyond pre-existent collective affiliations (HT, 107). In his reading, the Good Samaritan's compassionate response is the result of an ability to engage in a direct relationship, and to ignore the constraints imposed by traditions and institutions. The Good Samaritan internalizes the other's need and is willing to be transformed by it, as he not only dresses the victim's wounds, feeds him, and gives him a place to stay, but does so at the expense of his own initial plans.

Philosophers and political scientists often draw on the parable of the Good Samaritan when they want to present different types of social interaction, but they do not always read it the same way. Boltanski, for example, is concerned with how interaction can elicit compassion, and sees the parable as proposing a link between compassion on the one hand, and presence and particularity on the other hand. In his view, the Samaritan responds to the man in need because he has seen with his own eyes the pain and suffering of another human being, while the other travelers looked away and moved on. For Avishai Margalit, the story exemplifies the power of moral norms over individual actors—by aiding the wounded man the Samaritan acted in conformity with the moral imperative "Love thy neighbor as thyself" (Margalit, 44). Margalit explains the solicitude of the Samaritan as a manifestation of humanity defined in Kantian terms, as a fellowship predicated on sympathy for, and commitment to, one another. By contrast, Boltanski argues that the Samaritan decides what to do not in response to moral norms, but as someone who makes up his own mind in considering a particular task at hand. For him, the compassion to which the Samaritan attests is "inscribed in particular relationships between particular individuals" (Boltanski, 9).

In Ricoeur's reading, the parable of the Good Samaritan illustrates the priority of respect for the particular individual over respect for categories, "in the name of the solicitude that is addressed to persons in their irreplaceable singularity" (OA, 253). Thus fashioned, his interpretation is an interesting cross between the two accounts I have described so far, inasmuch as it capitalizes on the particularity of the agents involved, while also defining it as a derivation of the mutuality upon which their relationship is formed. Like Boltanski, he sees the Samaritan responding to a concrete problem, rather than acting out of general indiscriminate compassion. Yet like Margalit, he does not think the Samaritan chooses on his own when to be compassionate. The Samaritan is compelled to attend to the needs of the victim not by an abstract, external moral law but by an internalized Other who summons him to responsibility. Distinct from the Kantian moral norm, the summoning Other is part and parcel of the self—it does not make the Samaritan into a *moral* being but a *being,* and it is what defines him as an autonomous individual: "Never, at any stage, will the self have been separated from its other. . . . The autonomy of the self will appear then to be tightly bound up with solicitude for one's neighbor and with justice for each individual" (OA, 18).

Participation in community life, according to Ricoeur, is not "contingent and revocable" (OA, 181). At the same time, individuals are not "complete and fully endowed with rights before entering into society." Rather, they are shaped by the "*mediating* role of others," which allows them to make the journey from capacities to realizations (OA, 181). In Ricoeur's words, "life stories are so intertwined with one another that the narrative anyone tells or hears of his own life becomes a segment of those other stories that are the narratives of others' lives" (TJ, 7). At the same time, individuals carry specific responsibilities for their actions, which can be imputed to them alone but that are "inscribed in a context of *interaction* where the other figures as . . . antagonist or . . . helper, [are] in relations that vary between conflict and interaction" (TJ, 6). In such a context, individuals are autonomous, while also occupying various positions in relation to the other members of the community. Solidarity among them operates through consent rather than through consensus on a certain intervention or course of action.

Ricoeur explains the mechanism of consent in phenomenological terms as a combination of free will and necessity. When a person consents, she exercises her judgment on a given topic, while nevertheless regarding the decision she ultimately makes as necessary beyond an actual freedom of choice. The necessity, then, might seem to render the judgment irrelevant.

But conversely, to judge a necessity already assumes that its character is in question: if I debate with myself whether I "must do this," then I am also challenging the necessity of doing it, trying to demote it to a level of options rather than imperatives. If I say to myself "I must do this," it means that I simply recognize a necessity and deliberation becomes futile. But the act of consent is also self-transforming insofar as it requires, according to Ricoeur, "to take upon oneself, to assume, *to make one's own*" (FN, 344, my emphasis). On the one hand, analyzing the necessity creates a gap by opening up the possibility for embarking on different courses of action, adopting different beliefs, or drawing various conclusions. On the other hand, consent "seeks to fill the gap which judgment opens up" by zooming in on only *one* course of action, reflected on the side of necessity.

In the double articulation of judgment and necessity, consent creates a space defined by indetermination, an interstice where multiple, even conflicting beliefs can be entertained before some are discarded. In this space unfolds the critical self-examination that lies at the center of Hauser's conception of an emancipatory public arena. Sorting out one's convictions and beliefs is a step toward forming commitments, and can hence prevent indifference or political anomie. The commitment emerges not as an obligation to others but as a willingness to contribute to the creation of a good life shared with them.

The solidarity thus formed expresses a shared outlook, but is nevertheless different from Rousseau's general will, which binds individuals in the name of a virtual pact, and is hence an abstraction rather than a concrete expression of commonality. The general will, as defined by Rousseau, is comparable to Smith's impartial spectator insofar as both reflect a normative and moral perspective. As Andrew Levine explains,

> the "moral point of view," evident in Kant's categorical imperative but emblematic too of non-Kantian moral philosophy, is the standpoint of agent neutrality or impartiality. From this vantage point, individuals decide what do to on the basis of interests moral personalities share, in disregard of factors that distinguish particular agents from one another. Thus the moral point of view resembles the attitude Rousseau would have citizens adopt in the assemblies of the people, the perspective of generality. (Levine, 68–69)

Solidarity, on the other hand, is subsumed to an ethical point of view, which focuses on individuals in their particularity. Ricoeur maintains that ethics and morality are distinct, invoking their different intellectual lineages, Greek versus Latin. In his use, the term *ethics* is reserved for the *aim* of collective life, as sought out by agents who live together, while morality defines "the articulation of this aim in *norms* characterized at once by the claim to universality and by an effect of constraint" (OA, 170). For Ricoeur, the teleological perspective of ethics takes precedence over the deontological perspective of morality when it comes to making "immediate evaluations and estimations applied to action" (OA, 171). From an ethical standpoint, he views individuals as aiming at a good life lived "with and for others" (OA, 172), and at a good life as "the nebulous of ideals and dreams of achievement with regard to which a life is held to be more or less fulfilled or unfulfilled" (OA, 179). However nebulous, these ideals are established in accordance with others, as they reflect common values and principles. But the ethical aim remains at the latitude of each individual, and indeed must be not just adopted but individually discovered and formulated before it can be pursued.

Insofar as the ethical aim is based on a broad consent to participation, it creates conditions for empathy but also adds more specificity to how such empathy might be obtained. Looking more closely at the case of Polish Solidarity should reveal such conditions. Therefore, to ground the theoretical claims advanced so far and to demonstrate their explanatory power, I now turn to my case study, the text written by Michnik when he was a political prisoner in Poland in 1981.

"The Stone that Will Reverse the Course of Events"

On August 14, 1980, the workers at the Lenin shipyards in Gdańsk went on strike, protesting low salaries and poor working conditions. That strike was later credited as marking the beginning of a trade union movement that quickly became a much larger form of dissidence against the socialist regime in Poland. But the force of what happened at Gdańsk, then in Szczecin, Warsaw, Lublin, Silesia, and then in the entire country, lay in the very social interaction from which it got its name. The strike came to be seen as the expression of widespread solidarity among Poles, but it broke out as the solidarity of a group of workers with a particular individual, an employer who was laid off because she had spoken out against the officials. The person in question was a woman named Anna Walentinowicz, an outspoken person no doubt, but certainly not a charismatic leader. In only two weeks, the workers who came together behind her were able to mount so much pressure that on August 31 an agreement with the government was signed, officially recognizing the rights of workers and giving permission to the formation of independent trade unions. But the organization born at Gdansk was far more than a trade union: among the ten million members it included only during its first year of existence (1980–81) were a variety of people, from workers to intellectuals, who had different political priorities but one means of fulfilling them: consent to a common cause.

Even though created as an effort to counter official policies, Solidarity was not fashioned as a political organization. Instead, the movement focused on individuals, and tried to reach them in the plane of their commitment to a good life with and for others. Anchored in the practices of everyday life rather than in an abstract ideology, Solidarity's goal was to provoke a revolution in mentalities not just in politics. In Michnik's words, the movement attempted to "give advice to the people regarding how to behave, not to the government regarding how to reform itself" (Michnik, xxvi). To this end, unlike other underground dissident organizations created in the Eastern bloc during communism, Solidarity adopted a program that was both self-limiting and ambitious. The movement only sought to revise, not to dislocate, the existing regime, and hence did not fashion itself explicitly as anti-Communist. Its chief precepts included the willingness to sacrifice oneself for one's convictions, tolerance, and nonviolence. The leaders lobbied for reform to which individuals would subscribe freely, and envisioned social relations in highly personalized, almost intimate, terms. Solidarity, as viewed by the main protagonists, was predicated on a sense of closeness one usually finds outside the public arena, and as commentators noted, "that intense unity of thought and feeling which previously had been confined to small circles of friends—the intimate solidarity of private life in Eastern Europe—was now multiplied by millions" (Garton Ash, 32).

The links that cemented Polish Solidarity were firmly located in what Ricoeur would call the "realm of ethics and along the horizontal dimension." Because it was centered in individual consciousness, the movement managed to avoid the class divides characteristic that debilitated other dissident initiatives in many Eastern European countries, Poland itself in previous decades. Solidarity attracted and welcomed workers as well as intellectuals, and even though originally fashioned as a coalminers' union, it drew large support from academics and journalists, women and men, and the young and the old. One of its most respected and active leaders was Michnik, famous for his charisma and electrifying effect on individuals and crowds. By 1981, with the participation of people like him, Solidarity had not only attracted massive support from the Polish population, but also become critically involved in influencing public policy and official political decisions. The military dictatorship that took over in December 1981 under General Wojciech Jaruzelski sought to eliminate Solidarity from public life, and for this purpose it incarcerated its leaders, and then tried to talk them into signing a loyalty document, which offered them release from prison in exchange for the promise not to oppose the government's actions anymore. Michnik played a key role in maintaining the commitment and determination of the imprisoned Polish activists. Through texts written in minuscule script on cigarettes or on soap bars and circulated on both sides of the prison gates, he became a true custodian of the Solidarity consciousness.

In one of these writings, later published under the title "Why You Don't Sign, . . ." Michnik argues for the necessity to reject any pact with the Communist officials. The text is structured as a letter to an unnamed friend who has already decided to reject the offer and to remain in prison, but has to defend his choice to friends and relatives who want him to be free again, and would therefore expect him to sign. Michnik speaks as a counselor and confidante, someone who understands the dilemma but also the decision the prisoner has made. What gave the text so much power, as we find out from the memoirs of other Solidarity leaders who read it while imprisoned, is that it made no recourse to abstract demands and ideal imperatives, and managed to present the decision to remain in prison by not signing the loyalty declaration as an individual option, while at the same time conveying the sense that it was an unavoidable necessity.

Michnik's recourse to the epistolary genre facilitates a direct interpellation of the imprisoned men and women who are faced with this difficult decision. By repeatedly employing the second-person pronoun, the letter creates a basis of identification with the protagonist. But Michnik's focus on an individual receiver of his message goes beyond a convention of address and represents a philosophical credo (with political implications) that grounds civil society in individual consciousness. The goal of the letter is to awaken individual consciousness, and justification functions as the expression of accountability to others. Furthermore, framed as a justification of an already made decision, the arguments present the decision as a necessity more than a result of deliberation. Thus, what is in fact a question—whether political prisoners should accept the government's offer—is from the very beginning fashioned as a declaration: the detainees are not signing. What the letter articulates, then, is the prisoner's consent—as Ricoeur defines the term—a decision that once made appears as a necessity.

As a form of deliberation, this consent draws on spheres of justification that function within specific orders of recognition ("cities" in Ricoeur's terms). For Michnik, these are located at the level of private life, private values, individual choice, and destiny. The letter can be interpreted as Michnik's soliloquy, in which he reviews his own beliefs and convictions, and determinations and commitments. In part, the content of the text supports this hypothesis insofar as it includes information usually available upon first-person examination, such as feelings of loneliness, powerlessness, fear, or uncertainty. A perspective "from the inside" is thus created, conducive to trust. As Hauser notes,

> even if the arguments against the offer express Michnik's personal political beliefs, the ambiguity of *you* allows them to be read as the assessments of a confidante and friend who knows your commitments. . . . In this way, the text creates a profound identification with its readers, implicating them in a community of commitments and values populated by others on whom *you* can rely. (Hauser, "Prisoners of Conscience," 45)

The rhetorical efficiency of the text, then, depends on creating a sense of familiarity and communion. It does so at the level of style, as the tone is familiar, almost intimate in its use of direct, colloquial language. Closeness also emerges through allusions, allusions to actors identified only by their first names and by the initials of their last names, or details from the private life of the addressee, usually known only to a confidante. Michnik, according to Hauser, also makes belief statements *about another*, and creates arguments with an enthymematic structure, which "mention and depict in ways that leave the rest to be completed" (Hauser, "Prisoners of Conscience," 52). These strategies suggest a kind of intimacy that goes beyond friendship, extending into what Ricoeur would call the "hypersociological mutuality between one person and another," paradigmatically illustrated by the encounter between the Good Samaritan and the poor wounded. At stake in this mutuality is an ethical decision that reflects an individual's freely chosen and expressed attitude, rather than an obligation already exerted upon by someone else or by a collective.

Michnik's challenge is to argue for the necessity of staying in prison, without however advocating a heroic stance, according to which the prisoner is a savior of the Polish nation, or an exceptional individual willing to sacrifice his life for the good of others. Much of the text relies heavily on reconciling moral values like dignity, loyalty, and honesty to the individual concerns of survival and personal comfort. The most difficult argument to mount concerns the risk of being killed in prison. In a Communist country ruled by a military dictatorship, ad hoc executions and show trials were the rule rather than the exception. The safety of a prisoner is defined by the limits imposed on the safety of anybody who lives in a totalitarian society. Michnik emphatically rejects the possibility that he might be proposing a heroic stance:

> I know what you are thinking: he is reciting platitudes and banalities, demanding heroism; he is helplessly romantic. But this is not quite true. . . . You know that you are no hero and that you never wanted to be one. You have never wanted to die for your nation, or for freedom, or for anything else, for that matter. . . . This war surprised you in the company of a pretty woman, not while you were plotting an assault on the Central Committee headquarters. (Michnik, 10–11)

Arguing on the horizontal plane of ethics allows Michnik to describe the stakes of dissidence in individual terms rather than as a national duty or honor:

> Nevertheless, they did declare this war *on you* and over thirty million other people, and so you are forced to recognize that amid the street roundups, the ignoble court sentences, the despicable radio programs, and the distribution of leaflets by underground Solidarity you will not regain the normalcy that was based on *respect for yourself.* Now you must choose between moral and material stability, because you know that today's "normalcy" will have the bitter taste of self-defeat. . . . No, this is not heroism. It is mere common sense. . . . Heroism presupposes exceptionality. Today, Poles need normalcy and ordinariness if they are to resist the rule of the military and the police. (Michnik, 11)

The opposition between heroism and common sense is predicated on the assumption of a generalized necessity: to become a hero is a choice some, but not all, individuals make, whereas to actively resist the totalitarian regime is key to their own survival. Michnik's rejection of heroism was the hallmark of Solidarity's political program, which encouraged social resistance from the bottom-up, opposing it to the "romantic insurrectionism" of a few isolated individuals. Such a form of resistance relies on what many have in common, and not on exceptional, and hence hard to emulate, virtues. Yet it also relies on the consent of each and every one included in the anonymous mass of the "many." The unnamed "dear friend" to whom the letter from the prison at Białołęka is addressed is both a generic individual—one like many others—and a concrete, particular agent who controls his own destiny, and must be willing, rather than expected to participate in, the creation of a civil society.

Rather than historical narratives from a heroic past, Michnik relies on concrete, readily available examples in order to tell a cautionary tale about betrayal and sacrifice. The characters involved in this story are not heroes or villains from the past. They belong to a familiar network of interaction that also includes the protagonist of the letter:

> With your mind's eye you can see Andrzej M., the excellent literary critic, your friend, who while in jail wrote a brilliant essay denouncing people—proof of his moral death; Heniek Sz., an ambitious and intelligent man, who let himself be maneuvered into the role of chief informer on his friends; Zygmunt D., a charming companion and intelligent young man, who gave in once and then spent years denouncing his friends. So you remember with dread and terror this human debris, these people who have been battered by the police machine, and you will see that your own future, too, is an open question. The choice is yours, but your memory ceaselessly repeats in your ear: you, too, can be like them. No one is born an informer; you forge *your fate* daily, *at the price of your life*. (Michnik, 8)

Based on the distinction between one's life and one's fate, Michnik can define the profile of the Solidarity dissident at a level beyond issues of comfort or even survival. The examples of those who may have kept their lives but only as "human debris," are meant to indicate that betraying one's fellow citizens can destroy one's own identity. The brief captions characterizing the three individuals *before* their political compromise altered their very substance—"excellent literary critic," "ambitious and intelligent man," and "charming companion"—are in stark contrast with their depictions as "fallen" creatures—one misusing his talent to denounce people, another becoming a victim of manipulation, and finally the third one leading an undignified existence as a spy. The compromise is thus presented as an instance of self-negation, a sort of moral suicide that renders physical survival irrelevant.

Notice that the crime committed by two of the three compromised men was against their own friends, not against the generic Polish nation. Whether Michnik is referring to actual friends, or using the term metaphorically for the Polish people in general in order to convey a sense of widespread national solidarity and closeness, his notion of culpability is circumscribed in highly individualized terms. Correspondingly, the underlying ethical principles—violated by the compromise—are relative and concrete rather than absolute and abstract, experiential rather than theoretical. Michnik exposes specific traitors who have harmed people they knew rather than the rather abstract category of the Polish nation. This Hauser confirms in his observation that Michnik "abstains from a rhetoric of abstractions and ideological commitments" (Hauser, "Prisoners of Conscience," 51).

To stress the validity of the decision he is advocating, Michnik also includes in the letter information supposedly not known at the time of the decision-making, but available later, for instance, other prisoners did not sign the document either, and Polish dissidence did survive the military dictatorship. One would perhaps find it easier to make the sacrifice if one could have a guarantee that it was worthwhile. But Michnik deliberately makes only one category of reasons available to the "you" of his letter:

> You still don't know what will happen. You still don't know that people will begin to recover from the shock, that underground papers will appear, that Zbyszek B. will lead his Solidarity region from the underground, that in Wroclaw they will fail to capture Wladek F.; that Gdansk, Swidnik, and Poznan will again shake up all Poland; that illegal union structures will be formed. You still don't know that the generals' vehicle [allusion to the military government] is sinking in sand, its wheels spinning in place, that the avalanche of repression and calumnies is missing its aim. (Michniks, 14).

Notice that these are, again, concrete examples designed to support the teleological dimension of the ethical project at stake, one that defines the common good as a freely consented aim rather than an inherited obligation. Even by presenting this information as lacking, Michnik makes it available to the implied reader of the letter. But now he speaks to someone else than the *you* facing the decision to stay in prison. By now, as Michnik approaches the closing of his arguments, he can present the *you* who refuses to sign the letter as a moral being, capable of sacrifice and effort:

> But you do know, as you stand alone, handcuffed, with your eyes filled with tear gas, in front of policemen who are shaking their guns at you—you can see it clearly in the dark and starless night, thanks to your favorite poet—that the course of the avalanche depends on the stones over which it rolls. And you want to be the stone that will reverse the course of events. (Micknik, 14–15)

The letter, then, describes the consent to stake one's life for the common good. Michnik himself and many others like him chose to remain in prison, refusing to betray not a cause abstractly defined, but each other. The direct "hypersociological" engagement created in this letter was the trigger for a widespread solidarity among the Poles who dared to oppose a regime ready to kill in the name of a presumed rational concord. It is telling, in this respect, that the document the prisoner was requested to sign was entitled "a *loyalty* declaration." The efficiency—of Solidarity in general and of Michnik's letter in particular—in countering this discourse of national allegiance can be attributed to a deployment of moral values, as Hauser does. But we can only make such attribution as long as we understand that this was an emergent morality rather than one based on existing precepts that could have just as easily been manipulated by the government. This morality starts out as a commitment to the community hypostasized as one's neighbors, people one knows by their first names. Solidarity reached its political zenith when it could issue moral claims and expect adherence. But at the critical juncture of the 1981 imprisonment, moral claims had to be carefully couched in a language of political expediency and individual consideration.

Michnik managed to put forth profoundly moral arguments—such as self-sacrifice on behalf of human dignity—by creating a profile of the imprisoned Solidarity leader, for which the prison becomes a metonymy. He did so by arguing that the prisoner is not really deprived of freedom, but that in fact, outside the wired fences of Białołęka are the real prisoners, those who live under the constant surveillance of the secret police. Jaruzelski had declared, after all, national emergency, which in the Polish legal context amounted to a state of military occupation. Michnik points out that in such a world liberty can only represent a state of mind, not a state of affairs. To be free is to be free from fear and to be aware of your environment and the possibilities it both holds and precludes. The people outside Białołęka live the illusion of freedom but are in fact under the terror that they might lose it at any moment, and this fear limits and controls their mental and emotional mechanisms—suspicion, insecurity, and anguish. Inside Białołęka, "you need not fear anything . . . if one morning you are awakened by banging on the door you are not going to be afraid of the uniformed guests; it is only your good-humored jailer handing out the morning coffee. Here, you do not panic at the sight of the cynic with his darting eyes—a stool pigeon is not a threat" (Michnik, 4). Hence, the paradoxical conclusion: "Białołęka is a moral luxury and an oasis of dignity" (Michnik, 4). The Solidarity leader, privileged to reside in such luxury, and clearly superior to those who are only formally "free," has thus explained the necessity to remain in prison.

Conclusion

After a long tradition of political philosophy as well as rhetorical scholarship focused on social macrostructures and on the communitarian basis of politics, more recent work proposes a shift in the direction of the individuals and of their direct political engagement in public arenas. Ricoeur contributes to this shift a series of analytic distinctions. One such analytic distinction is between the horizontal and vertical levels of a public sphere. The asymmetry he finds between these axes—as the vertical tends to encroach upon the horizontal—explains the difficulty of anticipating to what extent increased political participation will indeed be emancipatory and hence benefit the entire community, or reactionary and hazardous. An additional important distinction concerns the modularity of the public sphere as a descriptive characteristic of social practices on the one hand, and the shared basis of social life, the free circulation of agents among different spheres or "cities," on the other hand. Without admitting that there is such a possibility of border-crossing it becomes self-refuting to plead for inclusion and an opening up across discursive fields, as it has been the case with some of Habermas's critics. Yet another distinction defines ethical relations as grounded in the commonality just mentioned, in the practices of everyday life shared *with* other individuals, and views moral obligations as based on abstractions and ideals that might vary across communities, just as the obligations of the two unsympathetic travelers differed from those of the Good Samaritan. At the horizontal level of ethical relationships individuals enter a direct contact that allows them to pursue common causes. Solidarity thus emerges from consent, not a temporary or strategic alliance, but rather a long-lasting affiliation and expression of individual identity.

The series of conceptual distinctions I have tried to articulate in this chapter represent not only a theoretically more coherent approach to the public sphere than alternative ones that rest largely on critiques of Habermas. Ricoeur's approach is also more historically sensitive, capable of explaining significant political moments in the formation and repression of democratic regimes. The case of Polish Solidarity is a key one because of its success in challenging a totalitarian state, a success rewarded in the first free elections after the collapse of communism. Concepts that can explain such cases have robust explanatory value, as well as social significance. Ricoeur's contribution, as I have outlined it in this chapter, comes from a politically engaged individual, who since the Hungarian uprising and the Algerian war spent many years matching concepts with political realities, measuring theory against practice, and refining ideas in a continuous search for understanding.

Conclusion

The protagonist of this book is a philosopher whose ideas I have tried to describe as another source of inspiration for a discipline already heavily indebted to philosophy. Indeed, of all the fields that have influenced it over the years, rhetoric has always enjoyed a particular closeness to philosophy, from which it has borrowed liberally but had to pay the high price of comparative marginality and, on occasion, explicit hostility. Does a field that has been so long in existence still need to lean upon contributions intended for another area, in order to clarify and enrich its own set of problems? Despite the current interdisciplinary climate in humanistic research, this question has special acuity for rhetoric, a field that has more than once called for a "defense." Are we asking rhetorical theory to admit to some sort of defectiveness by offering it a philosophical hand rather than help from within its own ranks in dealing with fundamental, core concepts such as the ones discussed in this book?

The rhetorical tradition, punctuated by large temporal gaps, and forced to be rather atheoretical throughout its history (Hariman, 38), is fraught with unanswered questions, loose ends, unresolved contradictions, tentative connections, and underdeveloped concepts. The most basic notions—such as the ones that I have explored in this book, to which one could add *kairos*, *enthymeme*, or *topoi*—remain the hardest to comprehend. The difficulty ranges from the translation of a foreign core vocabulary (Greek and Latin) to the relative scarcity of full-length treatments explicitly building on each other so as to articulate a coherent intellectual history. How can an outsider remedy this situation? As I have tried to demonstrate throughout the book, even though he does not seek to make a contribution to rhetoric, Ricoeur offers useful insights into its conceptual core by prompting fundamental questions, pivotal to the understanding of core concepts, while also discouraging an exclusive reliance on inherited definitions or getting bogged down in specious arguments and dichotomies. Thus, instead of spilling more ink on the question whether doxa (opinion) is inferior to episteme (certainty), Ricoeur encourages us to consider the ways in which rhetorical discourse can successfully incorporate and modify popular opinions. Rather than ponder the difference between ancient and modern practical reason, he supports an investigation of the type of reflection involved in *phronesis*, and of the specific ways in which it can unfold. In response to the proliferation of studies of national identity and historical commemoration, Ricoeur opens up a reevaluation of the ancient concept of epideictic not for the sake of its classical pedigree but for the analytic force it entails. Finally, instead of critiquing theories of the polis for their exclusionary consequences, he offers a heuristic that espouses the creation of an inclusive model.

To read rhetorical theory through Ricoeur's lens is to see what Henry James called "the figure in the carpet"—not so much details but an intellectual pattern that holds together beliefs and assumptions in a way that makes a discipline recognizable throughout its history. Such a privileged vantage becomes possible when rhetorical theory is approached holistically, as he does in the two essays that constitute my point of entry in this study, asking general questions of significance and distinctiveness. Where does rhetoric stand in relationship to other fields that study discourse? This is Ricoeur's main query, and unlike the "ruling comparisons" that Robert Hariman finds responsible for rhetoric's marginality, it sponsors—I have tried to show—a systematic redefinition of key rhetorical concepts. I have striven to make the focus and stakes of this investigation less about deficiencies in existing accounts—although I had to point them out when they were the source of conceptual confusion—and more about opportunities for improvement. The investigation, as I have attempted to frame it, is less a critique or exegesis and more a specific theoretical proposal. Because it is not an exegesis, my goal has not been to exhaust a body of work but to identify the pertinent ideas and to incorporate them in the overall theory Ricoeur sponsors. As a theoretical proposal, then, I expect this study to be taken to task on two fronts: its potential for integration with other theories in the larger intellectual context of the rhetorical tradition, and its explanatory power.

On the first front, I have tried to forge the integration by staging a dialogue between Ricoeur and renowned rhetorical theorists. In this respect, the book is not just about Ricoeur, but also about an entire coterie that includes classics like Aristotle and Perelman along with contemporary figures such as Michael Calvin McGee, Edward Schiappa, or Gerard Hauser. In bringing these scholars together in an "invisible college," I have followed Carole Blair's recommendation that we do not simply follow historical tracks, but also put together critical scenarios in our diachronic study of rhetorical theory. In her essay, "Contested Histories of Rhetoric," Blair argues that histories of rhetoric that seek to detect influences, predominant as they are in the field, are conservative attempts at maintaining a set of concepts and distinctions as they were intended at the time of their creation. But such preservationist efforts are in vain, she reminds us, because the perspective from which we read these concepts, as well as the use to which we put them, have inevitably changed. The alternative approach proposed by Douglas Ehninger, that of "systems histories," commits the fallacy of assuming that the passing of time marks an improvement in intellectual content, and hence seeks indications of progress in historical shifts that concepts may have undergone from Aristotle to, say, Kenneth Burke. What Blair would prefer to see instead is an approach she calls "critical," which takes into account that a theoretical vocabulary changes meaning and significance over time but seeks nevertheless to identify coherent conceptual trajectories and to focus on the explanatory value of a pedigree concept in response to culturally situated problems. Such measuring of theory against practice has also been my aim in selecting provocative case studies, whether well-known (for different reasons) examples of American oratory (like King's speech, "I Have a Dream," and Ronald Reagan's Bitburg address) or of European public and political discourse (like Hável's eulogy and the historians' debate in Germany). At the same time, by creating a dialogue between Ricoeur and rhetorical theorists I have not been preoccupied with establishing influences (though I noted them when they were useful for understanding the philosopher's allegiances). The concepts I have tried to elaborate on here—*doxa*, *phronesis*, *epideictic*, and *polis*—do not constitute Ricoeur's direct contribution. Rather, they emerge from a process of inquiry into inherited rhetorical theories, which starts from a set of premises and questions formulated by him, and continues to draw on his systematic and careful distinctions. It is in this respect that my theoretical approach follows the lines of a critical history.

There are major advantages to choosing such a path, which I hope have emerged throughout the book but deserve to be summarized in the conclusion. First, by unfolding as a dialogue among theorists, this study does not glorify Ricoeur into rhetoric's savior, as is too often the case with authors or ideas introduced across disciplinary lines. I have maintained a reverent and at times enthusiastic tone throughout the book, but not because there are no frustrating gaps in Ricoeur's explanations, expository obscurities, inconsistencies, or inconclusive demonstrations. To not zoom in on such pitfalls is not an indication that there is no critical perspective at work here, but simply a consequence of the fact that this study is not an exegesis. My argument has been that Ricoeur's thinking opens new avenues for rhetorical investigation, but the avenues themselves need additional consolidation. For example, the investigation of doxa sponsored by Ricoeur makes no provision for the difficulty of challenging an audience's conventional beliefs, and describes the tandem ideology-utopia in neat terms, without interest in how or when utopia might fail to counterbalance ideology. The conception of solidarity as grounded in a perfect equivalence among individuals who recognize themselves in the other is compelling but not frequently encountered in actual practice, except for special circumstances such as the ones that gave birth to Polish Solidarity. Ricoeur is silent on how such circumstances emerge or influence the discursive practices in question, or only has something very general to say, for instance: solidarity can be more easily achieved when the individuals feel that their existence as a community, rather than as separate members, is in danger. To recognize such limitations should not detract from the merit of the conceptions presented, but simply point to areas that need improvement and hence call for further research.

A second advantage of my approach concerns the possibility of seeing the concepts proposed not as an ad hoc list but as a coherent set that provides unique insights into the intellectual deep structure of that rhetorical theory. Presumably, the core vocabulary that rhetoric has inherited from the classics designates ideas and notions that fit well together in the original intellectual framework. But do they still form a coherent set in current usage and applications? Can the classical emphasis on the rhetor as an agent who could influence attitudes and behaviors still exist given our postmodernist skepticism that individuals have agency at all? What do these concepts have in common?

In their reflections on contemporary rhetorical theory, John Louis Lucaites, Celeste Michelle Condit and Sally Caudill insist on locating the field between the Scylla and Charybdis of modernism and postmodernism. Instead of joining the modernist search for truth and certainty or participating in the postmodernist perpetual critique, rhetorical theory, as they see it, "offers distinctive approaches to particular questions in social theory" (Lucaites et al, 611). Through its sustained focus on refining the notion of agency, the authors argue, rhetorical theory tries to understand how the social world is constituted in a way that makes possible visions of how lived experience can be improved. Rhetorical theory, by such an account, "denies neither the materiality nor the significance of the agency of speaker or audience, but it does contextualize the agency of all parties to a social interaction as bound in relationship, rather than as the solitary product of some sort of determinism (be it economic or biological) or autonomous free will" (Lucaites et al, 612).

Together, the four concepts I have developed here through recourse to Ricoeur's philosophy deploy a rhetorical theory similarly focused on the agency of individuals as bound in relationships. Agency is the link that makes these concepts, as discussed from Ricoeurian lens, coherent. The presentation of doxa in chapter 1 draws on Ricoeur to show how the beliefs that over time rigidify in conventions and gather around them communities can be modified by rhetors who have the ability to step outside the frame of conventions and encourage others to join them in contemplating new ways of existence. My discussion of phronesis in chapter 2 emphasizes the role of history in framing arguments, but it also tries to make clear that individual rhetors control their reliance on history through interpretive moves and explanatory strategies. In chapter 3 I use Ricoeur to develop a conception of epideictic that shows how national identity relies on positive images of its past, but I also demonstrate that such images do not prevent a national community from taking responsibility for the actions committed by its members at a given time. Individual agents play a crucial role in this discussion inasmuch as they are the ones who bear the brunt of the responsibility, allowing the communal space they inhabit to remain untarnished. As shown in chapter 5, Ricoeur enables us to see that even the social matrix that holds individuals together through recourse to history is constantly re-created from the bottom up, as the work of actual individuals who convince one another to pursue particular goals that are important in their everyday lives. Thus, chapter 5 argues that the "common good" often seen by rhetorical theorists as the foundation of a polis is not a normative abstraction but a concrete articulation of a particular community's beliefs and aspirations.

These four concepts, as deployed here from a Ricoeurian perspective, contribute to a theory of rhetorical agency, and notably, they do so against competing accounts that explicitly de-emphasize the ability of individuals to make effective discursive interventions. Take, for example, the case of doxa, which I approach through recourse to Ricoeur's conjunction of ideology and utopia. The conflation of doxa and ideology is not uncommon, and in this regard Pierre Bourdieu's contribution may be more familiar to rhetorical theorists. But an association with ideology can obfuscate more than clarify, as *ideology* is a notoriously difficult to define term, fraught with various premises of the diverse schools of thought that have employed the term. Nevertheless, the centrality of ideology to rhetorical discourse can hardly be overestimated, and it has been repeatedly noted by critics and theorists even when their subsequent goals have often been very different, from detecting and sanctioning ideology as a source of manipulation and corrupt discourse, to studying it as an empowering framework for activism and intervention. Many in rhetoric will share the reluctance to as much as use the term *ideology*. Such reservations go back to Burke, who flatly stated his preference for the concept of "myth" as a shortcut for explaining public and social phenomena. Burke subsequently forged an intellectual direction in rhetoric that actively sought to develop an alternative vocabulary and analytic categories, which led for a while to the concept's atrophy in the field of rhetorical theory and criticism. But myth and ideology equally de-emphasize the role of individual agency in effecting change, while their pervasiveness in discourse teeters on the brink of elusiveness. By contrast, Ricoeur's coupling of ideology with utopia explains the rhetorical resources that agents have in order to envision and then to create a world different from the ones they inhabit.

The alternative accounts sponsored by Ricoeur also have descriptive value and analytic purchase—they respond to problems and tendencies noticeable in public or political discourse. To explain the historicizing dimension of practical reasoning, for instance, is to address a recurrent discursive phenomenon in American political rhetoric and presidential speech particularly. Furthermore, to articulate a conception of epideictic that takes into account the possibility of, but does not reduce it to, propaganda offers a necessary conceptual tool for analyzing problematic cases such as the representation of the past in postwar Germany. Defining the polis as a possible site of solidarity that emerges among individuals engaging one another directly provides a conceptual setting for investigating what it takes to confront a nation-state, at a time when states begin to regain, indeed increase their power over citizens. In my own research I am also concerned with the creation of a diasporic polis—transnational political configurations that no longer have recourse to the usual state institutions and must establish their legitimacy by convincing each and every one of their members to participate in the pursuit of a common good. For such research, a model of polis that studies grassroot interactions carries much more analytic weight than normative theories.

Finally, a third advantage on which my approach in this book has counted concerns the handling of classical concepts. While operating with a technical vocabulary that has been long in use makes disciplinary specialization possible, the very historicity of the terms in question poses some risks. Jan Swearingen, for example, has convincingly argued against the frequent and misleading use of *ethos* synonymously with the modern concepts of "selfhood" and "identity" (in Baumlin and Baumlin, 1994). Such employment is anachronistic and deceptive, because the ancients had an understanding of individuality that was markedly different from what "selfhood" would seek to convey a few centuries later. Often hastily replaced with at best partial and at worst inadequate equivalents, the classical concepts retain value insofar as they can be systematically and coherently integrated in a broader theoretical framework. What gives me license here to employ terms like *phronesis* or *doxa* in order to discuss a contemporary rhetorical problem is the fact that I do not merely adopt the ancient term, throwing it casually in theoretical parlance. Rather, in each chapter I try to develop what linguists might call a semantic field, weighing in definitions and taking stock of the assumptions embedded in them before I allow Ricoeur to inform a new elaboration.

The main goal of this book has been to contribute to the ongoing efforts in rhetorical theory to refine its conceptual basis in a way that provides intellectual cohesion to the field as well as explanatory power. In an increasingly specialized and socially sensitive academic environment, prominence and respectability are rewards for theoretical maturity and sophistication, but are also rewards for a field's ability to address the problems of the world in which we live. I hope this book makes a convincing case that Paul Ricoeur can be a powerful ally in empowering rhetoric to acquire such a status.

Bibliography

Adorno, Theodor W. "On the Question: 'What Is German?'" *New German Critique* 36.4 (1985): 121–31.

Althusser, Louis. *For Marx.* Trans. by Ben Brewster. New York: Vintage Books, 1970.

Anderson, Pamela Sue. "Ricoeur's Reclamation of Autonomy: Unity, Plurality, and Totality," in *Paul Ricoeur and Contemporary Moral Thought*, eds. John Wall, William Schweiker, and David W. Hall. New York: Routledge, 2002 15–31.

Arendt, Hannah. *The Human Condition.* Chicago: University of Chicago Press, 1958.

Aristotle. *On Rhetoric: A Theory of Civic Discourse.* Trans. and introduction by George A. Kennedy. Oxford: Oxford University Press, 1991.

———. *Politics.* Trans. and introduction by C. D. C. Reeve. Indianapolis, Ind.: Hackett Publishers, 1998.

———. *Nichomachean Ethics.* Trans. by Christopher Rowe, introduction and commentary by Sarah Broadie. Oxford: Oxford University Press, 2002.

Asen, Robert. "Imagining in the Public Sphere." *Philosophy and Rhetoric* 35.4 (2022): 345–67.

Bender, John and David Wellbery. *The Ends of Rhetoric.* Stanford: Stanford University Press, 1992.

Benveniste, Emile. *Problems in General Linguistics.* Trans. by Mary Elizabeth Meek. Coral Gables: University of Miami Press, 1974.

Biesecker, Barbara. "Rethinking the Rhetorical Situation from within the Thematic of *Difference.*" *Philosophy and Rhetoric* 22 (1989): 110–30.

Bizzell, Patricia and Bruce Herzberg. *The Rhetorical Tradition: Readings from Classical Times to the Present.* Boston: St. Martin's/Bedford Books, 1990.

Bizzell, Patricia. "Editing the Rhetorical Tradition." *Philosophy and Rhetoric* 36 (2003): 109–18.

Blair, Carole. "Contested Histories of Rhetoric: The Politics of Preservation, Progress, and Change." *Quarterly Journal of Speech* 78 (1992): 403–28.

Boltanski, Luc. *Distant Suffering. Morality, Media, and Politics.* Trans. by Graham Burcell. Cambridge: Cambridge University Press, 1999.

Bourdieu, Pierre. "The Social Conditions of the International Circulation of Ideas," in *Bourdieu: A Critical Reader,* ed. Richard Schusterman. Malden, Mass.: Blackwell Publishers, 1999: 220–28.

Brockmann, Stephen. "The Politics of German History." *History and Theory. Studies in the Philosophy of History* 2.29 (1990): 179–89.

Browne, Stephen. "Reading Public Memory in Daniel Webster's Plymouth Rock Oration." *Western Journal of Communication* 3.57 (1993): 464–77.

Burke, Kenneth. *On Symbols and Society.* Chicago: University of Chicago Press, 1989.

Campbell, George. *Philosophy of Rhetoric.* Carbondale: Southern Illinois Press, 1963.

Campbell, Kohrs Karlyn. "An Exercise in Mythical America," in *Readings in Rhetorical Criticism,* ed. Carl Burchgardt. State College Pa: Strata Publishing Company, 1995, 442–56.

Castoriadis, Cornelius. *The Imaginary Institution of Society.* Trans. by Kathleen Blamey. Cambridge: Massachusetts Institute of Technology Press, 1987.

Clinton, William J. "Remarks to the Convocation of the Church of God in Christ in Memphis (November 13, 1993)," in *Public Papers of the Presidents of the United States: William J. Clinton 1993, Book II.* Washington, D.C.: United States Government Printing Office, 1994, 1981–1986.

Cloud, Dana. "Which Voices? Whose Democracy?" *Argumentation and Advocacy* 4.37 (2001): 210–13.

Condit, Celeste Michelle. "The Functions of Epideictic: The Boston Massacre Orations as Exemplar." *Communication Quarterly* 33 (1985): 284–99.

Conley, Thomas. *The Rhetorical Tradition in Europe.* Chicago: University of Chicago Press, 1990.

Copeland, Rita. "Rhetoric and the Politics of the Literal Sense in Medieval Literary Theory: Aquinas, Wyclif, and the Lollards," in *Rhetoric and Hermeneutics: A Reader,* eds. Michael Hyde and Walter Jost. New Haven: Yale University Press, 1993, 355–57.

Cox, J. Robert. "The Fulfillment of Time: King's 'I Have a Dream' Speech (August 28, 1963)," in *Texts in Contexts. Critical Dialogues on Significant Episodes in American Political Rhetoric,* eds. Michael Leff and Fred J. Kauffeld. Mahwah, N.J.: Hermagoras Press, 1989, 181–204.

Dallmayr, Fred. "Politics and Power: Ricoeur's Political Paradox Revisited," in *Meanings in Texts and Actions: Questioning Paul Ricoeur,* eds. David E. Klemm and William Schweiker. Charlottesville and London: University Press of Virginia, 1993, 176–94.

Daueunhauer, Bernard. *Paul Ricoeur: The Promise and Risk of Politics.* Lanham, Md.: Rowman and Littlefield, 1998.

Dilthey, Wilhelm. *Selected Writings.* Trans. by H. P. Rickman. Cambridge: Cambridge University Press, 1976.

Dosse, François. *History of Structuralism*. Trans. by Deborah Glassman, Minneapolis: University of Minnesota Press, 1997.

Eley, Geoff. *Forging Democracy: The History of the Left in Europe*, 1850–2000. Oxford: Oxford University Press, 2002.

Farrar, Cynthia. *The Origins of Democratic Thinking. The Invention of Politics in Classical Athens*. Cambridge: Cambridge University Press, 1988.

Farrell, Thomas. *Norms of Rhetorical Culture*. New Haven: Yale University Press, 1993.

———. "Knowledge, Consensus, and Rhetorical Theory." *Quarterly Journal of Speech* 62 (1976): 1–14.

Fraser, Nancy. "Transnationalizing the Public Sphere." Presentation at the Identities, Affiliations, and Allegiances conference, Yale University, October 3–4, 2003.

Friedländer, Saul. "Some German Struggles with Memory," in *Bitburg in Moral and Political Perspective*, ed. Geoffrey H. Hartman. Bloomington: Indiana University Press, 1986, 27–42.

Fritzsche, Peter. "The Case of Modern Memory." *Journal of Modern History* 1.73 (2001): 87–117.

Gadamer, Hans-Georg. *Truth and Method*. Trans. by Garrett Barding and John Cumming. New York: Seabury Press, 1976.

———. *Reason in the Age of Science*. Trans. by Frederick Lawrence. Cambridge: Massachusetts Institute of Technology, 1991.

———. *Praise of Theory*. Trans. by Chris Dawson. New Haven and London: Yale University Press, 1998.

Garton Ash, Timothy. *The Polish Revolution: Solidarity*, 3rd ed., New Haven: Yale University Press, 2002.

Garver, Eugene. *Aristotle's Rhetoric. An Art of Character*. Chicago: University of Chicago Press, 1994.

Gorgias, "Encomium on Helen" in Freeman, Kathleen. *Ancilla to the Pre-Socratic Philosophers* (Cambridge: Harvard University Press, 1948), 131–33.

Grondin, Jean. *Introduction to Philosophical Hermeneutics*. Trans. by Joel Weinsheimer. New Haven: Yale University Press, 1994.

Gross, Alan. *The Rhetoric of Science*. Cambridge: Harvard University Press, 1990.

———. "The Rhetorical Tradition," in *The Viability of the Rhetorical Tradition*, eds. Richard Graff, Arthur Walzer, and Jane Atwill. Albany: State University of New York Press, 2005, 31–45.

Gross, Alan and Ray Dearin. *Chaim Perelman*. Albany: State University of New York Press, 2003.

Habermas, Jürgen. "Apologetic Tendencies," in *The New Conservatism*, trans. Shierry Weber Nicholsen. Cambridge: Massachusetts Institute of Technology Press, 1989, 212–28.

———. *The Structural Transformation of the Public Sphere: An Inquiry into a Category of Bourgeois Society*. Cambridge: Massachusetts Institute of Technology Press, 1989.

Halbwachs, Maurice. *On Collective Memory*. Chicago: University of Chicago Press, 1981.

Halloran, Michael. "Text and Experience in a Historical Pageant: Toward a Rhetoric of Spectacle." *Rhetoric Society Quarterly* 31.4 (2001): 5–17.

Hariman, Robert. "Time and the Reconstitution of Gradualism in King's Address: A Response to Cox." In *Texts in Contexts*, 205–18.

———. "Status, Marginality, and Rhetorical Theory." *Quarterly Journal of Speech* 72 (1995): 2–17.

Hauser, Gerard. "Civil Society and the Principle of the Public Sphere." *Philosophy and Rhetoric* 31.1 (1998): 19–41.

———. *Vernacular Voices: The Rhetoric of Publics and Public Spheres*. Columbia: University of South Carolina Press, 1999.

———. "Prisoners of Conscience and the Counterpublic Sphere of Prison Writing," in *Counterpublics and the State*, eds. Robert Asen and Daniel C. Brouwer. Albany: State University of New York Press, 2000, 35–59.

Havel, Václav. *Open Letters: Selected Writings*. Trans. by Paul Wilson. New York: Knopf, 1991.

Hechter, Michael. *Internal Colonialism*. Berkeley: University of California Press, 1975.

Howard, Roy J. *Three Faces of Hermeneutics: An Introduction to Current Theories of Understanding*. Berkeley: University of California Press, 1982.

Hyde, Michael. *The Call of Conscience: Heidegger and Levinas, Rhetoric and the Euthanasia Debate*. Columbia: University of South Carolina Press, 2001.

Ihde, Don. *Hermeneutic Phenomenology: The Philosophy of Paul Ricoeur*. Evanston, Ill.: Northwestern University Press, 1971.

Iser, Wolfgang. *The Fictive and the Imaginary: Charting Literary Anthropology*. Baltimore: Johns Hopkins University Press, 1993.

Jarausch, Konrad and Michael Geyer. *Shattered Past: Reconstructing German Histories*. Princeton: Princeton University Press, 2003.

Jaspers, Karl. *The Question of German Guilt*. Trans. by E. B. Ashton. New York: Fordham University Press, 2000.

Judt, Tony. *Past Imperfect: French Intellectuals, 1945–1956*. Berkeley: University of California Press, 1992.

King, Martin Luther, Jr. "I've Been to the Mountaintop," in *Texts in Contexts: Critical Dialogues on Significant Episodes in American Public Address*, eds. M. C. Leff and F. J. Kauffeld. Davis, Calif.: Hermagoras Press, 1989, 311–21.

Kolakowski, Leszek. *Main Currents of Marxism*. Trans. by P. S. Falla. Oxford: Oxford University Press, 1978.

Lamont, Michel and Laurent Thevenot. *Rethinking Comparative Cultural Sociology: Repertoires of Evaluation in France and the United States*. Cambridge: Cambridge University Press, 2000.

Langsdorf, Lenore. "The Doubleness of Subjectivity: Regenerating the Phenomenology of Intentionality," in *Oneself as Another: Essays Inspired by Paul Ricoeur's Theory of Selfhood*, eds. Richard A. Cohen and James L. Marsh. Albany: State University of New York Press, 2003, 33–55.

Lathem, Edward Connery, ed. *Bernard Bailyn on the Teaching and Writing of History*. Hanover, N.H.: University of New England Press, 1994.

Lay, Mary M. *The Rhetoric of Midwifery. Gender, Knowledge, Power*. New Brunswick, N.J.: Rutgers University Press, 2000.

Leff, Michael. "The Habitation of Rhetoric," in *Argument and Critical Practice: Proceedings of the Fifth SCA/AFA Conference on Argumentation*, ed. Joseph Wenzel. Virginia: SCA, 1987, 1–9.

———. "Hermeneutical Rhetoric," in *Rhetoric and Hermeneutics*, 196–214.

Lefort, Claude. *Democracy and Political Theory*. Minneapolis: University of Minnesota Press, 1988.

Le Goff, Jacques. *History and Memory*. Trans. by Steven Rendall and Elizabeth Claman. New York: Columbia University Press, 1992.

Levine, Andrew. *The General Will: Rousseau, Marx, Communism*. Cambridge: Cambridge University Press, 1993.

Levkov, Ilya, ed. *Bitburg and Beyond: Encounters in American, German, and Jewish History*. New York: Shapolsky Publishers, 1987.

Loraux, Nicole. *The Invention of Athens: The Funeral Oration in the Classical City*. Trans. by Alan Sheridan. Cambridge: Harvard University Press, 1986.

Loreau, Max. "Rhetoric as the Logic of the Behavioral Sciences, trans. by Lloyd I. Watkins and Paul D. Brandes. *Quarterly Journal of Speech* 51 (1965): 455–63.

Lucaites, John Louis and Celeste Michelle Condit. "Universalizing 'Equality:' The Public Legacy of Martin Luther King, Jr.," in *Martin Luther King, Jr., and the Sermonic Power of Discourse*, eds. Carolyn Calloway-Thomas and John Louis Lucaites, Tuscaloosa: University of Alabama Press, 1993, 85–103.

Mailloux, Steven. "Articulation and Understanding: The Pragmatic Intimacy between Rhetoric and Hermeneutics," in *Rhetoric and Hermeneutics*, 378–94.

Mannheim, Karl. *Ideology and Utopia: Introduction to Sociology of Knowledge*. Trans. by Louis Wirth and Edward Shils. San Diego: Harcourt 1936.

Margalit, Avishai. *The Ethics of Memory*. Cambridge: Harvard University Press, 2003.

Marx, Anthony W. "The Nation-State and Its Exclusions." *Political Science Quarterly* 117.1 (2002): 103–26.

McGee, Michael Calvin. "The Ideograph: A Link between Rhetoric and Ideology." *Quarterly Journal of Speech* 66 (1980): 1–16. Reprinted in Carl Burchgardt, ed. *Readings in Rhetorical Criticism.* State College Pa.: Strata Publishing Company, 1995, 442–56.

Michnik, Adam. *Letters from Prison and Other Essays.* Trans. by Maya Latynski. Berkeley: University of California Press, 1986.

Müller, Jan-Werner. *Another Country: German Intellectuals, Unification, and National Identity.* New Haven: Yale University Press, 2000.

Murphy, John M. "Inventing Authority: Bill Clinton, Martin Luther King, Jr., and the Orchestration of Rhetorical Traditions." *Quarterly Journal of Speech* 83 (1997): 71–89.

Nora, Pierre. *Realms of Memory: Rethinking the French Past.* Trans. by Arthur Goldhammer. New York: Columbia University Press, 1996.

Osiel, Mark J. "Making Public Memory, Publicly," in *Human Rights in Political Transitions,* eds. Carla Hesse and Robert C. Post. New York: Zone Books, 1999, 217–61.

———. *Mass Atrocity, Collective Memory, and the Law.* New Brunswick, N.J.: Transaction Publishers, 1997.

Parameshwar, Dilip Gaonkar. "Rhetoric and Its Double: Reflections on the Rhetorical Turn in the Human Sciences," in *The Rhetorical Turn: Invention and Persuasion in the Conduct of Inquiry,* ed. Herbert W. Simons. Chicago: University of Chicago Press, 1990, 341–66.

———. "Toward New Imaginaries: An Introduction." *Public Culture* 141.1 (2002): 1–19.

Pavel, Thomas. *Fictional Worlds.* Cambridge: Harvard University Press, 1986.

Perelman, Chaim and L. Olbrechts-Tyteca. *The New Rhetoric. A Treatise on Argumentation.* Notre-Dame, Ind.: University of Notre Dame Press, 1994.

Phelps, Louise Wetherbee. *Composition as a Human Science: Contributions to the Self—Understanding of a Discipline.* New York: Oxford University Press, 1988.

Poulakos, John. "Toward a Sophistic Definition of Rhetoric." *Philosophy and Rhetoric* 16 (1983): 249–66.

———. *Sophistical Rhetoric in Classical Greece.* Columbia: University of South Carolina Press, 1995.

Ragin, Charles C. and Howard S. Becker, eds. *What Is a Case? Exploring the Foundation of Social Inquiry.* New York: Cambridge University Press, 1992.

Reagan, Charles. *Paul Ricoeur: His Life and His Work.* Chicago: University of Chicago Press, 1996.

Roberts-Miller, Patricia. *Voices in the Wilderness: Public Discourse and the Paradox of Puritan Rhetoric.* Tuscaloosa: University of Alabama Press, 1999.

Rousseau, Jean-Jacques. *The Social Contract and Other Later Political Writings.* Trans. by Victor Gourevitch. New York: Cambridge University Press, 1997.

Rousso, Henry. *The Haunting Past: History, Memory, and Justice in Contemporary France.* Trans. by Ralph Schoolcraft. Philadelphia: University of Pennsylvania Press, 2002.

Ryan, Mary. *Civic Wars. Democracy and Public Life in America during the Nineteenth Century.* Berkeley: University of California Press, 1997.

Schiappa, Edward. *Beginnings of Rhetorical Theory in Classical Greece.* New Haven: Yale University Press, 1999.

Sheard, Cynthia Miecznikowski. "The Public Value of Epideictic Rhetoric." *College English* 58 (1996): 765–94.

Simms, Karl. *Paul Ricoeur.* London: Routledge, 2003.

Sloane, Thomas. *On the Contrary. The Protocol of Traditional Rhetoric.* Washington, D.C.: Catholic University of America Press, 1997.

Smith, Adam. *The Theory of Moral Sentiments.* Cambridge: Cambridge University Press, 2003.

Stampp, Kenneth. *America in 1857: A Nation on the Brink.* Oxford: Oxford University Press, 1990.

Staniszkis, Jadwiga. *Poland's Self-Limiting Revolution.* Edited by Jan T. Gross. Princeton: Princeton University Press, 1984.

Swearingen, Jan C. "*Ethos*: Imitation, Impersonation, and Voice," in *Ethos: New Essays in Rhetorical and Critical Theory*, eds. James S. Baumlin and Tita F. Baumlin. Dallas, TX: Southern Methodist University Press, 1994, 115–48.

Taylor, Charles. "Modern Social Imaginaries." *Public Culture* 14.1 (2002): 91–124.

Thompson, John B. *Critical Hermeneutics: A Study in the Thought of Paul Ricoeur and Jürgen Habermas.* New York: Cambridge University Press, 1981.

Tocqueville, Alexis de. *Democracy in America.* Trans. by Arthur Goldhammer. New York: Library of America, 2004.

Todorov, Tzvetan. *Morals of History.* Berkeley: University of California Press, 1986.

Vernant, Jean-Pierre. *The Origins of Greek Thought.* Ithaca: Cornell University Press, 1982.

Walker, Jeffrey. *Rhetoric and Poetics in Antiquity.* New York: Oxford University Press, 2000.

Wallace, Mark. "The Summoned Self: Ethics and Hermeneutics in Paul Ricoeur in Dialogue with Emmanuel Levinas," in *Paul Ricoeur and Contemporary Moral Thought*, 80–93.

Walzer, Arthur. *George Campbell. Rhetoric in the Age of Enlightenment.* Albany: State University of New York Press, 2002.

Warnick, Barbara. "A Ricoeurian Approach to Rhetorical Criticism." *Western Journal of Speech Communication* 51 (1987): 227–44.

Zarefsky, David. *Lincoln, Douglas, and Slavery: In the Crucible of Public Debate.* Chicago: The University of Chicago Press, 1990.

Young, Iris Marion. *Inclusion and Democracy.* Oxford: Oxford University Press, 2000.

Bibliography of Paul Ricoeur's Works

Primary Sources: Books In English

History and Truth, trans. Charles A Kelbley. Evanston, IL.: Northwestern University Press, 1955. reprint, 1992.

Freedom and Nature: The Voluntary and the Involuntary. Evanston, Ill.: Northwestern University Press, 1966.

Husserl: An Analysis of His Phenomenology, trans. E. G. Ballard and L. E. Embree. Evanston, Ill.: Northwestern University Press, 1966.

The Symbolism of Evil, trans. E. Buchanan. New York: Harper, 1967. Reprint, Boston: Beacon, 1990.

Freud and Philosophy: An Essay on Interpretation, trans. D. Savage. New Haven and London: Yale University Press, 1970.

Tragic Wisdom and Beyond, with Gabriel Marcel, trans. P. McCormick. Evanston, Ill.: Northwestern University Press, 1973.

The Conflict of Interpretations. Essays in Hermeneutics, trans. D. Ihde. Evanston, Ill.: Northwestern University Press, 1974.

Political and Social Essays. Ohio University Press, 1975.

Interpretation Theory: Discourse and the Surplus of Meaning. Texas Christian University Press, 1976.

Main Trends in Philosophy (Main Trends of Research in the Social and Human Sciences. Selections). New York: Holmes & Meier Publishers, 1979.

Essays on Biblical Interpretation. Fortress Press, 1980.

The Contribution of French Historiography to French History. Clarendon Press, 1980.

Hermeneutics and the Human Sciences. Essays on Language, Action and Interpretation, ed. and trans. J. B. Thompson. Cambridge and New York: Cambridge University Press, 1981.

The Rule of Metaphor, Multidisciplinary Studies in the Creation of Meaning in Language, trans. Robert Czerny. Toronto: University of Toronto Press, 1981.

The Reality of the Historical Past. Marquette University Press, 1984.

Time and Narrative, Vols. 1–3, trans. Kathleen Blamey and David Pellauer. Chicago and London: University of Chicago Press, 1984–88.

Fallible Man: Philosophy of the Will (Ricoeur, Paul. Philosophie De LA Volonte), trans. Charles A. Kelbley. New York: Fordham University Press. Reprint, 1986.

Philosophy of Paul Ricoeur: An Anthology of His Work, ed. David Stewart. Boston: Beacon Press, 1990.

From Text to Action, Essays in Hermeneutics, trans. Kathleen Blamey and John Thompson. Evanston, Ill.: Northwestern University Press, 1991.

A Ricoeur Reader: Reflection and Imagination, Vol. 2, ed. Mario J. Valdes. Toronto: University of Toronto Press, 1991.

Oneself as Another, trans. Kathleen Blamey. Chicago: University of Chicago Press, 1992.

Figuring the Sacred: Religion, Narrative, and Imagination. Fortress Press, 1995.

A Key to Husserl's Ideas I (Marquette Studies in Philosophy, Vol. 10), ed. Pol Vandervelde, trans. Jacqueline Bouchard Spurlock. Marquette University Press, 1996.

Critique and Conviction: Conversations with Francois Azouvi and Marc De Launay, trans. Kathleen Blamey. Blackwell Publishers, 1997.

Tolerance between Intolerance and the Intolerable, ed. Paul Ricoeur. New York: Berghan Books, 1997.

The Just, trans. David Pellauer. Chicago: University of Chicago Press, 2000.

COAUTHORED BOOKS IN ENGLISH

The Phenomenology of Merleau-Ponty: A Search for the Limits of Consciousness (Series in Continental Thought, 3), Ricoeur, Paul and Gary Brent Madison. Ohio University Press, 1981.

Metaphoric Process: The Creation of Scientific and Religious Understanding, Ricoeur, Paul, Mary Gerhart, and Allan M. Russell. Texas A&M University Press, 1984.

The Religious Significance of Atheism, Ricoeur, Paul and Alasdair C. MacIntyre. Columbia University Press, 1986.

Lectures on Ideology and Utopia, ed. George Taylor. Columbia University Press, 1988.

A Ricoeur Reader: Reflection and Imagination (Theory/Culture Series), Ricoeur, Paul and Mario J Valdes. University of Toronto Press, 1991.

Critique and Conviction, Ricoeur, Paul and Francois Azouvi (Contributor), Marc B. De Launay and Kathleen Blamey. Columbia University Press, 1998.

Thinking Biblically: Exegetical and Hermeneutical Studies, Ricoeur, Paul and André Lacocque, trans. David Pellauer. University of Chicago Press. 1998.

Phenomenology and the Theological Turn: The French Debate (Perspectives in Continental Philosophy, No. 15), eds. Dominique Janicaud, Jean-Francois Courtine, Jen-Louis Chretien, Michel Henry, Jean-Luc Marion, Paul Ricoeur, Jean-Louis Chretien. Fordham University Press, 2001.

What Makes Us Think? A Neuroscientist and a Philosopher Argue about Ethics, Human Nature, and the Brain, Ricoeur, Paul and Jean-Pierre Changeux, trans. M. B. DeBevoise. Princeton University Press, 2002.

Martin Heidegger and the Problem of Historical Meaning (Perspectives in Continental Philosophy, 31), Ricoeur, Paul and Jeffrey Andrew Barash. Fordham University Press, 2nd rev. ed., 2003.

Books in French

Philosophie du mystère et philosophie du paradoxe, Gabriel Marcel and Karl Jaspers. Paris: Temps Present, 1948.

Karl Jaspers et la philosophie de l'existence, with Mikel Dufrenne. Paris: Seuil, 1947.

Philosophie de la volonté. I. Le volontaire et l'involontaire (Philosophie de l'esprit). Paris: Aubier, 1950.

Philosophie de la volonté. Finitude et culpabilité. I. L'homme faillable (Philosophie de l'esprit). Paris: Aubier, 1960.

Philosophie de la volonté. Finitude et culpabilité. II. La symbolique du mal (Philosophie de l'esprit). Paris: Aubier 1960.

Histoire et vérité (Esprit). Paris: Seuil 1955 (first edition), 1964 (second edition, with minor revisions), 1990 (third edition, with minor revisions), American edition Northwestern University Press, 1966.

De l'interprétation. Essai sur Freud (L'Ordre philosophique). Paris: Seuil 1965 (Points Essais) 1995.

Le conflit des interprétations. Essais d'herméneutique. (L'Ordre philosophique). Paris: Seuil 1969, American edition Northwestern University Press, 1974; English edition Athlone.

La métaphore vive (L'Ordre philosophique). Paris: Seuil 1975 (Points Essais), 1997; Canadian edition University of Toronto Press.

Temps et récit. Tome I (L'Ordre philosophique). Paris: Seuil 1983 (Points Essais), 1991; American edition University of Chicago Press.

Temps et récit. Tome II. La configuration dans le récit de fiction (L'Ordre philosophique). Paris, Seuil 1984 (Points Essais), 1991; American edition University of Chicago Press.

Temps et récit. Tome III. Temps raconté. (L'Ordre philosophique). Paris: Seuil 1985 (Points Essais), 1991; American edition University of Chicago Press.

À l'école de la philosophie. Paris: J. Vrin, 1986.

Le mal: Un défi à la philosophie et à la théologie. Geneva: Labor et Fides, 1986.

Lectures I: Autour du politique. Paris: Seuil, 1991.

Lectures II: La Contrée des philosophes. Paris: Seuil, 1992.

Lectures III: Aux frontières de la philosophie. Paris: Seuil, 1994.

La critique et la convinction, Entretiens avec François Azouvi et Marc de Launay. Paris: Calmann-Lévy, 1995.

Le Juste. Paris: Editions Esprit, 1995.

Réflexion faite. Autobiographie intellectuelle. Paris: Editions Esprit, 1995.

Autrement. Lecture d'Autrement qu'être ou au-delà de l'essence d'Emmanuel Levinas. Paris: Presses Universitaires de France, 1997.

L'idéologie et l'utopie (La couleur des idées). Paris: Seuil 1997.

Ce qui nous fait penser. La nature et la règle, with Jean-Pierre Changeaux. Paris: Editions Odite Jacob, 1998.

Penser la Bible, with André Lacocque. Paris: Seuil, 1998.

La mémoire, l'histoire, l'oubli. Paris: Seuil, 2000.

Le Juste I. Paris: Esprit, 2001.

BOOK INTRODUCTIONS IN ENGLISH

Metaphoric Process: The Creation of Scientific and Religious Understanding, Mary Gerhart and Allan M. Russell. introd. and design Paul Ricoeur. Texas Christian University Press, 1984.

Heretical Essays in the Philosophy of History, Jan. Patocka, introd. Paul Ricoeur. Open Court Publishing Company, 1996.

Saga and Philosophy: And Other Essays, Pall. Skulason. introd. Paul Ricoeur. University of Iceland Press, 1999.

Couples: Speaking from the Heart, Mariana Ruth Cook. introd. Paul Ricoeur. Chronicle Books, 2000.

BOOK CHAPTERS

"Between Rhetoric and Poetics," in *Essays on Aristotle's Rhetoric,* ed. Amelie Oksenberg Rorty. Berkeley: University of California Press, 1996, 324–84.

"Rhetoric, Poetics, Hermeneutics," in *Rhetoric and Hermeneuties in Our Time,* eds. Walter Jost and Michael J. Hyde. New Haven: Yale University Press, 1997, 60–72.

Secondary Sources: Books in English

Anderson, Pamela Sue, *Ricoeur and Kant: Philosophy of the Will (American Academy of Religion Studies in Religion, No. 66*. Atlanta, Ga: Scholars Press, 1993.

Boeve, L. and Laurence Paul Hemming, eds., *Divinising Experience: Essays in the History of Religious Experience from Origen to Ricoeur*. Leuren: Peeters Publishing, 2003.

Bourgeois, Patrick L, and Frank Schalow, *Traces of Understanding: A Profile of Heidegger's and Ricoeur's Hermeneutics (Elementa, Vol. 53)*. Amsterdam: Rodopi Bv Editions, 1990.

Clark, Stephen H., *Paul Ricoeur (Critics of the Twentieth Century)*. New York and London: Routledge. Reprint ed., 1991.

Cohen, Richard A. and James L. Marsh, *Ricoeur as Another: The Ethics of Subjectivity. (SUNY Series in the Philosophy of the Social Sciences)*. Albany: State University of New York Press, 2002.

Dauenhauer, Bernard P., *Paul Ricoeur: The Promise and Risk of Politics*. Lanham, Md.: Rowman and Littlefield, 1998.

Dosse, François, *Paul Ricoeur: Les sens d'une vie*. Paris: La Decouverte, 1997.

Dornisch, Loretta C., *Faith and Philosophy in the Writings of Paul Ricoeur (Problems in Contemporary Philosophy, Vol. 29)*. Lewiston, N.Y.: Edwin Mellen Press, 1991.

Evans, Jeanne, *Paul Ricoeur's Hermeneutics of the Imagination (American University Studies. Series vii, Theology And Religion, Vol. 143)*. Berlin: Peter Lang Publishing, 1995.

Fodor, James, *Christian Hermeneutics: Paul Ricoeur and the Refiguring of Theology*. Oxford: Clarendon Press, 1995.

Gerhart, Mary, *The Question of Belief in Literary Criticism: An Introduction to the Hermeneutical Theory of Paul Ricoeur*. Stuttgart Akademischer Verlag Heinz.

Greisch, Jean, *Paul Ricoeur: L'itinérance du sens*. Paris: Millon, 2001.

Gutting, Gary, *French Philosophy in the Twentieth Century*. Cambridge: Cambridge University Press, 2001.

Hahn, Lewis E., *The Philosophy of Paul Ricoeur*. Chicago and La Salle: Open Court, 1995.

Ihde, Don, *Hermeneutic Phenomenology: The Philosophy of Paul Ricoeur*. Evanston; Ill.: Northwestern University Press, 1971.

Jervolino, D., *The Cogito and Hermeneutics: The Question of the Subject in Ricoeur (Contributions to Phenomenology. Vol. 6)*. Dordrecht, Netherlands: Kluwer Academic Publishers, 1990.

Joseph, Peter, and C. M. Albano, *Freedom, Truth, and Hope: The Relationship of Philosophy and Religion in the Thought of Paul Ricoeur*. Lanham, Md.: Rowman & Littlefield (non-NBN), 1987.

Joy, Morny, ed., *Paul Ricoeur and Narrative: Context and Contestation*. Calgary, Alberta: University of Calgary Press, 1997.

Kaplan, David M., *Ricoeur's Critical Theory*. Albany: State University of New York Press, 2003.

Kearney, Richard, *Dialogues with Contemporary Continental Thinkers: The Phenomenological Heritage, Paul Ricoeur, Emmanuel Levinas, Herbert Marcuse, Stanislas Breton.* Manchester: Manchester University Press, 1988.

———, ed. *Paul Ricoeur: The Hermeneutics of Action.* London: Sage, 1996.

Kemp, Peter T., and David Rasmussen, eds. *The Narrative Path, The Later Works of Paul Ricoeur.* Cambridge: Massachusetts Institute of Technology Press, 1988.

Kenny, Maureen Junker, *Memory, Narrativity, Self, and the Challenge to Think God: The Reception within Theology of the Recent Work of Paul Ricoeur.* Münster: Lit Verlag, 2003.

Klemm, David E., and William Schweiker, eds., *Meaning in Texts and Action: Questioning Paul Ricoeur.* Charlottesville: University Press of Virginia, 1993.

Leeuwen, Theodore, *The Surplus of Meaning. Ontology and Eschatology in the Philosophy of Paul Ricoeur (Amsterdam Studies in Theology 2).* Amsterdam: Rodopi Editions, 1981.

Laughery, Gregory J., *Living Hermeneutics in Motion: An Analysis and Evaluation of Paul Ricoeur's Contribution to Biblical Hermeneutics.* Lanham, Md.: Rowman & Littlefield (non-NBN), 2002.

Lawlor, Leonard, *Imagination and Chance: The Difference between the Thought of Ricoeur and Derrida (SUNY Series in Intersections: Philosophy and Critical Theory).* Albany: State University of New York Press, 1992.

Lowe, Walter James, *Mystery and the Unconscious: A Study in the Thought of Paul Ricoeur.* Lanham, Md.: Scarecrow Press, 1977.

Marcel, Gabriel, *Tragic Wisdom and Beyond: Including Conversations between Paul Ricoeur and Gabriel Marcel.* Evanston, Ill.: Northwestern University Press, 1973.

Mongin, Oliver, *Paul Ricoeur.* Paris: Seuil, 1994.

Nordquist, Joan Paul, *Ricoeur: A Bibliography (Social Theory: A Bibliographic Series)* Santa Cruz, Calif.: Reference & Research Services, 1999.

Putti, Joseph, *Theology as Hermeneutics: Paul Ricoeur's Theory of Text Interpretation and Method in Theology.* San Francisco: International Scholars Press, 1994.

Reagan, Charles E., *Studies in the Philosophy of Paul Ricoeur.* Athens: Ohio University Press, 1979.

——— *Paul Ricoeur: His Life and His Work.* Chicago: University of Chicago Press (Trd). Reprint ed., 1998.

Simms, Karl, *Paul Ricoeur (Routledge Critical Thinkers).* New York and London: Routledge, 2002

Skousgaard, Stephen, *Language and the Existence of Freedom: A Study in Paul Ricoeur's Philosophy of Will.* Lanham, Md.: Rowman & Littlefield (non-NBN), 1979.

Thompson, John B., *Critical Hermeneutics: A Study in the Thought of Paul Ricoeur and Jürgen Habermas.* Cambridge: Cambridge University Press, 1981.

Van Den Hengel, John W., *The Home of Meaning: The Hermeneutics of the Subject of Paul Ricoeur.* Lanham, Md.: Rowman & Littlefield (non-NBN), 1983.

Vanhoozer, Kevin J., *Biblical Narrative in the Philosophy of Paul Ricoeur: A Study in Hermeneutics and Theology*. Cambridge: Cambridge University Press, 1990.

Vansina, F. D., *Paul Ricoeur. Bibliographie primaire et secondaire. Primary and Secundary Bibliography 1935–2000.* Leuven: Peeters, 2000.

Venema, Henry Isaac, *Identifying Selfhood: Imagination, Narrative, and Hermeneutics in the Thought of Paul Ricoeur.* (SUNY Series, *McGill Studies in the History of Religions*). Albany: State University of New York Press, 1992.

Wall, John, William Schweiker, and W. David Hall, eds., *Paul Ricoeur and Contemporary Moral Thought.* New York and London: Routledge, 2002.

Wetherbee, Louise Phelps, ed. *Pre/text:* Special Issue on Paul Ricoeur. 4 (1983).

Wood, David ed. On Paul Ricoeur: *Narrative and Interpretation (Warwick Studies in Philosophy and Literature).* New York and London: Routledge, 1992.

Book Reviews in English

'Aims of Interpretation'—Hirsch, E.D. TLS-THE TIMES LITERARY SUPPLEMENT, (3911): 216–16, 1977. Book Review. Times Newspapers Ltd. London, England.

Ways of Worldmaking—Goodman, Nelson PHILOSOPHY AND LITERATURE, 4 (1): 107–20, 1980. Book Review. Johns Hopkins University Press. Baltimore, MD.

Articles

Between Hermeneutics and Semiotics INTERNATIONAL JOURNAL FOR THE SEMIOTICS OF LAW-REVUE INTERNATIONALE DE SEMIOTIQUE JURIDIQUE, 3 (8): 115–32 1990, Deborah Charles Publications. Merseyside, England

The Golden Rule, Exegetical and Theological Perplexities NEW TESTAMENT STUDIES, 36 (3): 392–97 JUL 1990, Cambridge University Press, NY

On John Rawls 'A Theory of Justice'—Is a Pure Procedural Theory of Justice Possible? INTERNATIONAL SOCIAL SCIENCE JOURNAL, 42 (4): 553–64 NOV 1990, Blackwell Pub. Ltd, Oxford, England

Narrative Identity PHILOSOPHY TODAY, 35 (1): 73–81 SPR 1991, DePaul University, Chicago IL

History and Rhetoric: The Social Responsibility of the Historian DIOGENES, (168): 7–24 1994, Berg Publishers. Providence, RI

The Crisis of the Cogito SYNTHESE, 106 (1): 57–66 JAN 1996, Kluwer Academic Publishers, Dordrecht, Netherlands

The Erosion of Tolerance and the Resistance of the Intolerable DIOGENES, (176): 189–201 1996, Berg Books, Providence RI

Emmanuel Levinas—In–Memoriam PHILOSOPHY TODAY, 40 (3): 331–33 FAL 1996, DePaul University, Chicago IL

From Metaphysics to Moral Philosophy PHILOSOPHY TODAY, 40 (4): 443–58 WINTER 1996, DePaul University, Chicago IL

Obstacles and Limits to Tolerance DIOGENES, (176): 161–62 1996, Berg Books, Providence RI

Some Spiritual Sources of Tolerance DIOGENES, (176): 113–14 1996, Berg Books, Providence RI

Tolerance, Rights, and the Law DIOGENES, (176): 51–52 1996, Berg Books, Providence RI

To Think Tolerance DIOGENES, (176): 25–26 1996, Berg Books, Providence RI

ARTICLES IN GERMAN

Story, Metaphor and Interpretation Theory ZEITSCHRIFT FÜR THEOLOGIE UND KIRCHE, 84 (2): 232–53, May 1987, J C B Mohr, Tübingen, Germany

Objectivity and Alienation in Historical Research PHILOSOPHISCHES JAHRBUCH, 84 (1): 1–12 1977, Verlag Karl Alber. Freidburg, Germany

Hermeneutics of Law, Argumentation and Interpretation DEUTSCHE ZEITSCHRIFT FÜR PHILOSOPHIE, 42 (3): 375–84 1994, Akademie Verlag GMBH. Berlin, Germany

ARTICLES IN FRENCH

Structuralism and Hermeneutics ESPRIT, 322 (1963): 596–627. Paris, France

A Hermeneutic Phenomenology of the Individual ESPRIT, (3–4): 115–130 MAR–APR 1990. Paris, France

Patockajan and Nihilism ESPRIT, (11): 30–37 NOV 1990. Paris, France

Narrative Identity: Ipseity and the Discourse Revue Des Sciences Humaines (221): 35–47 1991. University Charles De Gaulle—Lille III. Villeneuve Dascq, France

Justice Falls between What Is Legal and What Is Good ESPRIT, (9): 5–21 SEP 1991. Paris, France

Heidegger and the Problem of History TEMPS MODERNES, 48 (552–53): 79–88 JUL–AUG 1992. Temps Modernes. Paris, France

Passing Judgement—The Role of the Judge in a Court of Law ESPRIT, (7): 20–25 JUL 1992. Paris, France

From Metaphysics to Morals: An Analysis of the Two States of Being from a Contemporary Point-of View REVUE DE METAPHYSIQUE ET DE MORALE, 98 (4): 455–77 OCT–DEC 1993. Librairie Armand Colin. Paris, France

The Concept of Responsibility—An Attempt at Semantic Analysis ESPRIT, (11): 28–48 NOV 1994. Paris, France

Moral Philosophy Written in English. Ricoeur, P; Cantosperber, M. REVUE DE METAPHYSIQUE ET DE MORALE, 99 (2): 147–147 APR–JUN 1994. Librairie Armand Colin. Paris, France

On the Spirit REVUE PHILOSOPHIQUE DE LOUVAIN, 92 (2–3): 246–53 MAY–AUG 1994. Inst. Superieur Philosophie. Louvain La Neuve, Belgium

When Human Suffering Warrants Military-Intervention ESPRIT, (2): 154–59 FEB 1994. Paris, France

Can Forgiveness Bring Healing ESPRIT, (3–4): 77–82 MAR–APR 1995. Paris, France

Dumas, André and His Assessment of Bonhoeffer, Dietrich Theology ESPRIT, (8–9): 197–99 AUG–SEP 1996. Paris, France

Mikel Dufrenne—In Memoriam REVUE D' ESTHETIQUE, (30): 12–14 1996. Editions Jean-Michel Place. Paris, France

The Three Levels of Judgment in Medicine + Therapeutic Aspects of Bioethics ESPRIT, (12): 21–33 DEC 1996. Paris, France

Memorial Tributes to Paul Fraisse Domenach, JM; Ricoeur, P. ESPRIT, (2): 190–92 FEB 1997. Paris, France

The Mark of the Past in Terms of Epistemology and Ontology REVUE DE METAPHYSIQUE ET DE MORALE, (1): 7–31 JAN–MAR 1998. Librairie Armand Colin. Paris, France

The Metaphor of Marriage in the 'Song of Solomon' ESPRIT, (5): 114–26 MAY 1998. Paris, France

Political Memory, DIVINATO, 6(1998): 27–37.

The Paradigm for Translation—A Comparison of the Approaches of Antoine Berman and George Steiner. ESPRIT, (6): 8–19 JUN 1999. Paris, France

Conversation with French philosopher Paul Ricoeur Descamps, C; Ricoeur, P. QUINZAINE LITTERAIRE, (796): 18–20 NOV 16 2000. Paris, France

La Mémoire, l'histoire, l'oubli'—The Origins of Memory, Letting Down One's Guard, Ricoeur, P; Macron ESPRIT, (8–9): 32–47 AUG–SEP 2000. Paris, France

La Mémoire, l'histoire, l'oubli'—The Respective Roles of Judge and Historian, Ricoeur, P; Macron ESPRIT, (8–9): 48–69 AUG–SEP 2000.Paris, France

Life Examined, Life Justified—Monique Canto-Sperber and the Topicality of Moral Thought. ESPRIT, (10): 120–35 OCT 2001. Paris, France

Paul Beauchamp, An Atypical Bible Scholar: A Study of His Critical Interpretations: Schlegel, JL; Ricoeur, P. ESPRIT, (6): 32–45 JUN 2001. Paris, France

Aristotle: From Anger to Justice and to Political Amity ESPRIT, (11): 19–31 NOV 2002. Paris, France

The Apostle Paul—Proclamation and Argumentation—Some Recent works ESPRIT, (2): 85–112 FEB 2003. Paris, France

Index

Books in the Rhetoric in the Modern Era Series

Thomas De Quincey: British Rhetoric's Romantic Turn
Lois Peters Agnew

Chaim Perelman
Alan G. Gross and Ray D. Dearin

Adam Smith: The Rhetoric of Propriety
Stephen J. McKenna

Paul Ricoeur: Tradition and Innovation in Rhetorical Theory
Andreea Deciu Ritivoi

George Campbell: Rhetoric in the Age of Enlightenment
Arthur E. Walzer